NEFERTITI

Books by Evelyn Wells

NEFERTITI

Evelyn Wells

GARDEN CITY, N.Y.

Doubleday & Company, Inc.

1964

DEDICATED TO

Judge Sylvester J. AND *Zora C. McAtee*

ACKNOWLEDGMENTS

For background material I am indebted to many books about Egypt whose authors will be found listed in the bibliography at the end of this book. Foremost among them are the works of James H. Breasted, every available line of whose writings I read with absorption many years before I thought of writing about the Akhenaton and Nefertiti he helped bring to life. Surviving later discoveries and newer authors, Breasted remains the greatest of all who have written of inexhaustible Egypt.

Much is owed to publications from various world museums, notably that of the Cairo Museum in Egypt, and to the splendid resources made available by the patient staffs of the Metropolitan Museum and the 42nd Street Public Library in New York, the Museum of Brooklyn, the Museum of Fine Arts in Boston, and the Peabody Museum of Natural History in New Haven, Connecticut.

My warmest thanks to Mrs. Louise Lawn for her friendly interest and her skillful final typing of a most difficult manuscript.

Affectionate tribute must be paid to the small stone Phi Beta studio in the forested grounds of the MacDowell Colony at Peterborough, New Hampshire. In that fairy-tale setting, deep in a snowy winter and divine isolation, this life of Nefertiti was written.

Contents

Illustrations

CHAPTER ONE

Afternoon in Egypt

Tell el-Amarna, 1912 A.D.

The discovery was made early in the afternoon of December 6, 1912, at the site of the long vanished city of Amarna, between Memphis and Thebes, in Middle Egypt. After the noonday meal of bread and dates, digging had been resumed in the Street of the Sculptor, and the picks and shovels of the fellahin rose and fell to a rhythmic chanting.

In his hut near the excavation Professor Ludwig Borchardt was still deep in his midday nap. He was a short man with a massive head covered with a shock of hair he made no attempt to control. He was one of the finest archaeologists ever to dig in Egypt and was in charge of the German expedition known as the Deutsch-Orient Gesellschaft which for two years had been excavating in the ruins of Amarna.

Amarna and its history had been lost for more than three thousand years. Only a legend lingered in Egypt of a magnificent ancient city that had once existed somewhere on the Nile. But no one knew where, nor why it had risen like a mirage between the two deserts, nor how it had mysteriously vanished.

Then, in the early 1800s, in this empty stretch of tawny sand, protected on the east by a semicircle of forbidding cliffs and on the west by the river, fellahin from the nearby village of El Amarieh began uncovering fragments of an interesting unknown pottery, small, beautifully modeled statuettes, and mud walls of buildings. The place became known, after the village, as Tell el-Amarna, later as Amarna.

Early nineteenth-century tourists rode camels to the spot and collected small but exquisite pieces of glassware, pottery, and faïence, statuettes from the nearby tombs, and cartouches and stone or clay tablets covered with a writing no one recognized. All were samples of an art unknown to Egyptian history. Much of Amarna's story must have been lost with these scattered souvenirs.

Some of these pieces bore the names of an unknown king and queen who were not listed in Egypt's historical records. Their names were intriguing; Akhenaton and Nefertiti. Nothing was known about them, nor the lonely place on the Nile where they had apparently lived.

The souvenir hunting served a purpose. It drew attention to the site. Archaeology was a new science, Egypt was an ideal country for such research. The dry warm climate and the sand acted as preservatives of the antique.

The catalyst who brought about the discovery of Amarna was that many-faceted genius, the German-born Alexander von Humboldt, who had added to his fame as naturalist, world traveler, statesman, and author by following Champollion, "the Father of Egyptology," in the translation of the hieroglyphs. At the end of his long, action-packed lifetime he learned of the discoveries at Amarna and persuaded King Frederick William IV of Prussia to send an expedition to the site. It was headed by Humboldt's brilliant and scholarly young friend Richard Lepsius, who became a great German archaeologist.

In 1843 the Prussian group began excavating. Three years of exploration revealed the foundations of a once great city of which nothing was known. Yet it had been one of the greatest cities of the ancient world. The leveled foundations indicated temples, palaces, public buildings, and princely villas as magnificent as had ever been erected in Egypt.

Steles, records, and markers revealed it to have been once known as the "city of the sun's horizon," the capital of Egypt when that country had been the world's most powerful empire. It had been built in the fourteenth century B.C. by a great religious reformer who called himself King Akhenaton, and whose queen was described on the fragments as having been beautiful beyond all other women.

So on this deserted site a legend began of a queen whose loveliness, intelligence, and grace had made her the most famous woman of her time. But her appearance and her story no one knew.

Her name had been stricken with her husband's from the

list of kings. Only once, in the Nineteenth Dynasty, which followed theirs, is Akhenaton found in the records, and then he is mentioned merely as "the criminal of Amarna."

All the discoveries emphasized the fact that Amarna had been built by and for this one man and woman. Fragments revealed labeled portions of their faces and bodies, an ear, hand, toe, his finely carved fanatic's mouth, her provocative lips, her graceful torso, her nose, a breast of hers in stone. Why were the monuments and statues and steles shattered and the names of Akhenaton and Nefertiti mutilated?

The city of Amarna had not been destroyed by time. It had not collapsed into itself, as happened to most lost cities. True, the mud walls had been worn down by centuries of abrasive sands, but first, the excavating revealed, Amarna had been razed to desert level.

No natural disaster, but the violence of man, had brought about the almost complete obliteration of the once great metropolis.

Amarna had been built—and wantonly destroyed—within a space of approximately twenty years!

Nothing could be found to explain such vandalism. A city that had been the richest, most cultured, and most beautiful in the world had been razed, almost at its beginning. No one could discover what manner of people Akhenaton and his wife Nefertiti had been, or why unknown enemies had tried to destroy all proof that they and their city had existed. Thousands had lived in the city. What had become of them?

Amarna's ruins were unlike those of other ancient cities. These were mostly built on many levels, as cities sank into the earth and others were built upon them. But Amarna consisted of one level. Its cement foundations had been poured on the sand much as foundations are today, and upon these had been erected a fabulous and unique city.

The Lepsius group sent their finds to Berlin. Interest grew in the mysteriously vanished king and his lost, beautiful wife. But souvenir hunters had rummaged for too many years. The low-walled rooms and the rock tombs in the nearby cliffs had been thoroughly ransacked. The German group decided Amarna had been ravaged beyond all hope of yielding any finds of value. They abandoned the site.

Archaeological discoveries were being made all over Egypt. Other sites yielded treasure. Amarna was forgotten.

But the name of Nefertiti was not forgotten. The beautiful lost queen was the most fascinating mystery of ancient Egypt.

In 1887 an Egyptian—Leonard Cottrell and several others believe it to have been a woman—from the nearby village was digging fertilizer in one of the excavated rooms. She dug into a cache of rotted wooden chests. Their alabaster lids had fallen off, and for a long time it was not known that these lids bore the names of King Akhenaton and his renowned father, Amenhotep III.

The chests were filled with printed clay tablets. The woman, and those to whom she took the tablets, did not recognize the symbols or know that the tablets carried the names of the two kings.

She was an unschooled countrywoman, but all Egyptians had learned that antique objects might be of value. She shoveled the hundreds of tablets into sacks, thereby damaging many, and took them to the village. At El Amarieh many of the larger tablets were broken into small pieces, rendering them undecipherable, on the theory that the more the pieces, the greater the profit.

The tablets were taken to the French-controlled Service des Antiquités, at the Cairo Museum, where the authorities examined them with little interest. So many beautiful, valuable finds were pouring into the museum from all over Egypt, and in an endless supply, that no one saw merit in the dull shapes of Nile mud, covered with small, almost obliterated signs, in a language nobody recognized. The museum experts dismissed them as forgeries.

French antiquarians in Paris sustained the Egyptian verdict: the tablets were worthless.

Bandied about, carelessly handled, and rejected, the clay shapes were steadily crumbling away. A dealer bought up all that remained for a trifling sum and hawked them around the country in sacks as "antique souvenirs."

By the time the Cairo Museum authorities woke to the fact that one of the greatest literary treasures of all time had slipped through their hands, and took steps to reclaim and recheck the tablets, many had been sold, stolen, or destroyed. With them was lost much of the history of Amarna and of Nefertiti and Akhenaton.

Only 377 letters remained. Of these about 60 were kept by Egypt, 180 went to the Berlin Museum and the rest went to the British Museum.

They are all that remain of the famous Amarna Letters, nearly all of which were written to King Akhenaton by the kings of Nineveh, Babylon, Canaan, and Mitanni in the reign of Akhenaton and Nefertiti and during their years at Amarna.

After the experts accepted the letters, a careful study began that took many years. The story of the tragedy that had overtaken Amarna was slowly fitted together. The wonder grew that the fragile clay tablets had been saved.

Perhaps some humble clerk risked his life to bury the royal correspondence. It may have been hidden by Aye, who, as former royal scribe, would have respected the kingly letters, many of which he had written. Or it may have been Nefertiti herself, proud and slender, goddess and monarch and heroine of the tremendous drama, who in face of the advancing enemy, surrounded by slaves, ordered the burial of the correspondence of the king she had loved.

If this is true, Nefertiti's was the final triumph. Her enemies and Akhenaton's must have believed all trace of the royal lovers had been destroyed. The translation of the tablets returned to life the personalities of a great king and queen, and with them one of the most important eras in ancient Egypt. A stirring period of history was recovered, complete with lost-long heroes, villains, intrigues, conquests, defeats, and heartbreak. Now it was known that at Amarna a man and woman had lived who loved deeply, who worshiped beauty and lived by truth, who had defied the ancient and terrible gods, and, led by a vision, had thrown their world away.

The tablets were small, of baked clay, and rather of the shape and size of modern dog biscuits. They were covered on all sides with fine print, done by hand. Many words were written in red ink and nearly all were neatly separated/in/this/fashion/by/lines.

On some of the tablets are fingerprints, and one wonders, could any of these be Aye's?

The Egyptians had no actual historians, but they were devoted keepers of records. In letters and on stone, in print and portraiture, the history of Egypt was kept in the recorded lives of its people. Notable deeds were posted in the tombs. The kings took full advantage of this means of recording their achievements, and their boastings saved much of Egypt's history.

When the Amarna Letters were written, writing had been in use in Egypt for thousands of years.

Cottrell has called writing, "the greatest of all Egyptian inventions." According to him, our own alphabetical symbols were "taken from the Romans, who adapted them from the Greeks, who took them from the Phoenicians, who, some scholars believe, took them and simplified the more complicated Egyptian writing." The twenty-six symbols that make up our daily reading "are remotely descended from the primitive pictographs invented by the inhabitants of the Nile Delta about six thousand years ago."

It was learned that the fine print was in the Babylonian cuneiform, and so for the first time it was known that the accepted diplomatic writing of Egypt in Nefertiti's time had been the Semitic Akkadian dialect. Only the letters from the king of Mitanni were written in Assyrian cuneiform.

While this information maintained interest in Amarna, it was felt that the discovery of the tablets had exhausted the site.

Then, in 1906, unique and beautiful objects in faïence, marble, and pottery began appearing in Cairo antique shops. They were so different from any artifacts previously found in Egypt that they again attracted the attention of German archaeologists who came to the exciting conclusion that Amarna must have been the center of a great lost art and its builder, Akhenaton, the Pericles of fourteenth-century B.C. Egypt.

The German archaeological expedition was organized under the leadership of Professor Borchardt, and in 1910 digging began in earnest in Amarna. The architectural level was thin, but it yielded marvelous treasures. It was discovered that Amarna had been carefully and lovingly planned by master architects; it was in fact the world's first planned city.

The winter of 1912 had been a tremendously successful season for the Germans. They had unearthed fabulous finds. They were excavating in the Street of the Sculptor and were exploring the ruined rooms of that treasure chest of antiquity, the Sculptor's House. Low, broken mud walls were all that remained of the atelier of Amarna's master sculptor, the great Thutmes. There under the sponsorship of King Akhenaton, surrounded by his school of talented apprentices, Thutmes had immortalized in marble, plaster, and limestone the great and near great who had lived in his time.

The studio itself, and an open space near the house known as the Sculptor's Area, where the school had deposited its rubbish, was an inexhaustible mine of artistry. Among other treasured finds were a statue of a horse and the head of an aged queen.

This last was of special interest, since the early Egyptians had been lovers of youth and age was seldom portrayed. Their lives were shorter than ours, just as their bodies were smaller. So the rare study of an older woman is important. It wears on the forehead the uraeus, the sacred asp worn by royalty, and is believed to have been a portrait of the fascinating Queen Tiy, who was the mother-in-law and close companion of Nefertiti, made during her historic visit to Amarna.

Many of the works were evidently incompleted discards. Others were apparently models of important statues that must have been displayed in public places in Amarna and destroyed by the enemies of Akhenaton and Nefertiti. And here, in the studio, surviving under layers of granite dust and the warm, safe sand, as miraculously as the Amarna Letters had survived, were the busts of many of Amarna's leading citizens, whose names were on the records and in the letters. By the inscriptions on the bust they were known, and their names were familiar.

Obviously portraits taken from life, many of these heads were signed, and their hieroglyphic captions were corrected in black ink by the hand of the master Thutmes. Their authenticity could never be disputed.

Also in the Sculptor's House were found drawings and small models of elegant funerary equipment. The importance of these would not be known for several decades, until the discovery of the tomb of King Tutankhaton at Thebes, for they were models of furnishings made at Amarna and found in his tomb. The tomb of the boy-king, originally planned for Amarna, would give the final, finest exposé of living conditions as they were in Nefertiti's time.

The Sculptor's studio was seemingly inexhaustible. The delighted Germans uncovered one after another of the lost faces of great and lowly, young and middle-aged, male and female. Fragment by fragment the banished citizens of Amarna were being fitted back into history. Personalities were lifted out of the dust of centuries. Shards were found of the strange, gentle, fanatical features of Akhenaton, and tantalizing bits of statues of his beloved Nefertiti. But none gave complete proof of her vaunted beauty that had stimulated artists and poets thirty centuries before.

So we come to Amarna on the afternoon of December 6, 1912, and to Professor Borchardt sleeping on his cot after his noonday meal and dreaming no doubt of even more dazzling finds, as all archaeologists must dream to make the long, dusty efforts worthwhile.

Remember the name of their foreman, Mohammed Ahmes Es-Senussi, who was the first to see the almost human gleam of golden flesh-colored fragment in the sand!

He cried out and raised his hand. Picks and shovels were lowered, and the workmen drew into a circle and waited while a dirt-carrier ran to the professor.

Professor Borchardt came scudding on short legs up the dusty Street of the Sculptor and into the excavated square. Shaking the thick shock of hair back from his high forehead, he knelt at the spot indicated by the pointing finger of Mohammed.

With trained, sensitive fingertips, with reverent breath, Professor Borchardt moved the sand from the buried object, grain by grain. This was the moment for which men of his stamp dig and suffer and pray.

Under the feather-light touch of his hands appeared first the slender throat, so exquisitely tinted it seemed to be alive. When the last grains of the sands of the millennia were blown away the head lay bared, life-sized and beautiful. It was Nefertiti, destined to become the most celebrated, copied, and admired bust in the world, the most famous face of all the Egyptian queens.

Across the space of three and a half thousand years her serene gaze met the eyes of Professor Borchardt, and even without the authorized signature of her name on its base it seemed to offer her final testimony: "I am she, Nefertiti, the beloved one, the all-beautiful."

Here, in limestone and plaster, was a woman and a queen as poised and dignified as she was lovely. The head, under the crown with its sacred royal asp, was held proudly on the lotus-stem throat. The eyes under kohl-marked brows were large, liquid, serenely questioning. The exquisitely molded face was tinted a pale golden apricot with a coloring made of red chalk and lime. One of Nefertiti's eyes was missing. The other was rock crystal painted a deep dark brown.

For a time there was horrible doubt—could the queen lauded as the most beautiful in history have had but one eye? Also missing and never found were pieces of Nefertiti's ears, which had perhaps broken away under the weight of heavily jeweled earrings.

Professor Borchardt reached the conclusion that the bust had been a study piece and had been discarded before the insertion of the missing optic. Had the final head been made from the model, and graced some palace or temple in Amarna? And if so, had enemies destroyed it along with so much else that had belonged to Queen Nefertiti?

Or was it still hidden somewhere in the preservative sands of Egypt?

The decorative articles, like the bust itself, would be widely reproduced and sold. Nefertiti's gold necklace was deep as a collar and set with a variety of gems. The links were petal-shaped, indicative of her well-known love of flowers. The blue head-dress was her own distinctive crown. Flaring back from her delicately contoured face, it was embroidered and begemmed, centered with the serpent emblem of supreme power, and tied unexpectedly and girlishly at the back with gay red ribbons.

Under the headdress the small skull may have been shaven. Both Egyptian men and women were given to shaving their heads for comfort. Wigs were worn in public, and it is known that Nefertiti wore them. On her Amarna head no hairline mars the pure classic lines of face and skull.

The excitement in the Sculptor's House must have been so-
bered by realization of the importance of the find. Professor
Borchardt and his associates knew it would open regions of history that had been kept in darkness for thousands of years. They
were digging at Amarna under a permit issued by the Egyptian
Service des Antiquités, which was under the direction of the
French Government. Technically, all archeological finds in Egypt
were the property of the Egyptian Government.

The Nefertiti bust, therefore, belonged to Egypt.

But all governments know that archaeologists will go to the
expense and labor of excavating only if permitted to share in the
finds. It had early been decided in Egypt and other countries
under study that a certain percentage of any discoveries belonged to the discoverers. In the early stages of the science of
archaeology the delicate problem of who got what had been
determined for all time by fair if primitive means—often by
simply tossing a coin.

The Germans had dug patiently for two years in the hope of
such a find. It is difficult to believe that on this sunny December
afternoon at Amarna when Professor Borchardt lifted the bust in
his trembling hands, that he did not recognize it at once as one
of the greatest archaeological discoveries of all time, and hoped
to keep his find for Germany.

The German scientists would argue later that when the bust
was found it was badly stained with earth and broken into two
parts, so that it was not recognized then as being the first authentic portrait of Queen Nefertiti.

Fortunately for them, during this same historic winter at
Amarna they uncovered another tremendous find, the magnificent altarpiece showing Akhenaton, Nefertiti, and three of their
children exulting under the beneficent rays of the sun god, Aton.

At the end of their Amarna season, when Borchardt and his
group displayed their finds to the Egyptian authorities for the
final selection, evidently both sides regarded the altarpiece and
the bust as being of equal importance. The final decision as to
which of the two finds should remain in Egypt was made, according to Professor Borchardt, on January 20, 1913, a little over
a month after the bust was found.

Monsieur Lefevre of the French-controlled Service des Antiquités personally passed upon the finds and decided the group portrait was the most valuable. It was turned over to the Cairo Museum, while the Nefertiti bust, "with remarkable speed," was dispatched to the Museum of Berlin.

Little was printed concerning the arrival of the bust in Germany. But in Egypt protest began.

The English Consul General at Cairo at this time was none other than the renowned Lord Kitchener, the avenger of "Chinese" Gordon at Khartoum. Kitchener was a firm believer in keeping Egypt's treasures in Egypt—or perhaps in the British Museum.

He voiced an indignant query: Why had Nefertiti's bust been permitted to go to Germany?

Egypt reached the belated realization that after losing the major share of its priceless Amarna letters, it had now given away its most beautiful find. Egypt was indignant. Cairo authorities fumed. Berlin protested. The world press reported the argument, and the feud made headlines.

In Berlin, museum authorities defended their right to the Nefertiti. They argued that Professor Borchardt and his associates had toiled for years in Egypt before finding the head, that its value had not been suspected by either side at the time of the allotment, and that the museum had papers to prove the bust had been fairly and honestly awarded the Germans by the Egyptian authorities.

The publicity made Nefertiti's bust the most celebrated object in the Berlin Museum. A popular movement swept Europe, demanding its return to Egypt. The beautiful little crowned head that had remained high under so much storm and change was once more a center of contest.

Professor Borchardt was anxious to return with his group to Amarna and resume digging. He begged the Egyptian authorities for a permit. It was refused.

"Return the bust of our queen to Egypt," the Cairo authorities informed Germany, "and we will gladly permit you to dig again at Amarna."

Berlin refused. Egypt made another offer.

"Return our Nefertiti," the Egyptian authorities pleaded, "and we will not only grant the German scientists the right to excavate again at Amarna, but as an added bonus we will send to Berlin two rare statues of Egyptian Pharaohs!"

German newspapers hooted by way of refusal, "Are two kings worth a queen?"

It is believed that it was due to this refusal that German archaeologists were denied all rights to dig again in Egypt, and before long World War I put an end to the controversy and, for a time, to all excavating at Amarna.

Egypt's anguish over the loss was soothed by subsequent discoveries at Amarna. Rubbish heaps far out of the town, which had evidently been the "dumping ground" of the great palace, yielded endless treasure in pottery and glassware, and rings stamped with royal names, and, strangely and never to be explained, human bones.

In the rubbish heap near the great Temple of Aton was found what is supposed to be the death mask of King Akhenaton. It was unquestionably made after death, for no orifices show the nostrils, and the eyes are half open. A cloth fillet banding the forehead prevented plaster getting in the hair. It does not show the pendulous jaw so many of Akhenaton's cartoonlike portraits accentuate. Set in death, tragic and unyielding, one might say this is a good, a *lonely* face.

Nor is the Cairo Museum bereft of the presence of Nefertiti, for many paintings of her have been found, and most important, a second bust of the queen was discovered at Amarna. Like the first, it is a trial piece left unfinished for some reason by the sculptor, but if completed, it would surpass the first in artistry. The lines are more classic, the throat fuller, the expression warmer. As in all Nefertiti's portraits, the queenly head is high.

Place on this bust the Nefertiti headdress and it is far more beautiful than the bust in Berlin.

The first bust served to bring into full recognition a great and legendary age, and restored a banished king and queen to their rightful place in history.

From other parts of Egypt came reports of finds that helped round out the histories and personalities of Akhenaton and Nefertiti. Heliopolis yielded evidence; Aswan contributed. At Thebes, the dramatic discovery of the tombs, particularly that of

King Tutankhaton, King Amenhotep III, and the scribe Aye and his wife, helped authenticate what for centuries had survived as a glamorous legend.

It is a rash undertaking to attempt the biography of a woman who has been dead thirty-four hundred years.

The experts do not always agree. Many questions remain unanswered in Egypt. Fresh discoveries are constantly being made that refute much that was believed before. Not only the use of names, but the dates of the dynasties are disputed, although within a limited space of time.

One can only balance the opinions of the most respected authorities against the newest finds, and say, This may have happened, or, perhaps . . .

Still, we know a great deal about Nefertiti.

Sir Leonard Woolley has pointed out, in *Digging up the Past*, that archaeological work has recovered the whole history of Egypt in astonishing detail.

"I suppose," he observes, "we know more about ordinary life in Egypt in the fourteenth century before Christ than we do about that of England in the fourteenth century A.D."

That was Nefertiti's century.

Ancient records and artifacts, writings on papyrus, clay, and stone, statues and steles and monuments and walls and tombs have served to re-create the woman whose face is one of the best known in the world. Since Borchardt's discovery other renowned archaeologists raked the sands of Amarna. Sir Flinders Petrie, Howard Carter, John Pendlebury, Thomas Peet, Henri Frankfort, and Leonard Woolley in turn have helped contribute to the understanding of Nefertiti and her beautiful city.

Thanks to the testimony of the finds, we know the games Nefertiti played, the songs she loved, the dresses and jewels and flowers and perfumes she chose, the foods and wines. We know of the palaces Nefertiti lived in. We know ancient Thebes, and Amarna, her city, which was as brilliant and beautiful as her own existence.

We know she was deeply loved, for carved in stone remain many poetic tributes such as this written for her by Akhenaton, her lover who was poet, priest and king:

". . . . the great royal wife, his beloved,
Mistress of the Two Lands,
Neferneferuaton (Beautiful is the beauty of Aton),
Nefertiti
Living and flourishing forever and ever."

But she was more than a creature of poetry. She walked in the effulgence of a great love and a great destiny; she was the most powerful empress in the world. She suffered, struggled, connived, playing a long and dangerous game, with princesses and kings as pawns, in a despairing fight to hold Egypt. More than any of the Egyptian queens, she was her country, and to know Nefertiti one must know Egypt and the times in which she lived.

Two Children of Thebes

In the Palace, 1372 B.C.

In the time of the empire, when Thebes, the "hundred gated," was the capital of Egypt, somewhere around the year 1372 B.C., two children were growing up together like brother and sister in the Theban palace on the Nile.

We believe Nefertiti to have been eleven years old in this year. She was already marked by destiny, for she was the favorite companion of the twelve-year-old prince upon whom the hopes of Egypt were centered. He was the fourth Amenhotep, named for his father, but we shall call him by the name he chose for himself, Akhenaton.

He was the sole male descendant of the most powerful family in the world. This was Egypt's imperial age and the peak of the Eighteenth Dynasty, the richest, most cultured, and most powerful Egypt would ever know. The boy was descended from a line of aggressive kings who had enlarged and consolidated Egypt into the world's leading empire. As the first-born and only son of King Amenhotep III and Queen Tiy, he would shortly be called upon to rule Egypt.

The narrow-faced, narrow-bodied lad was capable of a fanatic's concentration. We know that burning attention was focused early on the golden slip of a girl who was Nefertiti.

Nefertiti's legendary reputation for beauty has been confirmed. She was probably beautiful as a child. She is also reported to have been affectionate, intelligent, graceful, and possessed of a joyous disposition. She evidently had attributes beyond those of extraordinary good looks to have won the love of the young Prince Akhenaton and the approval of that strong-willed empress, his mother, Tiy.

At this time Nefertiti must have been a sweet-tempered, happy little creature, already charmingly feminine. Like all Egyptian

children, she would have worn the forelock of youth, coquettishly twisted into a curl over her right ear, and delicately fashioned childish jewelry such as bracelets and rings and necklaces
made of gold and silver beads and colored seeds that dangled
tiny amulet images of the gods. She went barefoot, or wore
beautiful little sandals. She may have worn a single, almost transparent garment of the thinnest and finest linen, hand-woven from
the Egyptian flax, but most of the time she was not ashamed to
go naked even in the royal presence.

Nudity was considered an honest and natural state in the hot
climate of Egypt, where all children and even adults went naked.

She would have had many toys—rag dolls to be cuddled,
wooden dolls with painted heads and movable arms and legs,
doll-sized beds and chairs, jumping jacks and puppets that
worked on strings, and wooden animals with jointed parts that
wriggled when she dragged them over the painted floors of the
palace. There were games she could share with the king's son,
such as jacks, running and jumping games, and one resembling
checkers played with interesting little carved figures, like chess-
men, which were kept in carved ivory boxes.

The two children owned many tiny images, given them as
presents. All Egyptian children had these figurines, which might
be miniature replicas of the gods or of the sacred animals. Small
figures of this kind have been found that belonged to the boy
Akhenaton. Other toy images, made in his time but later, in
Tutankhaton's childhood and found in that boy-king's tomb,
were of a lion, deer, birds, snakes, frogs, fish, scorpions, scarabs,
and even flies.

They played in the large, magnificently furnished rooms of
the great palace and in the gardens around it that swept down
to the Nile. Egyptian children were never excluded from family
circles, and Akhenaton had small but important roles to play in
the ceremonial rites that were part of royalty's daily routine. At
present it was Nefertiti's duty to observe, hovering in the regal
but amiable presence of Queen Tiy. Due to the merry personality
of the queen, the atmosphere in the palace was cheerful, and
since Egyptians had a special devotion to children, we may be
certain the early years of Nefertiti and Akhenaton were happy
years.

Wherever the two children went they were accompanied by a small, loyal retinue. The boy's was headed by Aye, whose wife, Tiy, "the Great Royal Nurse" was in charge of the little girl.

They were surrounded by pets. It is impossible to understand the ancient Egyptians without understanding their attitude toward animals, which to them were an extension of humans—and the gods. Many animals were divine, and could be played with and sometimes be made to work (or even eaten) but they must still be respected since they were of the stuff of gods. Cat was the goddess Bastet, who honored even a royal family by living in their palace and catching their mice, and was personally loved for her grace and charm. (Cat's common name was Miw; a sheep was known as Baa.)

Herodotus would write, centuries after this, "An Egyptian will let his house burn down to save his cat."

As for Dog, he was not only the animal of Anubis, god of the necropolis, but had been since earliest times an honored member of the family. He had his own affectionate and flattering name and handsome collars, and slept at night on his mistress' bed.

There were several popular breeds. Hounds came of ancient stock. They wore wide protective collars and leashes and went hunting with their masters. Large, fierce dogs were trained to guard their masters in war. Others were the basset type and the greyhound, now known as the saluki, which was supposed to be close kin of the jackal, scavenger of the desert. A favorite small, short-legged dog resembled the Welsh corgi.

These were dogs born to high fortune, like their masters. Others were less tenderly treated. The farmers had dogs that helped guard the harvest and herds, and in the vast kitchens of the palace and in all wealthy homes, menial dogs patiently turned the spits to brown roasts they dared not touch, as their canine ancestors had for centuries.

Still, every dog was respected. The wild desert dogs roved the streets undisturbed. Dogs and other pets were mummified at death to share the hereafter with their masters. There were cat and dog cemeteries. Many cat and dog and bird mummies have been found in Egyptian graves. On the walls of the tombs their virtues were cited, and the dog was invariably praised for his fidelity in guarding his master in death and in life.

For added protection, black dogs were painted on the outer
doors of tombs. Prayers on tombs were addressed to Dog, and
he even had his own city in Egypt, Cynopolis, City of Dogs.

In one grave the dead boasts: "I have taken care of ibises,
falcons, divine cats and dogs, and I have buried them according
to the ritual, anointing them with oil and wrapping them with
cloth."

Guarded by their retinues, human and animal, but free to go
where they willed, the boy-prince and his girl companion shared
childish pleasures in a great palace and a great city. They took
part in the court amusements, learned the rituals that would be
required of them in the great Temple of Amon on the other side
of the river (crossing with the king and queen in the royal barge)
and rode in chariots with the royal parents through the narrow
streets of Thebes, a city overcrowded with people and gods.
And beyond Thebes on every side was the Egypt that would
be theirs when they left the untroubled world of childhood.

They may have spent their happiest hours in the palace garden. All Egyptians loved gardens, which were designed for
beauty, pleasure, love, and for the fortunate old who could enjoy idleness. Theirs was the immense palace park, tended by
armies of gardeners, servants, and slaves, under the authority
of an impressive chief gardener. Fig trees and date palms and
rare trees and plants and flowers from foreign countries surrounded the artificial lake. The two children were amused by
the antics of the monkeys and baboons in the trees, and the
ostriches, giraffes, and other curious creatures that were part of
the tribute sent to Akhenaton's father by the Negroes of
Kordofan. The ostriches were caged and could be dangerous; so
were the lions whose roars were outdone by the hippopotamus
pool where huge clumsy beasts bellowed in monstrous play.

Another favorite amusement place was the Nile.

The children had their own small decorative boats woven of
reeds. Drifting between the papyrus clumps, armed with child-
sized fishing poles, nets, and spears, they filled baskets with the
fish so plentiful that they turned the river waters to roiled silver.
With bows and arrows and boomerangs they brought down the
ducks and other water fowl that, rising out of the reeds, clouded
the skies over the Nile.

They were growing up in a virtually untouched Eden.

The boy had slingshots like those his father's soldiers carried into battle. But while theirs slung lead pellets that could kill men, his only hurled lumps of clay at birds. His kingly father, and his forefathers, had been mighty bowmen and hunters, but Akhenaton would never distinguish himself as a sportsman.

He was a thoughtful, gentle, affectionate boy.

He would be that kind of a man.

The banks of the Nile where they played were green with the feathery papyrus, which has almost vanished. Like a green ribbon, the river ran through the center of Thebes in Upper Egypt and on through the heart of Egypt, flowing strangely down-river as few rivers run, to the north, or Lower Egypt.

On either side stretched the kingdom the two children would inherit.

"To-mery" the Egyptians called it, their "beloved country."

The world then was Egypt. Were there other lands as secure, cultured, civilized? The Egyptians did not know of them. They did not know that other civilizations had been slowly evolving elsewhere in the Middle East, in China and India.

Their long and narrow country, barriered on either side by deserts, had cradled the first civilization.

There is a new and steadily strengthening theory that Egypt may have been the original Garden of Eden (or one of several) and that prehistoric man first raised himself on shaggy legs beside the Nile. Later he built huts of reed mixed with mud, and chipped axheads of stone, and with crude wooden implements began tilling the soil.

The huts appeared in clusters as families drew together for mutual protection. Fields were planted, cattle domesticated; the agricultural settlements grew. The birth of civilization was taking place along the Nile.

That had been in Neolithic times, four or five thousand years before Christ.

Leonard Cottrell has written, in *The Anvil of Civilization*, that no civilization on earth existed until 4000 B.C. "Eight hundred years later one such community had begun in Egypt . . .

about five centuries later another civilization—that of Sumer—was established in Lower Mesopotamia."

These two valley civilizations developed independently. Both were ruled by kings, worshiped many gods, invented an alphabet and developed writing, developed agriculture, learned the use of metals, and built ships. Egypt was the stronger and more stable. It was not invaded until the Eighteenth Dynasty, whereas Sumer, Akkad, and Babylon were frequently molested.

Now, in Nefertiti's and Akhenaton's time, dynastic Egypt had attained a level of security, prosperity, and content it was not likely to know again. The cultural leap forward from the Stone Age to their era is one of the most extraordinary in the history of human development. Actually, we are not much farther removed from Nefertiti and Akhenaton than they were from the people of the Stone Age.

Their era was the imperial age. In it life was being lived in Egypt much as it had been for the past thousand years.

The rich land was under heavy cultivation. As far as the children could see, looking up and down the river, fields of wheat and corn and barley, orchards, and vegetable gardens were tended by workers with wooden tools and watered by canals cut to the Nile.

With scythes now edged with copper, the mowers cut the grain-wheat for making bread, barley for making beer. Papyrus was gathered to make paper. Goats and sheep were raised for their flesh and their wool; though little wool was worn in a country as warm as Egypt it was valued for filling mattresses and pillows and weaving into wall hangings. Vast areas of land were planted with the flax that supplied linen for the cool, simple one-piece garments worn by all.

The long- and the short-horned cattle belonging to the clergy or the nobles or the king were branded. They were herded, as were the sheep and goats and hogs, and butchered for the dinner tables or the altars.

The country was still agricultural, but the Neolithic farming communities had grown into cities, and the greatest of all was Thebes. It was the capital of Egypt, and Egypt was the leading country of the world.

Due to the energy of Akhenaton's forebears, Egypt had become the strongest kingdom in existence. As the center of world trade, it was open on every side to culture and all the known lands paid tribute and homage to Egypt. It stretched from the Euphrates in Northern Syria south to the Sudan.

The two children of Thebes knew vaguely of lands apart from their own. They knew of Nubia, where the boy's father had been forced to punish quarrelsome tribes when Akhenaton had been a year old, and Punt in the south, which yielded the perfumes Nefertiti loved and the incense that wreathed their heads when they were worshiping with the royal family in the great Temple of Amon. They knew that somewhere "down" the Nile to the north was Lower Egypt, and of cities there less great than Thebes named Memphis and Heliopolis, and of the great pyramids in the north. Beyond these, they knew, were the Mediterranean and a strange island named Crete; to the northeast in Mesopotamia was Mitanni, from whence came the beautiful princesses, and to the west the mysterious "Green Sea" (the Atlantic), which everyone knew was the watery rim of the earth. There the world ended.

The two children of Thebes would hear of other cities. They knew of Babylon, Nineveh, and Tyre (all doomed to ruin, as Thebes would in time be doomed). They may have heard of a small but important mud-walled trading post that, four centuries after this, would be established as a city by King David under the name of Jerusalem.

But no other city compared with Thebes.

Memphis in the north had once been supreme, but its power had waned. Now Thebes had been the capital for six hundred years, and it was the world's richest and largest city, and the center of world power.

It was the first great metropolis.

It was colorful, crowded, swarming with traffic and trade. Ships pulled up to its stone wharfs bearing tribute from the vassal lands which made up the rest of the known world. Tyre, Sidon, Byblos, and cities of Canaan yielded annual tribute to Thebes, and much of this went to Amon, whose richly robed, besashed priests swarmed in the city.

At this time the city was known as No-Amon and it was dedicated to Amon, who was the god of all the gods of Egypt.

They grew older.

Nefertiti might watch admiringly while with other lads of the court Akhenaton took part in the youth games. Egyptian lads played a form of handball using a stuffed leather ball stitched much as baseballs are now. Akhenaton probably learned to wrestle, fight duels with blunted wands, lift weights, run races, and play at mock battle. He drove his own chariot when very young and may have entered it in the races in which young nobles competed, as auto racers do today. He hunted from his chariot with his dogs, bows and arrows, and spears, which was fine training for war, as all the nobility, when fighting, fought from their chariots.

But it is doubtful that Akhenaton gave any thought to war. He and Nefertiti were growing up in a reign notable for peace. He was a boy and would become a man who delighted in the company of women. At this time of approaching puberty he was under the influence of his mother and closest, among all the children in the Theban court, to the child Nefertiti.

Was Thebes wondering even then—who was she? Was the child a mystery to the Egyptians who saw her first as the chosen companion of the adored young prince who would in time be their king? In her time, Egypt may have known the truth about Nefertiti, but later all traces of her would be lost until the day her bust was discovered at Amarna.

The experts would dispute the theories of her origin. They would offer the same opinions, and ask the same questions, concerning Akhenaton's mother, the fascinating Queen Tiy.

Some of our leading authorities once believed that both Nefertiti and Tiy were originally princesses from Mitanni. The theory rose from a curious political agreement made between Egypt and Mitanni before either of these women were born.

Farther back in the Eighteenth Dynasty, enmity of long standing had existed between the two countries. The Egyptian frontier had been kept in a state of harassment for more than a hundred years. Then, sometime at the beginning of the empire, in the reign of Amenhotep II, the Mesopotamian country found itself endangered by those perennial invaders, the Babylonians and the Hittites. The Mitanni reached the conclusion that politics could be more profitable than war, and sued all-powerful Egypt for protection.

In token of the new friendship, the Mitanni kings sent shiploads of treasure up the Nile to the Egyptian kings. Decorated barges flying the bright pennants of foreign royalty anchored off the long stone wharf at Thebes to disgorge fortunes in treasure of every kind—rare animals, horses, chariots, slaves. And with these, as supreme tribute from their royal fathers, came Mitanni princesses to serve as "extra" wives in the harems of the Egyptian kings. They were the crowning pledges of Mitanni's pact with Egypt.

Three generations of Egyptian kings married these royal daughters of Mitanni. Akhenaton's grandmother had been one of them, sent to Egypt by her father, King Artatama of Mitanni, to become the bride of Thutmose IV. There she took the Egyptian name of Mutemuya, honoring the goddess of truth. Thutmose made her his "great queen" and she became the mother of Amenhotep III, Akhenaton's father.

Mutemuya was noted for her beauty and her kindness. When her son Amenhotep chose Tiy as the girl he wished to marry, Mutemuya welcomed her into the royal family and was a devoted mother-in-law. In her turn Queen Tiy showed notable affection for the child Nefertiti who was the choice of her own son.

The royal family of Mitanni were Aryan, of Indo-Iranian descent. They worshiped the gods of India. Through Mutemuya and the other Mitanni princesses Aryan blood was introduced during the Eighteenth Dynasty into the already mixed Egyptian blood. Akhenaton therefore was part Aryan. The kings of Egypt and Mitanni since the time of his grandfather had addressed one another as "brother."

The Mitanni princesses were still being sent into Egypt while Akhenaton and Nefertiti were growing up. The two children must have been watching wide-eyed at the wharf as the royal ambassadresses of love alighted from their barges on jeweled feet, while after them came their colorful retinues of brightly clad ladies in waiting, (all chosen, as was the princess herself, for beauty) and hundreds of servants, and slaves leading rare animals and bearing the trousseaus and bridal gifts.

While these princesses were accepted as subsidiary wives by Amenhotep, Tiy was his one and only beloved "great king's wife." We know of at least one sent to Akhenaton when he was very young. He may not have accepted the gift, for in all that remain of the records, Nefertiti is listed as his only love.

But the presence of these princesses in Thebes so confused future historians that more than three thousand years later both Tiy and Nefertiti would both be suspected of having been Mitannian. One princess was reported as having been the original of both Nefertiti and Tiy.

This was the Princess Tadukhipa, a daughter of King Tushratta of Mitanni, from whom a great deal would be heard. As a correspondent he had no peer, and his letters to Amenhotep, and later to Akhenaton, crowded the Amarna archives. He sent a sister and several daughters to Thebes, which gave him the right to become one of the most interfering in-laws in history.

The princess brought with her an impressive dowry, listed in the Amarna records, which included, along with the usual treasure, a wealth of magnificent household furnishings. Among them were costly bedspreads. For the first time they would have been placed on beds, for Egyptian royalty slept in splendidly carved and gilded beds. But in Mesopotamia, even royalty slept, like poor Egyptians, on the floor.

The Mitannian princesses and their dowries were not tax-exempt. In return, the Egyptian king was expected to send royal treasure by return barge. King Tushratta contributed another daughter to Akhenaton's father and felt free to unleash more exorbitant demands.

"My brother, my son-in-law, who loves me and whom I love," he wrote King Amenhotep, ". . . let my brother send gold in great quantities, without measure. . . . for in my brother's land gold is as common as dust."

This was almost true. Egypt was rich in gold, which was valued for its beauty and because it was known to be of the flesh of the sun. There were mines in the desert and in the eastern and southeastern mountains where slave and convict labor dug and washed and melted the gold. Additional gold came as tribute from the vassal states of Nubia and Syria. As a result gold appeared everywhere in Egypt, on the persons of the rich, on furniture and chariots and coffins. Gold was piled throne-high before the kings and filled chests stacked in the royal treasury. Palaces, temples, and tombs were literally lined with gold.

Amenhotep III did send gold "in great quantities" to insure peace on his frontiers, and in time this would be considered as a sign of weakening on the part of mighty Egypt. His son Akhenaton would learn that loyalty can not be bought.

A curious scandal in the Theban harem at this time is revealed in the Amarna Letters. King Amenhotep had accepted as an "extra" wife one of the sisters of King Kadashman-Bel of Babylonia, who wrote demanding word of her. His ambassador in Egypt, the Babylonian king complained, had been to Amenhotep's palace, but had not been permitted to see the princess. In fact the ambassador from Babylonia had reported that a woman dressed as a queen had been pointed out to him, but at a distance, and he had not been allowed to get close enough to make certain of her identity.

King Amenhotep's answer to this was decidedly testy. He suggested that since the emissary was evidently "not infallible," a trusted eunuch who knew the sister should be sent to Thebes.

No more is found on this touchy subject, but it is not an amiable correspondence between brothers-in-law.

There is another curious letter in the Amarna files from King Tushratta. Written to Queen Tiy, it begs her to give his greetings to "his daughter and her daughter-in-law." This is apparently the sole hint that Akhenaton may have had an "extra wife," and gave rise to the legend that Nefertiti may have been one of the Mitanni princesses.

The great Egyptologist James H. Breasted wrote that the origin of Nefertiti was "mysterious," and that she may have been "foreign."

He wrote before the testimony of the tombs.

Until certain discoveries in the Valley of the Kings at Thebes and the tombs at Amarna, the same theories concerning the origin of Queen Tiy were accepted to explain Nefertiti. Although a generation lay between them, both were believed to have arrived in Thebes as tender tribute from Mitanni, and won there the love of their separate kings.

In a sense, the legend is true. The origins of Nefertiti and her
mother-in-law were curiously alike. Both rose out of obscurity
to win the love of the world's leading monarchs.

Until fairly recently nothing was known of Tiy's origin. Attempts were made in turn to prove her a daughter of a king of
Mitanni, a king of Syria, and a king of Babylon. One authority
believed her to have been a sister of King Tushratta's.

The truth is, Akhenaton's mother was humbly born. Tiy's story
is that of Cinderella and Cophetua's beggar maid—centuries before either of these romances were told.

When King Amenhotep married Tiy he issued the first of the
Egyptian commemorative tablets to announce their union. The
announcement was written in cuneiform on stone tablets in the
shape of the sacred beetle the scarab. These must have been
issued in great quantities, as many have been found, even as far
away as Greece.

Contrary to all royal precedent, no mention was made of the
bride's ancestry. The scarabs merely announced that Tiy was
now "the Great King's Wife, Queen Consort, the Great and Right
Heiress, Mistress of Many Lands." This emphasis on her new
exalted station would certainly have discouraged any of Tiy's
subjects from hinting that she was not to the manner born. From
her wedding day on Tiy was always shown standing or sitting
beside the king, and her name was affixed next to his on all royal
documents and monuments.

Her influence over King Amenhotep was recognized. Her
power was absolute.

It is with a start of recognition that one meets in museums
with the portraits and statues of Amenhotep III and Queen Tiy,
for this happily smiling, lustily handsome pair are in some way
people known to us. They are so very human, so obviously delighted with one another and their station in life. They had the
good fortune to be the supreme rulers of Egypt at its triumphant
apex. The Eighteenth Dynasty would in time be known as "the
Golden Age," and theirs would be its most peaceful reign.

Even in stone, in gigantic shape, we recognize the innate content of this regal pair. They share an aura of well-being, gustiness,
and mutual esteem. Amenhotep smiles, but his bearing is touched
with sternness; Homer would write of him as "one of the stateliest

of men." He is obviously aware of his tremendous responsibilities as the world's leading monarch.

Tiy on the other hand is a creature of the earth and delighted with all its holdings. She is obviously the king's equal. Previous Egyptian queens, with a few notable exceptions, had been kept in oriental seclusion and if pictured were usually shown small-sized and doll-like, often grasping one of their lord's legs to demonstrate their right to his protection. Tiy leans on no one. She sits squarely on the throne, leaning forward, alert and eager and deliciously feminine. Hers is a bold, complacent charm. Her body is slender but sturdy, of a "country" healthiness, and her fine features are wreathed in gaiety. There is much sweetness in the broad, dimpled, good-natured smile, and even in stone she is revealed as having a rich appreciation of the great lord she has married and her own value as a woman and a queen.

Eighteenth Dynasty royalty has been held exceptional for superb health and sanity. Tiy and her king were outstanding examples. Painted portraits show Queen Tiy to have been blue-eyed and fair of skin. There had been fair queens in Egypt before her. Back in the Fourth Dynasty, the era in which the Pyramids were built, there were recorded two blond queens, one of whom had hair of a reddish shade. A legend handed down from ancient Egypt told of a celebrated fair-haired courtesan.

Such women and Tiy may have been descended from a lost tribe of blue-eyed people who many centuries before wandered down into Egypt from southern Europe.

We can see in her portraits the qualities that won for Tiy the love of the world's leading king. But we do not know how this lusty creature, without wealth or rank, first came to the attention of King Amenhotep, and nothing was known of her origin until certain excavations were made in 1905 in the Valley of the Kings at Thebes.

There, in the burial area reserved for royalty, Theodore Davis found a magnificent tomb belonging to an Eighteenth Dynasty man and wife who were not even of the minor nobility.

According to the inscriptions, this pair had been commoners, without titles or honors of any kind. Their names were Yuya and Thuya (another form of Tiy).

They were Queen Tiy's father and mother and the grandparents of Akhenaton. Tiy's father was a priest. Amenhotep made her brother, Anen, a high priest of Amon.

The greatest honor a Pharaoh could pay a beloved subject was to have a costly tomb prepared for him during life and his body embalmed after death. The love Amenhotep held for his wife and the respect shown her parents is displayed in the splendor of the tombs prepared for Tiy's father and mother. The funerary equipment found in their graves gave the finest concept of Eighteenth Dynasty luxury until the later discovery of Tutankhaton's tomb.

Akhenaton came from a long line of aggressive ancestors, which in his father's case had been tempered by a great capacity for love. Akhenaton and Nefertiti were being reared in an atmosphere of deep affection. In his every act as a monarch Amenhotep III showed his devotion to Tiy, who was his confidante and companion as well as his queen. Strong, affectionate, and kind, he set a pattern in fealty that would be followed by the young prince who would be king of Egypt.

The reign of Amenhotep III, like his domestic life, was marked by its serenity. Only once, when Akhenaton was a year old, had Amenhotep been forced to revert to the ancestral role of warrior, mount his gold chariot, and lead an army southward out of Thebes and into Nubia to quell a disturbance there among the tribes. He returned with much bounty and seven hundred black slaves, a victory that obviously did not deserve the lavish panegyrics awarded it by the priests of Amon, who were always made vocal by shared wealth.

King Amenhotep was a reluctant warrior but he was an enthusiastic hunter of lions and wild cattle. Hunting had always been the favorite sport, next to war, of Akhenaton's ancestors. He and Nefertiti would remember how as children they watched King Amenhotep set out from Thebes on one of the royal safaris. A boat would be provisioned with food, hunting chariots and equipment, horses and dogs, and the king and his fellow sportsmen, all of the nobility, would be rowed to some spot on the Nile where wild game had been sighted. Once Akhenaton's father killed 170 wild bulls in a single day, and a scarab commemorates his having slain more than 100 lions. These he shot from his chariot with arrows, which was no sport for the timid.

Queen Tiy's name is found beside her husband's on such scarabs, and it is suspected Akhenaton's energetic mother accompanied her husband on the dangerous excursions.

Their son took no more interest in hunting than he would in war. Akhenaton would never be shown wearing the copper cuff that protected the arm of the dedicated archer from the rebound of the bow string. But his father and grandfather were master archers; Amenhotep II was portrayed as being the mightiest bowman of his time. Other ancestors were shown holding sickles with which they slew "chiefs of all foreign lands."

From the beginning Akhenaton was a prince of peace. His chief inheritance from his lusty parents was a love of beauty and of architecture.

Amenhotep and Tiy ruled in an Egypt economically and politically secure, and were free to develop its architectural glories in ways intended to make their names live forever. Queen Tiy was an enthusiastic supporter of her husband's construction plans and later she would help advance the architectural works of Akhenaton and Nefertiti.

The hopes of this interesting pair and of all Egypt were centered on the boy Akhenaton who had been born in the fourth year of Amenhotep's reign. At the appearance of a male heir to carry on the Eighteenth Dynasty, festivals were held everywhere in Egypt and bread and beer was distributed to the people. The proud father, holding the emblem of life, the Ankh, uttered the most solemn wish an Egyptian father could make for a newborn child: "May you exist for millions of years, like the sun."

The sun was of supreme importance to Akhenaton by the time he was twelve years old.

The young prince was the adoration of all Egypt.

Akhenaton did not greatly resemble his father and mother. They were sturdy; he was apparently frail. They were joyous extroverts; he was thoughtful and withdrawn. His features faintly resembled Tiy's, although her face was round and his elongated, but he lacked her gusty good humor. He did not have his parents appetite for energetic living.

As their first-born and evidently only son Akhenaton's authority in the palace was undisputed.

He had one full sister, Beketaton, who would follow him to

Amarna. There is mention of another sister, Isis, and Queen Tiy may have had other children who did not survive.

There were other royal children in the palace at Thebes. King Amenhotep married the princesses sent him by their royal fathers for political reasons. Their positions and their children were respected, and several were to fill important places in Nefertiti's and Akhenaton's lives, but unless these children married royalty they could never hope to rule. The only recognized children of King Amenhotep were those born of his "Great Royal Wife," Queen Tiy, and among these the boy Akhenaton was closest to his parents and the sole heir to Egypt.

And Nefertiti—who was she? A petted, pampered, exquisite little pawn, she was being pushed forward on the chessboard of Egypt by irresistible forces. For a long time it would not be understood why this was done to her, and by whom.

As many theories have been offered concerning Nefertiti as once clustered around the name of Queen Tiy. Like Tiy, her origin was veiled. Unlike Tiy, no scarabs commemorate the great days of Nefertiti's life. But, as with Tiy, there came eventually the testimony of the tombs.

One authority argued that the only possible explanation of Nefertiti was that she was born to King Amenhotep and Queen Tiy and therefore was a full-blood sister to Akhenaton. This cannot be true. Unlike the lives of Nefertiti and Akhenaton, those of Amenhotep and Tiy were amply documented and the records remain. If a daughter of Tiy, Nefertiti's birth would be registered somewhere on the many monuments honoring that queen.

Another, more plausible, suggestion held Nefertiti to have been Akhenaton's half sister, born to his father Amenhotep by one of the Mitanni "extra" wives. This would explain the persistent belief that she was of Mitannian blood.

These theories had adherents since it was argued that only royal ancestry could explain the power achieved by Nefertiti; that only a sister or half sister would have been considered divine enough to have married the son of the king.

Still, Tiy was non-royal, and she achieved absolute power.

It must be kept in mind that the mores of ancient Egypt were not like ours. The family was all-important. Brothers and sisters married to preserve the ancestral strain. This was customary amongst the poor and even more common in royal circles. It was especially prevalent during the Eighteenth Dynasty. The right to succession was through the female line, and a hereditary princess could transmit her divine powers through marriage and make a king of a husband who was not even of the nobility.

Matriarchy was strongly felt from the palace to the tenements. A wife and mother had influence. In the home she was given deference. Abroad, she was a first-class citizen. A woman could own, inherit, buy, and sell property. She could testify in court. Inheritance was through woman; a mother passed on property and titles to her oldest daughter.

But it was a woman's greatest triumph to be loved by her husband, her own and her husband's family, her children, and the gods. Her position was made the more enviable by marriage to a beloved brother. The closer the blood ties, it was believed, the deeper the love.

The results were often genealogically confusing.

The term "sister," or "brother" did not always mean a family relationship. It might be a term of endearment. In the love songs which delighted the Egyptians and which became especially tender during the Eighteenth Dynasty, the woman singer sang to her love as her "brother," while the male singer addressed his "sister." A favorite concubine might be called "sister" by her lord as a special mark of esteem.

Centuries later, Solomon would sing in his Song of Songs to "my sister, my bride." (Incidentally, many concubines married and attained respectable positions in their communities.)

We can be certain Nefertiti was no child of Tiy's, but she did follow the example set by Akhenaton's mother. Queen Tiy was one of the outstanding personalities in a long line of brilliant Eighteenth Dynasty queens. Her qualities were more subtly expressed in Nefertiti.

Each achieved supreme power through the love of the pampered oriental potentate she married.

And Nefertiti, like Tiy, was humbly born.

All attempts to prove her of royal ancestry have failed, as they failed in the case of Tiy. Apparently Nefertiti held no title in childhood beyond her own musical name.

She had a little sister, four years her junior, whose name was

Nezemmut, and who would be referred to as a princess. That title may have been given her after Nefertiti ascended the throne. No records give any premise of nobility to the two little sisters met with first in the Theban palace.

We must look elsewhere for a solution to the mystery of Nefertiti.

Wherever we follow her we meet with the brooding presence of the "powerful and mysterious Aye."

Chief scribe of the court of Thebes, as we see him first, he was to play a curious role in the life of the boy Akhenaton and cast a portentous shadow over the small figure of Nefertiti. So before attempting to solve the problem of her identity we must find the answer to another question, for who was Aye?

CHAPTER THREE

Beware the Grand Vizier!

Thebes, 1372 B.C.

The great leaders of early Egypt were ambitious men. Aye has been called "the man of destiny." He was the hero of the world's first success story—the poor boy from the country who worked his way and won.

His statues show his determination. The stark, strong features might be cast in iron. The lines of the face are deeply drawn. Under level brows the indomitable look seems to repudiate the canard that such a man could ever die.

Through five reigns, during the Eighteenth Dynasty, he was the all-powerful personality who towered and seemed to vanish and rose again.

Literary detective work is needed to follow Aye under his many names and titles in many histories. He would be an incredible man-myth in any age. His achievements are registered on stone and his name is always linked with those of the great leaders of his time.

We cannot exaggerate his importance to Nefertiti.

One of the puzzles of Egyptology has been the way authority was achieved by a man as humbly born as Aye!

He began life as the son of a commoner, one Hapu of Athribis in Lower Egypt. (At this time there were no family names in Egypt. A person was "son of," or "daughter of." A cousin would be described as "the son of the brother of the father.")

While Aye appears under other names, he himself never dropped the identifying "son of Hapu." Perhaps to honor his royal patron, Akhenaton's father, and with his permission, he lived for some years in Thebes as "Amenhotep, son of Hapu." His wife, Tiy, "the Great Nurse" also may have taken her name to honor the queen whose son she nursed.

Aye's drive to power became evident when he was a boy.

Egypt was an absolute monarchy, but in many ways it was curiously democratic, and an ambitious boy could rise from the level to which he had been born. As a rule, a son followed in the footsteps of his father. The farmer's son tended the flocks and fields, the cook's baked bread and roasted meats, the weaver's stuck to the loom and the potter's turned the wheel. Their fathers had been poor, and they would be poor and live, most of them, in crowded slums and never quite know what it was like not to go hungry.

Poverty is seldom desirable, and certainly it was not in Egypt where the privileged were fabulously rich and the majority incredibly poor. Not in money, for although gold and silver rings and strings of beads were used, money would not make its appearance for another thousand years. Purchasing power was in the produce of the land which was the Egyptian means of barter. The rules of trade were carefully laid down, weights and measures were standardized, and a man knew exactly how many sacks of goat wool and bushels of wheat would buy meat and beer for his family. The peasants tended the lands and the herds and gave much that they produced to the priests and the king.

It was only during festivals, when, due to the kindness of the king, bread and beer were distributed to the populace, that a humble Egyptian would be likely to know the pleasure of a full belly.

But if a poor boy could by some means learn to read, he need not remain poor. He could become a scribe. He would be given every opportunity to advance. Then neither he nor any of his family would ever again have to work at menial labor or know hunger.

There was a popular saying, A scribe never knows poverty!

In other countries the warrior would be the national hero. Egypt, whose people have been termed "the least warlike of antiquity," had its war heroes, but the scribe was greatly respected for he represented knowledge. The Egyptians were agriculturalists and organizers of good government. Above all they were keepers of records. Scribes kept the tally of the crops, the taxes, the official records of rich and poor. Scribes wrote the love letters, the letters sent from the living to the dead, the panegyrics on the tombs, the correspondence of the kings. Egypt owes its recorded history to the scribes.

There were no heights to which a scribe might not aspire. He could enter the government or the army. He would be invited to feasts in the palace. He might even attain in time to the position of Vizier and become a threat to the throne. Advisers of ancient Pharaohs had handed down a warning: "Beware the grand vizier!"

In time, Aye would be grand vizier.

His career began when he made up his mind to learn to read and write. This necessitated years of such arduous study that few Egyptian boys aspired to learning. Somehow Hapu's son obtained admission to one of the religious colleges run by Theban priests of Amon on the west side of the Nile.

He studied under a master scribe, who taught him first the twenty-four sign pictures of the Egyptian alphabet, of a language based on the Semitic and Nilotic, then, one by one, the more than seven hundred hieroglyphic signs, which symbolized words or, when placed together, made words. All these, once memorized, had to be used correctly in written compositions.

Essays thousands of years old have been found in Egypt, written in copybooks by students and corrected in ink by their master scribes.

The boy Aye practiced patiently over a period of years, writing first on clay tablets, then on palettes of slate, wax, wood, or ivory. As his skill improved he was permitted to write on the thin, expensive sheets of paper made from the pith of the papyrus. He carried a pen case with a sliding cover, in which were his pointed metal stylus, brushes and pens made of palm fiber, or alfa grass, or pointed sections of reeds, and small vials of the red and black ink the Egyptians had invented, using soot or red ochre with a gum base.

He must have been a serious student, this lad from the provinces. He evidently took to heart the voluminous advice handed down to generations of students by famous old-time scribes.

These were Chesterfieldian essays of "advice to the young man."

One warned the ambitious student against indulging in excesses, such as the overuse of "wine or tankards of beer," that in some cases had been followed by such reprehensible acts as "performing acrobatics on a wall . . . learning to play the flute or pluck the lyre . . . frolicking about with a bad lot of girls . . . [lying] beside a pretty girl, drenched in perfume, a garland of flowers round your neck, beating on your stomach, reeling and rolling about. . . ."

The picture this evokes evidently had no appeal to Aye. Drunkenness was no disgrace, but it interfered with ambition.

He would have been more likely to have memorized the terms of advice laid down by another ancient teacher who listed famed Egyptian scribes "whose names became everlasting."

This homily urged young men: "Be a scribe. Put it in thy heart, that thy name may fare similarly. More effective is a book than a decorated stone wall . . . A man is perished, his corpse is dust, and all his relations are cast to the ground . . . it is writing that makes him remembered."

Aye would be remembered not only for his writings which were to preserve much of Egypt's history but also by stone walls and costly tombs, for his would be the singular honor of possessing two graves.

The homily lists the great and ancient scribes including the greatest, Imhotep, who wrote the first of the "wisdom literature." His maxims, once revered, have not survived. He was also astronomer, magician, physician, and architect, and as secretary of state and chief architect to King Zoser (or Djoser,) in the Third Dynasty, about 2700 B.C., Imhotep designed and had built for the king Egypt's first pyramid, the magnificent Step Pyramid at Sakkara in its complex of walls and temples and courts. It stands today, an architectural triumph left us from the ancient world, the world's first structure built of stone.

Imhotep's statues show him to have been a strong and purposeful man. He holds no emblem of power, only the roll of papyrus paper that was the symbol of a scribe. This was modesty, as while living he achieved power second only to that of his king and after his death he was worshiped as a god by physicians and scribes. Young scribes anxious to get on in the world sought the ghostly influence of Imhotep, and it is certain that the ambitious Aye offered up many prayers begging for his intervention.

Aye would also have addressed many fervid prayers to Thoth,

the god of learning and patron of scribes, since he had invented writing and served as secretary to the other gods. It was Thoth who had written down the wisdom of the gods in sacred writings the students had to copy endlessly.

Thoth must have granted special favor, for when we first meet with Aye he had become the Imhotep of the Eighteenth Dynasty.

Thoth appeared in many forms, so his images might be shaped as a bird-headed man, as that sacred bird the ibis, as a solemn, sagacious-appearing ape, or as a dog-headed baboonlike animal. Aye kept sacred images of the god in his offices, archives, or palace schoolroom, and small good-luck amulets of the god would be prudently tucked into a fold of his kilt at the waist.

Aye learned to take the scribe's oath, swearing "by the ka of Thoth." Every Egyptian god and citizen had his "ka," which was the vital force, a sort of *Doppelgänger,* or duplicate of self. A person was not likely to meet this second self face to face, although it was firmly believed this could happen. It was not an experience to be desired.

Learning to write took Aye many years, but there was a great deal more for him to learn before he was awarded the scroll of the scribe. He had to master mathematics. The Egyptians had a form of "everyday" arithmetic that served them well. They were experts in fractions, even those of large denominations. Examples have been found written on papyrus that would be acceptable in modern classrooms. One begins: "If so many loaves of bread are to be divided between so many men . . ."

Aye took courses in geometry. A scribe was obliged to know the Egyptian formulas that included the square root of the triangle, cone, cylinder, and pyramid, and to be able to square eight ninths of the diameter of the circle. This may have led Aye's facile mind to the study of architecture.

He was obliged to study astronomy, which was one of the most respected of the sciences. Contrary to popular belief, astrology was unknown in early Egypt. Futures were forecast, not by stars, but by a study of days, dreams, and other influences, such as portents, that might be considered lucky or unlucky. But interest in the heavens was based on pure science. Our knowledge of Egypt's history is due to the Egyptians' having set their dates by the stars. The solar calendar of 365 days was invented by Egyptian astronomers in the year 4241 B.C. It has been called their greatest scientific achievement. It was not exact, but it served the Egyptians well, and, introduced to the Romans by Julius Caesar, became in time the ancestor of our own.

Above all, Aye had to memorize the endless lists of the gods, the complicated religious faith of Egypt, and the interminable rituals, prayers, and hymns. He had to copy accurately the sacred writings set down hundreds of years before.

The years of study and the prayers were well repaid, for when Akhenaton and Nefertiti were children in the palace at Thebes, one of its chief dignitaries was Aye, son of Hapu, who held, among other important offices, that of chief royal scribe to King Amenhotep.

At any hour of day or night Aye might be summoned into the godlike presence of the king. He walked with dignity, empty-handed, while a slave came behind him bearing the pen case and palette. Seated cross-legged before the king, balancing his palette on his knees, Aye took down in elaborate hieroglyphs, writing from right to left, the profundities uttered by the king. In turn he might question, suggest, even advise. He had charge of the royal archives where he filed the king's correspondence. He knew all the court secrets. No other non-royal person was so close to the throne.

Carved on his statue is Aye's own explanation of his rise to power. It is the frank confession of an opportunist and diplomat. Before his determined advance opportunities opened, and he took advantage of them all.

And always, as we see him, he is pushing before him a gay, delightful little creature whose promise he was first to recognize, and whose advance would be his own.

Aye credited his own success to his "exceptional knowledge" of the hieroglyphs and the sacred writings.

"I was initiated into the affairs of the sacred book," the text runs. "I beheld the spiritual matters of Thoth and I was versed in their mysteries. I unfolded all their intricacies. One [King Amenhotep] took counsel of me in events that pertained to him."

Aye was not content with being chief royal scribe and having the confidence of the king. His plans, for himself and for Egypt, stretched far ahead of the man and his time.

Now, in the childhood of Nefertiti and Akhenaton, Aye was well on his way. He was a priest of Amon who led processions in the sacred festivals. He was a courtier with the right to hold his own gold baton in the presence of the king. In the court processions he carried the royal ostrich feather fan "on the right of the king." He was, in effect, secretary of state to Amenhotep, and entrusted with all military and state affairs. He became ambassador and went on mysterious missions to far-off places, "even as far as Babylonia."

He received from Amenhotep the high ranking military title of chief master of the royal horse. This made him head of the king's cavalry, an impressive show of chariots, horses and men. He was also chief military commander, in charge of all the king's armies. One of his duties was that of chief conscription officer.

Conscription was new in Egypt, and may have been initiated by Aye, as it had been unknown before the Eighteenth Dynasty. Now an ordinary sight in Thebes was the searching of homes by soldiers for young men of draft age, who were marched rapidly off by hundreds through the streets by officers brandishing battle-axes, to be trained for military duty. All this was by orders of Aye.

"I mustered the young men," he proclaimed in his tomb.

His military duties had been assumed soon after Akhenaton's birth. Of King Amenhotep's sole war sally into Nubia, Aye boasted: "I showered the peasants with the best of the booty which his majesty had taken on the battlefield."

Now that Akhenaton and Nefertiti were twelve and eleven, they must have taken pride in the military spectacles staged by Aye on the plains outside of the city to demonstrate the power of the Egyptian Army. The dazzling central figure of this tremendous display that covered an area of miles, was the kindly, familiar presence of the boy's father, majestic and terrifying in the flashing panoply of war. In his gold chariot, perhaps wearing gleaming mail, King Amenhotep was surrounded on every side by the officers of the elite troops, all splendidly outfitted for battle, all driving chariots of electrum (which was a mixture of silver and gold).

These chariot battalions represented mechanized warfare as organized by Aye. Chariots, invented by the Sumerians circa 3000 B.C. had been introduced into Egypt about four hundred years before. Now Egyptian chariotry was the most famous in the world, in display, sports, peace, and war.

The most splendid chariot, next to the king's in position and in grandeur, was that of Aye, commander of all the king's armies and of Nefertiti's destiny. Lined up around them, in formidable array, was a well-organized standing military force of many divisions that guaranteed the peace of Egypt. The thousands of foot soldiers had been trained to march as one. Some were black troops from Nubia. All were skilled in the craft of war. Some carried spears and battle-axes and slingshots, but the majority were archers trained to fire their arrows in volleys, wave on wave, during an advance. All wore brief kilts and wigs and were barefoot and only the spearsmen were protected with painted shields.

The weapons were bronze and copper. The king might wear at his belt a dagger made of iron. Iron was newly discovered and more valuable than gold.

The soldiers, trained to the quick, must have strained in their ranks during these demonstrations, eager to be off to battle and sever the hands of fallen enemies that could be brought back to Thebes and exchanged for gold. Equally tense were the lean-flanked, broad-collared hounds, and lions brought from Africa and Mesopotamia, all trained to follow their king into battle, and standing quivering and taut-throated against their leashes, held back by powerful slaves.

Akhenaton and Nefertiti would see fewer of these military demonstrations during this time of their growing, for there would be no more battles for King Amenhotep. He disliked warlike display even in times of peace. The boy's parents were devotees of peace. Their magnificent empire did not need defending. But beauty can always be built on beauty, and Amenhotep and his queen had plans for displays that would be more lasting than any wars.

Since they had no need to add to the dominions of Egypt,

they returned to the dream of every Egyptian Pharaoh, to create monuments that would make his name endure forever.

Aye read the hearts of his royal sponsors. Aye, the pragmatist, proceeded to give aid to the furtherance of the dream.

He was that type of genius, rare in any generation, who seemingly absorbs with ease all the knowledge of his time. Leonardo da Vinci was such a man. Aye found time away from his many duties to study architecture. He mastered that knowledge. King Amenhotep and Queen Tiy made him their chief royal architect and put him in charge of all their projects.

Of this new responsibility, Aye wrote, "I acted in accordance with what he [the King] said and I accomplished what he placed in my care. I found it beneficial . . ."

Beneficial to Aye, to Nefertiti, and to all who have shared the lasting beauty he gave to Egypt!

The ruins of Thebes are the most magnificent in the world. How much of this splendor do we owe to Aye?

The city, the country, the man and woman on the throne, and the growing interest and influence of the boy-prince, were exactly right for such a man as Aye. During his time as chief royal architect Thebes became the world's first great monumental city. The tremendous surge of construction began when Akhenaton and Nefertiti were children.

As chief architect, Aye was not content merely to draw the plans for the temples and monuments that were to preserve the memories of the boy's father and mother. He took charge of their construction. He was given free rein by the king. He had at his command inexhaustible supplies of slave labor and building funds. Evidently one of his duties was to insure the supply of such funds, for he writes in his memoirs: "I assessed the houses. . . . my pen recorded the number of millions . . ."

The people paid for the glorification of Thebes with taxes or their working lives.

The stone monuments of Egypt bear the names of kings, and memories of the nameless thousands who were their builders. Architecture had come a long way since Neolithic man built his first mud huts beside the Nile. Since the country was virtually treeless, the Egyptians were the first people in the world to build in stone. Imhotep had been first, with his Third Dynasty Step

Pyramid at Sakkara, but in the Fourth Dynasty (about 2500 B.C.), other Egyptian architects built the Great Pyramid at Giza for King Khufu (known to the Greeks as Cheops,) which alone remains of the Seven Wonders of the World.

For twenty years, to the whir of the lash and sounds of human humiliation, 100,000 men toiled, strained and died, raising 2,300,000 blocks of chiseled stone averaging 2½ tons each, to a pyramid laid with such precision, to a fraction of a degree, that a blade could not pass between the stones. Mechanical aid was of the simplest—levers, probably, and wooden rollers.

This was raised to honor the king, whose sacred mummified body was hidden deep in a maze of underground rooms filled with treasure under the stone mountain where it was presumed to be safe forever.

But when archaeologists finally found their way to the underground palace and discovered the secret of Cheops, the rooms had been looted, and the granite sarcophagus was empty.

When Akhenaton and Nefertiti were children, Egyptian architecture was approaching the height of its glory, and that glory centered in Thebes. It was a city of temples and monuments. The Egyptian architects had mastered the values of symmetry and line. They had created the pylon tower, the so-called Roman arch, the colonnade and the soaring, floral columns that were to become symbolical of Greek architecture. Both Greece and Rome would owe much to Egypt and its pioneer skills in architecture, art, and science.

Aye was carrying on in Thebes in the great tradition of his idol, Imhotep.

In every way Aye was imitating the career of the scribe turned architect who had accomplished in the Third Dynasty what Aye was doing for the Eighteenth. Both men were fortunate in serving kings who were passionately interested in advancing the architectural beauty of Egypt.

Aye was a perfectionist. He had driven himself without mercy into an understanding of many professions and now he drove thousands of workmen into construction work as splendid as it would be lasting. The Theban monuments were built by the finest stonemasons to be found in Egypt. Blocks of sandstone or granite weighing 200 tons each were lifted into walls of temples intended to stand forever. On the outer walls were carved in relief scenes of the king in battle, and the inner walls showed him offering homage to the gods.

Aye struck terror into the hearts of the foremen and their gangs as he drove about the construction areas in his chariot, representing in his sturdy person the majesty of the king.

With him on these trips would be a small, slight, gravely interested boy who was Akhenaton. And perhaps, since the boy and girl were seldom separated, another fascinated child passenger would be Nefertiti.

All construction in the city appealed to the imaginations of the two children. In turn Akhenaton and Nefertiti would build, as the boy's parents were doing, but on a wider, more extravagant, unprecedented scale.

Most of the magnificent building done at Thebes at this time was planned and constructed for King Amenhotep by his chief royal architect who was also his "favorite and friend." In his tomb Aye would claim credit for much that was completed before Akhenaton was twelve.

Amenhotep and Tiy were not content with keeping Egypt prosperous and at peace. Their reign was marked by its serenity and security and without war threats of any kind, and they were free to throw their tremendous energies and resources into the projects planned by Aye. As a result they became famed builders of temples. Not only in the capital, but as far north as Memphis and south as Nubia, temples and statues were raised that bore the names of Amenhotep III and Tiy, and that of their chief god, Amon.

There was already a splendid temple to Amon in the northern section of Thebes which was known as Karnak.

Its ruins are haunted by memories of many dramatic events in the lives of Nefertiti and Akhenaton. In its dim and cavernous hall they worshiped as children, awed by a knowledge of all that had taken place there that had influenced the history of the Eighteenth Dynasty. Here Aye presided over his own synod of priests of Amon. And here Nefertiti and Akhenaton were prepared in solemn ritual for the responsibilities they must assume.

The boy's father was grateful to Amon for the successes of his reign and his personal life. He did not think the temple to the god was adequate in a city as large as Thebes. He conferred with his chief architect. In Luxor, the southern section of Thebes, stood the ruins of a small temple that had been built to Amon back in the Twelfth Dynasty. Using this as a base, King Amenhotep had Aye rebuild upon it the greatest of all the king's monuments, the Temple of Luxor, dedicated to Amon. "Built on ground covered with silver and placed on a bed of incense," this temple possessed halls and colonnades of a new beauty. Magnificent stone columns lifted far above the eyes and burst into the shape of flowers, the predominant being the lotus. We may be certain the girl Nefertiti was present at the dedication of this temple, and that Akhenaton and his parents led the rituals, and that Aye was there, with his wife, to take pride in the stone miracle born of his energetic brain.

"The divine master of works," was one of Aye's new names.

The Theban ruins show us why such architects as Aye were paid every honor by their kings, and even deified.

And Amenhotep ordered the building of still another temple, dedicated to the goddess Maat, which still stands. He and Queen Tiy, and later Akhenaton and Nefertiti, had a special devotion to this female deity who was in charge of much that is respected by good people, such as truth and law and order.

Maat's temple was near the great Temple of Amon at Karnak, which was linked to the Temple of Amon at Luxor by a garden one and a half miles long. In the garden the king had ordered excavated a large artificial lake, fed by water from the Nile.

Between the two Amon temples and running down to the Nile through the park was the Avenue of Rams, sentried on one side by images of the sacred animal, which was Amon's, carved from stone. The other side was lined with sphinxes.

All Thebes, on both the east and west banks of the river, was one unbroken expanse of garden. Every building had its garden save the stone graves that concealed the bodies of the dead. Armies of peon labor tended the trees and plants, many of which were descendants of rare specimens brought back from foreign lands by Akhenaton's conqueror ancestors, that had changed and acquired new beauty in the soft climate of Egypt. It was said that every Egyptian loved flowers. Nefertiti's passion for them is shown in her portraits and the flowerlike jewelry she wore.

Out of miles of bloom, plumaged with palm and acacia, rose the columned temples and the palace, the obelisks flashing their gold sheathings in the sun, the elegant châteaux and villas of the nobles, and the royal funerary temples with their doors of gleaming gold. In the east beyond the city were the peaks that shielded Thebes from the desert, and beyond the city to the west other clifflike peaks hid the Valley of the Kings.

With unlimited wealth and man power, Akhenaton and his forebears made Thebes into the most magnificent of cities.

Like all Egyptian cities, it showed the influence of Babylon. As in Mesopotamia, even the homes of the rich were built of mud bricks, but the Egyptian architects had added to the flat-roofed adobe structures such distinctive flourishes as stone floral columns, red granite pillars shaped like papyrus, and paneled walls.

Theban artists had combined with the architects to further the city's beauty. The once glorious colors of ruined Thebes have been scoured away by centuries of wind-driven sand, but the areas of brilliancy that remain hint at a beauty that cannot be imagined.

Across the river from Luxor, in the western section of Thebes, King Amenhotep and Queen Tiy presided over a cheerful royal household in their large, comfortable, and handsome palace. Here Nefertiti spent her childhood.

Her appearance in the palace is as mysterious as the man who placed her there.

As easily as he did all else, the determined Aye was directing the course of the beautiful little girl Nefertiti.

CHAPTER FOUR

In the Palace

Thebes, 1372 B.C.

The palace at Thebes where the two children were growing up was a place of beauty. Akhenaton would attest to the happiness he had known there when he built a palace for Nefertiti at Amarna that would be almost a duplicate of the one built by his father for Queen Tiy.

Aye designed and built the Theban palace.

A house constructed for the world's leading family might be expected to be made of stone. Temples and tombs were of stone since they were intended to last forever. But life was temporary, so the house in which one lived need serve the owner only through his lifetime. Egyptian architecture had reached its peak, but the Pharaohs continued to build their palaces of wood or sun-dried mud bricks. Since they loved beauty, these modest structures were made enchanting with stone pillars, painted wooden beams, floors and ceilings, and pillars and door frames of stone.

The Theban palace was built of wood, but it made a magnificent appearance with its gaily painted outer walls and tall cedar staves planted before the entrance that flew the blue and white pennants of the king. Over the front entrance hung a columned balcony where the royal ones could loll at cushioned ease and watch the colorful craft move, north and south, along the Nile.

This was the "window of appearances" that was part of every Egyptian palace. On it the royal personages made their ceremonial appearances before the public, or held presentation affairs for their favorites. These were gift-giving sessions, where the ones to be rewarded, standing on the ground below, caught the gifts tossed down to them by their royal benefactors.

There were many apartments in the palace. King Amenhotep, Queen Tiy, Akhenaton, the princesses, and the "extra wives," each had separate quarters, completely staffed. Nefertiti's and Akhenaton's sister, had their own apartments.

There were many state rooms, offices, stores and courts. The palace was not only the royal residence; it was the seat of government.

Every room in the family section of the palace was a masterpiece of color and design.

Ceilings and walls were not frescoed but painted with distemper, with such realistic scenes as papyrus marshes, so that a room seemed to be an extension of the outside world. The green walls were relieved by the realistic flashing bodies of birds in flight.

Other walls were tiled a wonderful deep blue, traced with designs in gold. The floors on which the two children played were brightly painted with designs of the animals and birds these people loved.

And every article of furniture in this palace marked it as lived in by a people set apart from all others in their time by an appreciation of luxury and comfort and beauty. Each article in use had its own individual beauty; others were designed for beauty alone.

Every window and door opened upon gardens.

Before the palace, and sweeping down to the west bank of the Nile, was the park Amenhotep had built for the pleasure of Queen Tiy, and to add to her amusement he had constructed within the garden an artificial lake, six thousand feet long.

That had been a few years before, and since children were always included in family celebrations, Akhenaton and Nefertiti were surely present at the jubilee that took place when the lake was completed and filled with water channeled in from the Nile. This was a new festival, introduced by the king to please Queen Tiy, and featured a great procession making its way to the lake, where, after formal ceremonies, the royal family boarded the new pleasure barge, built for the queen, and named "The Aton Gleams," in honor of the sun. While the barge made its first triumphal tour of the lake, the court musicians followed on shore, singing and playing to the sweep of the oars.

The occasion was considered of such importance that the king had scarabs issued commemorating the completion of the lake and the festival, which from that time on was celebrated every year and may have been the first of the lake festivals that were so popular in Egypt. It was repeated every October 4, with feasting, merrymaking, and the ceremonial tour of the lake, and was known as the Festival of the Solar Disk.

To the Egyptians, who loved festivals and were blessed by at least two a month, this was just one more joyous holiday. The priests of Amon may have grumbled even then.

The naming of Queen Tiy's pleasure barge for the sun disk has raised some suspicion that she may have been responsible for Akhenaton's devotion to Aton. Queen Tiy, following in the tradition of the iron-willed Eighteenth Dynasty queens, was an honest woman and frank in showing her interest in the god of the sun. She had built a small temple to the Aton near the palace, and the two children would have worshiped there with her, Nefertiti rapt and wide-eyed, following the queen's every ritual movement, and Akhenaton with a strange, spiritual intensity. By this means Queen Tiy may have fostered the seeds of a rebellion that would in time rive Egypt and exile her only son in centuries of oblivion.

It was in ways such as this that the boy was introduced to the disastrous rivalry between Amon, the chief god of Thebes, who, when combined with Ra, was Amon-Ra the Sun, and Aton, a hitherto minor Theban god who was the actual face of the sun.

The average Egyptian did not dispute this delicate theological difference, which only a mind as acute as Aye's might be expected to understand.

But the boy was not an average person and it would not be long before it would be shown that when very young he had made up his mind to understand the ways of the gods. Many and curious were the questions he must have asked of Aye. As for King Amenhotep, he never wavered in his devotion to Amon. All that was being built in Thebes carried his name and Tiy's and that of "Amon, his father." The image of Amon was raised in a thousand places by Aye in the name of the king.

It is known that Aye, while chief architect of Amenhotep III, built for the king the royal palace at Thebes, the colonnaded temple at Luxor; had carved for the royal family many statues, reliefs; ordered wall and funerary paintings, and built for Amenhotep his greatest monument, the splendid funerary temple Kom el Haitan.

The temple was Amenhotep's crowning achievement. It was planned as the eternal home where he and his beloved Tiy would play host to the gods and still be able to keep a protective watch over living Egyptians until the end of time. Nothing was left out that might be desired after death by way of comfort, luxury, and beauty to delight sealed eyes, for it was part of the magic of death that one regained youth by dying, and all the awareness that goes with youth. So a king's mortuary was his future palace, and was not built of wood, like the one lived in, but of everlasting stone.

Amenhotep and Tiy were a hearty middle-aged couple enjoying life, but they knew that death was merely an interruption to present happiness, and once its slight annoyance was over and the soul weighed, life went on more joyously than ever. So the eternal palace Aye planned for them was an object of beauty all the family enjoyed, and we may imagine many royal excursions were taken before its site was established, north of the family palace, and toward the western hills where was hidden the Valley of the Kings.

Akhenaton's ancestors, all the kings of the Eighteenth Dynasty, were buried in the Valley of the Kings. Since times unremembered Egyptian royalty had been buried there hastily and in secret, in rock crypts carefully concealed. The bodies were hidden, mummified, and covered with jewels; it was the "ka" or other self that would continue to visit in the mortuary temples away from the graves. The bodies were hidden to protect them from the robbers who even then were the curse of Egypt, but the graves were systematically entered and despoiled.

Many of the kings were as forgotten as their graves. Who could know all their names! One had ruled only three days.

Many royal mortuary temples stood before the Valley of the Kings, among them, against the cliffs, Deir el-Bahari, built by the strongminded Queen Hatshepsut, who in the preceding dynasty had usurped all the privileges of a king, including that of building her own magnificent temple. It remains today as one of the most beautiful of all Egypt's ancient buildings. Amenhotep III chose the site of his own eternal home to the northeast of his

own palace and nearer the river, and after Kom el Haitan was
completed by Aye, the king described it in his own words as:
"An august temple on the west side of Thebes, an everlasting
fortress, a possession of eternity, of fine sandstone worked with
gold throughout."

Completed, the enormous building was oriental in splendor.
Aye not only built the temple, but he furnished it sumptuously.
Years later, not far from this place, he would hastily furnish a
grave for the boy-king Tutankhaton.

It is known that the huge, bronze-hinged doors were of costly
cedar from Lebanon, overlaid with sheets of bronze that were
damascened in silver and gold; the center motif was the figure
of Amon. And within, other monuments in silver and gold were
set to the glory of Amon, and statues and steles and obelisks of
silver and gold, encrusted with "every august precious stone." All
these were for Amon, that he might watch forever over the bliss-
ful after life, as capably as he did the present, of King Amenhotep
and Queen Tiy.

And it was Aye who saw all this was accomplished without
flaw, and who placed before the temple the boulevard leading
up to the splendid doors that was known as the Avenue of Jackals,
guarded by stone images of this animal of Anubis, who was god
of the dead. Amenhotep, Akhenaton, and other Egyptian kings,
saw themselves as larger than human and ordered themselves per-
petuated on gigantic scale. Aye ordered carved and raised before
the temple the two gigantic seated statues of Amenhotep that
were the wonders of the age and which the Greeks were to call
the Colossi of Memnon (Amenhotep). To this day men wonder
how Aye, "divine master of works," raised those mammoth statues
to their stone feet. The Colossi awe now as then. Each was about
fifty feet high and carved from a single block of sandstone
hauled by sledges and man power from Red Mountain almost
438 miles away. One statue, by some means the Egyptians
placidly accepted as the usual miracle, reputedly had the power
of making strange musical sounds when warmed by the first rays
of Aton, the sun. It became famed as "the singing Memnon."

Aye boasts of the completion of this project: "I ordered statues
to be hewn from stone and had them set up. I built a ship and

transported it upstream, and it was erected in the great temple, to endure like the sky."

This must have been one of the funerary boats built for kings to carry them on their journey into the underworld.

All this was done in Akhenaton's boyhood, when his parents were still young enough to take joy in their building. The two children, standing dwarfed under the towering Colossi, must have been impressed by the immensity of this presentation of the king who was to one the lenient father-king and to the other the tender king-father-image. The gigantic statues of the Egyptian kings exaggerated only in size. In actual portrayal they were true to life, as mummies of the originals have shown. The immense head of Amenhotep III in the British Museum is considered one of the finest existing portraits made in ancient Egypt, while Akhenaton's retention of the colossal convention has been shown by the heads discovered at Karnak.

Nothing is left of the magnificent funerary temple of Amenhotep III but its sandstone foundation, the discovery of which was one of the great triumphs of archaeology. But it had been built, as was all that was built in Amenhotep's name, to last in his own words, "for a million millions of years."

Aye did his best to carry out that order.

Behind the towering Colossi and at the entrance of the great temple was a jewel-encrusted stele bearing the figure of Amon, and words that must have burned into the consciousness of the boy Akhenaton. They were written by his father the king:

"My majesty has done these things [to last for] millions of years, and I know they will abide in the earth."

These words by King Amenhotep are often compared to those on the fragment described by Shelley as bearing the name of Ozymandias, king of kings, and the command:

"Look on my works, ye Mighty, and despair!"

Nothing remained but the fragment.

Nothing remains of King Amenhotep's temple that Aye built to last forever save the two battered figures of the Colossi in the lonely field; tribute to a great king's glory, and the genius of Aye.

We now find the mysterious figure of Aye far on the road to eminence. He was the most powerful man in Egypt after the king. He was royal scribe, priest, courtier, fan bearer, ambassador, keeper of the royal archives, commander of the king's armies and his chief architect.

He was many men in one and was said to be the wisest man in Egypt. As a seer, he was believed to foretell coming events. This may have been due to his analytical knowledge of politics and people.

He had one more responsibility which was the most important of all. He was the tutor of Akhenaton.

King Amenhotep and Queen Tiy showed their confidence in this extraordinary man when they placed their only son in his care. The thoughtful boy was the future of Egypt, and that future, along with the lad's mental and moral development, was turned over to Aye.

Aye would be given credit for this, and also for guiding Nefertiti to her high destiny.

He was a dominant personality to the two children, and he would always be with them, mysterious, ruthless, implacable, guarding their rights and his own.

So, during these important early years, he was adviser confidante, and teacher, and a power behind the throne.

The two playmates were approaching maturity. Children grew up rapidly in the hot climate of Egypt. There was much for Akhenaton and Nefertiti to learn in preparation for the august place they would shortly occupy. Thebes was the city of a thousand delights, but their lives would not be all pleasure. Tremendous responsibilities would be theirs, both in marriage and on the throne.

The bird eyes of the image of Thoth watched over the palace schoolroom (there would be such a room later at Amarna) where the boy-prince bent his studious head over papyrus and palette and Aye took time from his other manifold duties to revert to his original role of scribe and instruct Akhenaton in the reading and writing he had been taught when he was a boy.

It is likely that Nefertiti sat, small and demure, clutching her own dainty writing palette, at the side of the boy-prince during these lessons. Girls in royal households were often taught to read and write, as Nefertiti's own daughters would be later at Amarna, either by Aye or under his jurisdiction. It is a fair guess that she was given adequate education in preparation for the exalted role she was to play.

She was a lovely, flowerlike child, and ambition was planted in her early by Aye, with the encouragement of the king and queen. At present she was pliable and amiable, a true child of happiness. Only disaster, far in the future, would reveal the core of iron in this delicate girl. But Aye knew. He was her mentor, councilor and guide, and he was a man whose eye was always on the future. He knew her way to power was through the reedy boy who, in a land where people married early, had already chosen her to share his future throne.

Aye's shrewd, stern authority would have kept Nefertiti to her lessons. Equally watchful, and always with her, was his wife, whose chief duty was to keep close watch on the girl who was their special charge; hence her title, Tiy the great royal nurse. Actually she acted as governess to Nefertiti.

The entire Theban court must have kept knowing watch over Nefertiti at this time. Farsighted flattery and fawning would have been hers. Those who were her sponsors must have been satisfied as she continued to bud in charm and beauty. Among the watchers none was more keenly observant than Aye. His plans for her were limitless. They were not only for her. He knew this petted, adorable child could be his future wand to power. And beyond his advantageous position as Nefertiti's mentor, he had another, more intimate hold over the girl that would not be revealed for many centuries, and then by the testimony of the tombs.

It is not likely that Nefertiti spent more time in the schoolroom than it would take to ground her in a rudimentary knowledge of reading and writing. She had more important lessons. Slipping out of the stern presence of Aye, with Tiy the nurse at her heels, Nefertiti would find herself happier in Queen Tiy's perfumed and luxurious section of the palace, where Tiy's palace steward, her personal scribe (secretary), slaves, and personal maids—literally hundreds of them—milled about in joyous confusion preparing the imperious, volatile Tiy for her ceremonial appearances, public or private, at the side of the king. The wide, innocent gaze of Nefertiti would absorb the lengthy rituals of bathing and dressing, all done before an absorbed audience, un-til the final breathless moment of adjusting on the shaven queenly head the crown with its emblems of the two Egypts. All this was carried on to the sounds of song and music and lively chatter, and a bright little girl of eleven, listening to the gossip of court and boudoir, could learn far more of things a young queen should know than ever she would in the schoolroom, taught by Aye.

But Akhenaton, left alone with Aye, was drinking in the wis-dom offered by the wisest man in Egypt.

The prince was a boy who thirsted for knowledge. Aye as teacher was the parents' perfect choice. Centuries later, young scribes preparing for examinations would tip preliminary glasses to the ghost of Aye, beseeching aid, with the splashed libation of wine, from this scribe of scribes in the other world. Akhenaton, Aye's most celebrated pupil, was the first to revere him, for from Aye the boy would learn many things that would make him into the sort of man and king he was to be.

In all matters civic, temporal, religious, and moral, Aye was the chief instructor of Akhenaton. Akhenaton would profit from his father's example and his mother's shrewd advice. But much that would influence the future of Akhenaton and Egypt could only have been taught to him by Aye.

He doubtless gave the boy a smattering of astronomy and, from the cushioned balcony outside the palace in the dark-blue Egyptian night, pointed out the patterned movements of the stars all knew were torches set by the gods.

It was from Aye, as well as from his parents, that Akhenaton absorbed much of the passion for architecture he would be able to indulge when he became king. The boy was fascinated by the magnificent buildings rising around them in Thebes, and Aye, as their architect, instilled in Akhenaton a love of building that would have far-reaching and poignant results.

Out of his own endless store of knowledge, Aye shared with the youthful future king many interests, art, architecture, poetry, nature, the solar manifestations, and the mysteries of the gods. It was in this last study, that of religion, that Akhenaton would uncover forces that were to shake the foundations of Egypt.

Akhenaton as king was to be the religious leader of Egypt under
Amon. He would preside over the religious ceremonies in the
great Temple of Amon, across the river at Karnak. As a priest of
Amon, it was Aye's duty to instruct the young prince in his future spiritual responsibilities. And these were serious teachings,
which were intended to guide Akhenaton, not only through life,
but into the next world. There were ceremonies, chants, invoca-
tions, and rituals of many kinds to be learned, and each had its
special implication, its sacred inner meaning.

So Aye taught the boy-prince the intricate religious pattern set
down by Amon, as voiced by generations of Amon's priests.

We can imagine Aye, iron-jawed, flint-eyed, seated cross-
legged before the boy whose power over him was actually that
of life and death, exhorting Akhenaton out of his own inexhaustible wisdom and listening in turn to the long, slow thoughts of
the boy.

And Aye, the all-wise, must have known from the beginning
that this Akhenaton was not like other boys. The thoughts of the
long-jawed, serious stripling were unlike those of other Egyptian
schoolboys. Not only Akhenaton's royal birthright made him different, but a spiritual arrogance—a difference of heart and mind.
Akhenaton was a ponderer. An asker of questions. A doubter,
a dreamer, a writer of poetry. He told his poems to Aye—who
wrote them down and saved them. The slender, serious boy
pinned Aye with sharp questions. He could not accept certain
dogma accepted by all others in Egypt. He trained against it a
weapon new to royal authority. It was known as logic.

And Aye, the wise one, listened and apparently encouraged the
boy to find his own answers. Watching the long, thoughtful, un-
boylike features, the deep, questioning, fanatic eyes, Aye must
have recognized the strangeness of which this charge of his was
made and respected his uniqueness. He must have seen in the
boy the almost maniacal urge toward a greatness that would out-
distance that of all his ancestors, including his father's—ancestors
who were the outstanding leaders of all the Egyptian kings.

By listening, answering, suggesting, Aye won the confidence
of the boy Akhenaton and made himself indispensable to him as
he was to the parents, King Amenhotep and Queen Tiy. And Aye

had another more intimate and powerful claim to the royal family, through the girl-child Nefertiti.

We have gone deeply into answering the question, Who was Aye, for great authorities accept him as Nefertiti's father.

We know more about Aye than about most men of his time, for he was honored, as a king would have been, by having two graves. The first was begun for him at Amarna and never completed, but the one found at Thebes was built and furnished by Aye in his own lifetime, and both have yielded much information on Aye and his strong influence over Akhenaton and Nefertiti.

The graves testify to the hold he had on Egypt.

Aye's lists of his titles, honors and good deeds begin with his claim to being "father of the king." (Father-in-law?) In another translation he claims paternal authority over Nefertiti and her little sister Nezemmut. Other sources refer to him as having been related in some manner to Queen Tiy, perhaps a brother, and even as having been a cousin to Akhenaton.

But the formal acknowledgment that he was born the son of one titleless Hapu seems to discredit the theory that he had any blood relationship to Akhenaton's people. In his claim to being "father of the king" Aye may have been taking advantage of the deference paid him by Akhenaton as father-in-law. Certainly Aye had a strong hold over Akhenaton that he could boldly claim relationship on enduring stone.

The first of the leading archaeologists to accept the theory that Nefertiti was the daughter of Aye was Professor Borchardt, who discovered her bust. He believed Nefertiti came from "a middle-class Egyptian family," and that her father, Aye, was "a man of mystery and tremendous power."

There are other theories. One, harking back to the Mitanni princess legends, suggests Aye was the father of Nefertiti by one of those tender hostages sent by their royal fathers to Akhenaton and his father. Another, that as ambassador Aye was often sent on long confidential journeys by King Amenhotep, and on one of these into Mesopotamia he met with the infant Mitannian and recognized in her the potential qualities that made Nefertiti a great queen.

These are guesses made at hazard. Aye was chief of the forces that brought Nefertiti to the throne of Egypt. We are certain that he brought her as a child into the palace, and watched over her growth there under the personal supervision of his wife, Tiy the great nurse, and that firmly and swiftly, aided by her own inborn talents, he channeled her way to the throne.

The graves yield evidence that Aye and his wife were awarded singular honors and affection as the "lifelong favorites" of Akhenaton and Nefertiti.

We know far less of Tiy the nurse. Her portraits show a comfortable, hearty-looking woman, with none of her husband's drive to power. Her honors are listed along with Aye's, and while not as many as his, still they reveal Tiy to have been the handmaiden of greatness. Among her titles are listed:

"Lady of the House (Aye's wife), Great Nurse, Nurse of the Great Queen (Nefertiti), Tutoress of the Goddess (Nefertiti), Favorite of Nefertiti, Great Favorite of Akhenaton." She is also given the curious honor of having been Akhenaton's "handmaiden," or "concubine." Elsewhere she is cited as having been his nurse as well as Nefertiti's. She makes no claim to having been Nefertiti's mother.

It has been theorized that Nefertiti and Akhenaton were brought up together from infancy and nursed from the same breast, that Aye watched over the boy and Tiy the nurse over the girl. We know of many ways in which Aye guided the fortunes of the two children and saw that they were prepared to keep their rendezvous with destiny.

Centuries after the Eighteenth Dynasty ended, Aye's wise and witty sayings were quoted in Egypt. Some time around 140 B.C., a thousand years after his death, Aye was deified, as his idol Imhotep had been before him, as a god of healing. A chapel was built to Aye at Deir el-Medina, and to this magical shrine sick people came to be cured from all over Egypt. Ambitious young scribes prayed to him to advance their fortunes, and offered libations, as once he had prayed to Imhotep.

It is mainly due to Aye's writings that so much of Nefertiti's life is known. He brought her out of obscurity. He prepared her for the part she would play. She listened to him; was he not the wisest man in the world? Fortune had awarded Nefertiti a mentor whose ambitions for her were as great as the role she was to play in history.

Aye's plans soared in the year 1372 B.C. when Akhenaton was twelve years old and took his place on the golden throne under the name of Amenhotep IV, King of Egypt.

CHAPTER FIVE

The Girl and the Throne

In the Palace, 1369 B.C.

Akhenaton was made co-regent by his father in 1372 B.C. The next four years were important years for the two children. Akhenaton was preparing for the assumption of absolute authority; Nefertiti, for the sharing of that authority.

During those years they grew up.

There is a suspicion that King Amenhotep III had begun to show an increasing lack of interest in the world around him, and that for a time Queen Tiy acted as co-regent with her son, strongly supported by Aye, who was chief adviser to Akhenaton.

We can imagine how carefully Nefertiti was being attended at this time. With Tiy as her model, Tiy the nurse as instructress, and the perfectionist Aye as critic and guide, she continued to develop in distinction and grace. The attention of all Egypt was fixed on Nefertiti, and she was surrounded by eagle-eyed observers who watched every move made by the boy-king's chosen love. While from his new exalted position on the throne Akhenaton watched her growing and was stirred to the depths of his strangely secretive and passionate nature.

She was being prepared for all the future might demand of her as his companion in the royal bedchamber and at public appearances where she would be the cynosure of thousands. As wife, hostess, priestess, and regent, she would be required to have beauty and charm.

Beauty above all was demanded of her, and it grew with her knowledge of her womanhood. There were other requirements to be met, such as a knowledge of religion and politics—the two curiously intermingled in Egypt—to make her a fit companion to the world's leading monarch. But her chief endowments were given Nefertiti at birth—a face and body that pleased Akhenaton beyond those of any other woman.

Nefertiti had chosen wisely her setting and her time. It was a fine thing to be a woman during the Eighteenth Dynasty, when even a girl of humble background, as in Tiy's case, and Neferti-ti's, might become a queen. And a queen, if she so minded, could even assume total monarchy! Queen Hatshepsut in the previous dynasty had done so.

It was Nefertiti's additional good fortune to live in the reign of such a queen as Tiy, to come early under her patronage, and to be chosen by Tiy's only son. Let Aye take the credit for their romance if he must, but strong-willed Tiy must have approved the choice.

Now the family of Akenaton were not only the foremost family in the world, but one exceptional in its family devotion. The trait was strong in Amenhotep, and would be in his son Akhena-ton.

Both were surrounded from their earliest years by every appeal to the senses an oriental potentate can command. The most beautiful princesses in their world were offered to add to their pleasure in life. Every Pharaoh, every rich man, had his harem.

Egypt, to the fortunate, was a land of many delights. Much of its pleasure, charm and relaxation was supplied by women. In the banquet halls of the noble or wealthy, the dancing and singing and music were provided by women. The palace had its own orchestra and its own troupes of entertainers. All were women.

Women danced before the incense-wreathed altars in the temples.

In the palace and the great houses, the kitchens, storerooms, wine cellars, archives, and weaving rooms were all presided over by men!

It was Nefertiti's duty to be not only a beautiful woman but the most beautiful in her world. Only such a woman could hope to hold such a king as Akhenaton.

Under the capable guidance of her sponsors, the little girl in the Theban palace was being reared as a thing of beauty and joy forever.

Her day began when Aton, the many-armed face of the sun, lifted above the eastern cliffs and its warmth-filled hands moved across the night-chilled city of Thebes and over the river, touching the gleaming shafts of the Colossi of Memnon with light and bringing strange music from the one that sang.

Out of the towering Temple of Karnak came trooping the sleepy-eyed priests, heavy with much good eating and drinking the night before, to bathe with purification ritual in the sacred artificial lake before the temple. Steps ran down into the lake, to be used when the waters from the Nile were low. Physical purity was stressed in the Amon priesthood. The priests bathed four times during the twenty-four hours; their heads were shaven and their beards plucked and they were circumcised. They wore wigs and on occasion, masks. Their robes were of linen only. Garments of wool or leather were forbidden, as being of animal origin, although they did wear capes of leopard skin.

In their white robes and the sashes of Amon, the priests returned into the tremendous temple hall and massed in groups under the columns to celebrate the solemn lighting on the altar of the sacred fire. In the dim, cavernous place the golden image of Amon gleamed through rising clouds of incense. The priests were its servants; they tended the god. They chanted hymns to the morning and the renewed greatness of Amon; they beat loudly on the sacred gongs, they poured myrrh on the fire. "Burn—shine like Ra on the horizon!"

To the crashing of the gongs, the city roused from sleep. Out of the crowded districts of the poor came the workers, tumbling from their humble homes, gulping the last fragments of their unleavened bread soaked in barley beer. In jostling hordes they threaded the narrow streets and scattered to their various duties in the city or in the fields. Work hours were regular and followed ancient rules. Men went to work when the sun rose and stopped work when it set. Time in Thebes was set by that not too popular god, Aton, who was the face of the sun.

The ancient, narrow streets filled with people, confusion, and loud sounds. Burdened trains of camels and donkeys jockeyed for place against carts and sledges, and chariots drawn by fiery horses that a pedestrian must make room for lest his life be the penalty. There were thousands of chariots in Thebes.

The great market places filled with vendors, the shops opened their doors, and trays and baskets of goods and produce were set out in the streets. The bargaining began that was the lifeblood of trade, in shrill, high, oriental-sounding voices. And all over Thebes was heard, night and day, the high keening of song and the music of street musicians. Children raced under-foot, cats walked with feline dignity, and hundreds of hungry dogs scavenged the streets and were respected as the representa-tives of the god Anubis.

To foreigners visiting the city the most remarkable sight was the presence in the streets of women. Nowhere else in the world did women have the freedom they were permitted in Thebes. They were to be seen everywhere. Wearing the single white sheathlike garment that was almost universal in Egypt, and head cloths folded becomingly across the brow, they went on domestic errands in the shops and market places, carrying, or having their servants carry, large baskets and jars. They argued with the shopkeepers and pinched fruit in the market places; their manners were as relaxed as if they were men. But they were mothers and wives, and very feminine. Their voices were gentle and they behaved with dignity.

Visitors, especially from Asia, could not get over the wonder of this. In other countries women remained in hiding and spoke only to men of their family. Respectable Egyptian women were never self-conscious about appearing in public either with or without their men. Centuries later, Herodotus would be shocked by the way Egyptian women went unescorted in public.

In the great palace over the river Nefertiti woke to the sound of music and the scent of flowers and perfumes.

In their various luxurious quarters in the palace the members of the royal family were wakening to a day that would be principally given over to pleasure but which had a rigid under-lying base of responsibility. Theirs was a luxurious and leisurely existence, but protocol was strictly observed and those in power had to behave accordingly. At this moment King Amenhotep, in his royal suite, was probably considering the events of the day and choosing the most appropriate of his many crowns.

As for Nefertiti, she opened her eyes in a bed carved and painted and gilded by one of the great Theban artists, with pillows and mattress of the softest goat's wool, which was used principally for bedding. (No Egyptian, in that climate, would wear wool next the skin, and wool capes were reserved for cold desert nights.) The bed sheets were of the softest, silkiest, hand-woven linen, and her later to be celebrated cheek rested on a crescent-shaped headrest, such as is still used in Japan, of carved and painted wood or colored glass. The smiling face of Tiy the nurse might be over hers for a moment as Tiy bent to blow out the flame in the lucent alabaster night lamp that burned with a twisted cotton wick in oil.

Every article Nefertiti opened her eyes upon would be a museum treasure today.

Like every other room of the palace, hers was large and magnificently furnished and cooled by a ventilating system perfected by the Egyptians.

As in all fine Egyptian homes, rooms and halls and courts were heavy with perfumes.

Hanging on the painted walls or spread on the floors were rich tapestries and finely woven mats. Others hung at the windows to keep out the heat of the sun or the sand from the desert when the wind blew. There were many tables, small and large, and beautiful little taborets and footstools and chairs, some as stately as thrones, bull-footed, lion-footed, gilded, painted, and inlaid with marquetry. There was furniture of rare cedar brought from Lebanon, and ebony overlaid with ivory on gold leaf, or studded with gold, made by master craftsmen, without nails, but studded as fine furniture would be, centuries later, in Europe. There were carved ivory and ebony boxes, and, against the walls, magnificent ornamental chests, used for storage.

On every gleaming surface were set large, handsome lamps, and vases filled with flowers, and colored glass bowls where bright, live fish swam. And scattered everywhere were the small, exquisite bibelots Egyptians cherished and exchanged as gifts, such as tiny statuettes of the gods and the divine animals, in wood, faïence, pottery, alabaster, silver, or gold. There were goblets and small vials and vases and bottles and jars and bowls of every possible size and kind, of copper, silver or gold, faïence, alabaster, or crusted with jewels.

Many of these would be presents given her by Akhenaton. Every Egyptian lavished all the gifts he could afford on the girl he was to marry.

All the palace was furnished in this fashion, but even more

splendid were the queen's headquarters, the king's, and the princely suite where the boy-king Akhenaton was also undergoing the processes of purification, bathing and grooming before a large and appreciative audience.

But if Nefertiti's rooms were not, as yet, the most splendid in the palace, they were splendid enough to serve as attraction to hundreds of sycophants who milled about her rooms as soon as it was known the little queen-to-be had wakened from sleep. The people of the court who had once filled Queen Tiy's rooms of a morning were not slow to recognize the potential power of the girl. It is unlikely that Queen Tiy minded this desertion, for she was a generous woman. She regarded Nefertiti as a daughter, and at this time she was preoccupied with the care of the failing King Amenhotep.

So it was Nefertiti's suite that was crowded now. Her own personal staff was enormous and we do not know how many ladies in waiting attended her even after she became queen, but one of Amenhotep's minor queens had more than three hundred women in her train.

Every royal person, even a young girl, had her own steward to attend to her household, her own scribe to take down any messages or letters she might dictate, her own governess or nurse, and hundreds of other serving women, servants, and slaves. Filling the suite in addition were Nefertiti's morning visitors, courtiers and their ladies willing to dispense, or gather, the gossip of the palace.

All of them rushed about, chattering at the top of their voices, the musicians played loudly, and Tiy the nurse tried to maintain a semblance of order and oversee the preparation of her beautiful charge.

The noise was emphasized by the trilling of the caged birds, the barking of the excited dogs, and the plaintive voices of the many cats that were cherished members of Nefertiti's intimate circle. Each pet had its special name and attributes, but, as usual, Miw the cat was given the most deference.

Stored away now, but not discarded, since Egyptians treasured their toys as mementos of childhood, were Nefertiti's little-girl playthings, the dolls and puppets and games. In their places were her hundreds of beautiful treasures.

Many of the bibelots had to do with her personal appearance, for she had been trained from childhood in the rituals that made a lovely woman even lovelier. Queen Tiy would have taught the girl her own personal arts, and Tiy the nurse would have assisted in imparting lore that was part of the heritage of every Egyptian woman.

To this day the beauty secrets of ancient Egypt are respected. The shadowing of brows and lids, the delicate touches of rouge, the application of ointments and perfumes were arts practiced by both men and women, and the men lost none of their masculinity in the practice. Nefertiti's first make-up boxes would have been given her when she was very young.

The toilette of any great lady was an elaborate ceremony. Nefertiti's required the rapt attention of many personal women. Each had her special knowledge, materials, or implements, and a high-sounding title indicative of her duties. So there was a supervisor of the bath, a first lady of the eye pencil, an attendant of the long-handled, decorative unguent spoons, a keeper of the myrrh, a guardian of the jewel boxes, a tender of oil jars. Tweezers, combs, scissors, kohl stick, rouge pot and eye pencil, eye paint, eyewashes, depilatories, razors for shaving the head, pins, needles (one type of needle had two eyes so that threads of two colors could be used) hair pins of bronze and ivory, and the many hand mirrors of highly polished silver, gold, or bronze with handles shaped like animals, people, or gods—all had their guardians.

The toilette accessories of Nefertiti's time are the pride of modern museums. Graduated sets of painted pottery or alabaster jars and jugs and flasks and vials held costly unguents and perfumes, rouge for the lips, coloring creams for the lids, blue and green, such as both men and women wore, made of powdered malachite or lapis lazuli, and kohl, to add dark mystery to brows and eyes. The application sticks and spoons for these cosmetics were smaller works of art, and so were the great painted pottery jars that held the perfumed oils.

To judge by paintings of such ceremonies, Nefertiti breakfasted on breads and fruits, perhaps a glass of mild pomegranate wine, while carrying on a running commentary of chatter, and submitting to everything that had to be done before this fair, fresh young beauty was ready for public view.

The all-important bath was first. Even the poorest Egyptians bathed daily, in the Nile if necessary, and lavished upon their bodies afterward any attars and oils they could afford. In their arid climate the skin shriveled without oils, and the Egyptians used many kinds.

All homes of the well-to-do and even modest homes had bathrooms, and separate lavatories where seats of wood or brick were placed over removable earthenware pots. The bathing place was usually a stone slab, hollowed out to receive the body of the bather. Slaves poured water from large jars and the water ran down into a huge removable pot set in a pit in the floor.

Many comfort-loving Egyptians had these "lustration slabs" in their dining rooms.

Nefertiti's bathroom would have been a lustration shrine. The bathing slab would be of alabaster, the water jars larger and more ornate, and the containers of oils and unguents works of art made for her by leading artists.

The perfumes, unguents, and oils rubbed into the naked, child-like body were heavily scented with attars expressed from roses, lilies, lotus, and other flowers. Perfumes were worn by women and men. Egyptians made lavish use of perfumes. Their bodies and homes were saturated with fragrance and the very streets of Thebes held, amongst a myriad of less desirable odors, the penetrating citrus scent of myrrh. The myrrh, known as the "incense tree," was a favorite source of incense and perfume. Some perfumes were made from formulas centuries old and took months to prepare.

Nefertiti would walk through life in clouds of costly fragrance. Considering the skimpiness of the attire worn, Nefertiti's dressing took a remarkably long time. She slipped into a single garment. For centuries the kilt had been the accepted costume for Egyptian women and men and no costume could have been simpler. It consisted of a square of linen wrapped around the body from waist to knee and fastened by folding in a flap at the waist.

But the Eighteenth Dynasty was richer and more sophisticated than any that had gone before and along with much else it had changed the style of dress for both women and men. Now only the gods were pictured as wearing kilts. Some men and women still wore them upon occasion, but the leaning was toward long, full, flowing robes, white, or dyed in glowing patterns or stripes.

Wardrobes had grown elaborate. Nefertiti owned many changes of clothing.

Her favorite garment appears to have been the new popular sheath. This was a tube of sheer linen, upheld by a single shoulder strap. She was also fond of the modish full-skirted dress, of linen so finely woven it was as transparent as veiling, that was strapped under the breast and both flared and clung, revealing every line of her body. The skirt might be pleated or draped. Since it was popular to appear nude, even if not wholly nude, this was the only garment she wore. She might still wear no dress at all at times. Nudity continued to be a natural state even to grown-up Egyptians in a country where Aton laid his burning hands almost every day of the year.

Still, at this stage of her career, we may assume Nefertiti made her public appearances dressed.

Her clothing came from the carved and painted chests set along the walls. A separate wardrobe room was lined with wooden benches under which articles could be stored, and atop these were boxes, jars, small chests, and woven baskets that held more of her personal effects.

The brief act of dressing over, the greater part of Nefertiti's morning ritual was given over to the application of make-up.

At this point Queen Tiy might drop in on her way to her morning public "appearance" beside her two kings. Cheerful and energetic, she would cast her trained eye over proceedings, exchange opinions with Tiy the nurse, and offer basic earthy encouragement to the girl her son had chosen.

Nefertiti's morning make-up procedure was watched as carefully as if a masterpiece were being created to live forever. Woe to the lady in waiting whose hand might tremble now! Breathlessly the women watched while kohl was darkly streaked under lashes and over brows, the full, provocative mouth reddened, the hair dressed and made heavy and fragrant with myrrh, and body and dress touched everywhere with perfume.

It is probable that until her marriage Nefertiti continued to wear the forelock of youth, and we can imagine Tiy the nurse

watching with jealous care as the ornamental comb was run
through the black silky waterfall. She would by this time, however, own a chestful of wigs, for all great Egyptian ladies, and
their gentlemen as well, had wigs for every occasion and changed
them often, permitting heads to be shaven for the sake of
coolness. The wigs were usually dressed in page-boy style, with
becoming bangs.

Another chest would be given over to sandals. Sandals became
universally popular in this dynasty. They were made by carefully
trained craftsmen and were so comfortable and elegant that their
duplicates are sold in fashionable shops today. They were of
leather, cloth, metal, and of woven and tinted strips of papyrus,
like raffia. Some were gilded with gold leaf or with silver. Others
were elaborately beaded, like the moccasins of American In-
dians. Some were tied around the ankles with thongs, others
held by a strap between the toes. Should she choose, Nefertiti
might go unsandaled. Men and women could wear ornate jewels
and (elaborate) jeweled headdresses atop their wigs, and still go
barefoot.

Lastly, the decorated jewel chests were opened.

Never, until this the fourteenth century B.C., had such ornate
jewelry been seen in Egypt. It could be heavy, elaborate, set
with large gems, or made in designs as fragile and flawless as
snowflakes. Some of the jewels worn by Nefertiti are in museums,
and sold in duplicate today. A popular favorite is the deep-collar
necklace petaled with jewels.

Nefertiti's ears were pierced. (So were Akhenaton's; both men
and women had taken to wearing earrings which made their
appearance during this dynasty.) Nefertiti was one of the first
women in the world to wear earrings. They were in such forms
as large loops, pendants, buttons, or studs made of a single gem.
Nearly all were of gold; almost all were jeweled, as was most
jewelry; bracelets, amulets, earrings, necklaces, many of these so
wide they lay on the shoulders. Jewelry was often stamped with
the wearer's name and perhaps the image, name, or "animal" of
a god. Aye, for example, probably wore a signet ring with the
image of the wading bird, the ibis, the sacred image of his patron
god, Thoth. Signet rings were first used during this dynasty and
some used as seals by dead kings and queens have helped

identify for us many of the names and dates of Egypt. They had originated as cylindrical seals.

Nefertiti was almost ready. There were more cries and final ecstatic touches, bright ribbons were tied at her head and under the breast, more perfume applied, and fresh, sweet-smelling flowers pinned at waist and throat and on the full transparent skirt. Nefertiti's was an era of frivolity and coquetry—no girl was better equipped to live it to the full.

She stood at last among her women, an image of artistry from her small, proudly held head to the small, slender, perfumed feet. Confronting with her sweet, serene gaze her circle of critics— the sycophants, the servants, the worshipful ladies in waiting, the narrowed, critical eyes of the two Tiys, she was the perfect emblem of loved womanhood, small and slim, petal-soft, flower-scented, and around her like an aura the gleam of jewels.

Now she could walk with assurance, head high, knowing no woman in Egypt was lovelier. For palace or temple or abroad by chariot in the streets of Thebes, she was prepared, armored in loveliness. A chorus of whispered accolade followed her from her rooms. Walking with small steps in the tightly clinging skirts, her head high, Nefertiti went to meet her destiny.

Nefertiti! "Behold, the beautiful woman . . ."

In another part of the great palace Aye was keeping a shrewd and appraising eye on the development of Akhenaton, who was being bathed by priests in water brought from the sacred lake. Time was racing to meet time in the scribe's calendar, and Aye's plans were made.

All knew the day was nearing when the boy-king would be given complete charge of the country. King Amenhotep III had ruled wisely and long. His reign, notable for prosperity and peace, had lasted almost twenty years. He was readying now to turn authority over to his only son.

As co-regent, the grave and thoughtful boy was revealing a promising awareness of Egypt's importance in the world. With a gravity worthy of an older person, he had shown himself able to share in decisions and judgments. He was gradually assuming powers of state.

With his father as leader and Aye as mentor, Akhenaton learned the religious-political mechanics of his country.

Egypt, a monarchy, had developed into a self-sustaining nation, now enriched by tribute from its conquered lands. The king maintained this satisfactory state by supreme authority. Only the priests of Amon dared dispute his rulings.

The king presided over an Egypt that had centralized government control (centered in Thebes); a complicated and highly effective tax system; an impressive foreign policy, a foreign service attended by ambassadors, consuls, and other officials; a civil service; a rapid postage system, a police force; and an army and navy.

The postage service operated from official stables where fine horses were always waiting, harnessed to chariots, with couriers to speed the mail on its way. Love letters were sent by messenger.

The police force was the pride of Egypt. The smallest village had its constabulary. Egyptians boasted that a traveler could sleep by the side of the road and be as safe as on his floor at home.

The frontiers were rigidly drawn and patrolled. Customs officers checked the points of egress and entry, and collected customs fees for the king and Amon.

All treaties were signed, agreements made, oaths taken, and important documents sealed, in the name of the chief god and the king.

Diplomacy had reached a high level. The diplomatic correspondence in the Theban Foreign Office was in Aye's charge as court scribe. The official tablets would eventually be the nucleus of the Amarna Letters. Justice was seriously imposed. Its official dispenser for the king was the grand vizier.

The grand vizier held a position of tremendous authority. He wore a long judicial robe, fastened under the arms, and was always pictured as of a stern, forbidding appearance. It was his first responsibility to make himself respected.

His orders ran: "Inspire fear of thyself, so that men may fear thee. . . . The official is an official of whom men are afraid, because the dread of the official is that he should do justice."

Above all else, he must be fair. His instructions were clear: "The abomination of the god (Amon) is a show of partiality. . . .

thou shalt look upon him who thou knowest, like him who thou dost not know . . ."

The viziers of the Eighteenth Dynasty took pride in being conscientious dispensers of justice. They rested their reputations on fair-mindedness, and laid claim to their success in their tombs.

The palace was the seat of government as well as the home of the royal family. Each morning there was a formal opening of the royal offices. It began when Akhenaton and his father took their places on the two golden thrones in the great hall of the palace for the official morning visit of the grand vizier. This was the first public "appearance" of the day and one of the chief duties of a king.

A brief but formal ritual was carried out; then the vizier, leaving the royal presence, led his entourage to the front of the palace. Pausing under the bannered cedar staffs, he held brief conferences with the chief treasurer. That formality over, with a flourish of his wand of authority he ordered the opening of the great front doors crested with the image of Amon.

The palace was now officially open for the day.

Now the grand vizier at this time was one of the most upright of men and his name was Ptahmose, in honor of Ptah, who was the god of the city of Memphis. He had first appeared in history as the superintendent of the royal house, under Amenhotep III and Queen Tiy.

In proof of the hints that Akhenaton had the example of protest against the priests set for him by his own father, is the curious fact that Amenhotep III advanced his palace superintendent to the country's highest office, that of grand vizier.

For the first time in history, Egypt had a vizier who was not a priest of Amon!

Ptahmose evidently had a close understanding with Aye, and was one of the earliest admirers of Akhenaton. As the old king's powers lessened he could be seen gradually shifting his strong support to his son. (In time, to please Akhenaton, he changed his name to Ramose, and became a staunch and powerful aide to the boy-king.)

Ptahmose proceeded with his procession into the palace and to the Hall of Viziers, also known as the Great Council Room.

Other cities and towns had local courts, but this was the supreme court of Egypt. Here, every morning, a docket of prisoners
awaited trial. Here, too, came the poor, the frightened, the irate,
pleading for the right to be heard. And none were turned away.
This was the sanctuary of Maat, goddess of justice and order
and the law, and any Egyptian, rich or poor, might ask aid of
her. Women could appeal here, testify, take oath: "May I be
sent to the back of the house if I speak not truth."

In Maat's name, the grand vizier listened, weighed evidence
and passed judgment. Justice was a public matter. All complaints
and evidence was presented, and all verdicts rendered, in open
court. Closed sessions were forbidden. The vizier's law read:
". . . the official who is in public view, wind and water make
report on all that he does, so that his acts cannot be unknown."

The penalties awarded those found guilty were severe. A man's
possessions might be taken from him, or at least in part, and
awarded to one he had harmed. Punishments were by flogging,
banishment to the mines, or, in extreme cases, death.

Serious charges were referred by the grand vizier to the king,
but this was a mere formality. Amenhotep III himself had laid
down the legal code followed in his court. One of the king's
titles was that of "establisher of law." He would lay proud claim
to the fact that not once did he interfere with the judgments
given by his grand vizier, although he must often have been
tempted. In fact, he did describe a case in which: "The law
stood firm; I did not reverse judgment, but in view of the facts
I was silent . . ."

Even conspirators against the king received fair trial and were
not put to death unless their treason was proved beyond a
shadow of doubt.

More often now, Grand Vizier Ptahmose presented his final
judgments for approval, not to the aging King Amenhotep, but
to the solemn boy on the second throne.

And Akhenaton, in his turn, had no quarrel with the law as
carried out by Ptahmose. His interest was in a higher justice,
dispensed in another world.

Still, Akhenaton took seriously his position as co-regent of
Egypt. He observed conditions as they existed under the form
of government laid down before him by his forefathers and his

good father, and saw that since his great country was smoothly, peacefully run, with such administrators as Aye and Ptahmose to see to its running, that there was little left for him to do by way of developing Egypt.

Other ambitions grew in Akhenaton.

Apparently Egypt was smoothly running as a river. Aye was chief adviser to the throne; Grand Vizier Ptahmose was in effect secretary of state and secretary of the treasury. His was the highest official rank under the king. All legal contracts were deposited in Ptahmose's court and it was his officials who taxed the properties and collected from the people, in behalf of the king, oxen and other cattle, sheep and goats, linen, grains, and articles of gold and silver, including the gold-bead necklaces that were highly valued, and which served as substitutes for the nonexistent money.

The priests of Amon also had their representatives in every village and town who were industriously collecting taxes from every Egyptian to maintain the glory of Amon.

Centering around the core of power that was the king were three powerful classes. They were the priests, the officials, and the military. Among these the most strongly organized were the priests of Amon.

Most of these were of noble lineage. A poor young man might achieve the Amon priesthood, as Aye had done, by royal favor. But the majority inherited their positions, usually from a father or uncle, and the hierarchy of the temple was a confusing tangle of relationships. Thousands of Amon priests were living in luxury in the great Temple at Karnak, and their ranks and wealth and power were increasing day by day.

There were people in the palace who were beginning to resent the priests on the grounds that their claims to authority and to the country's taxes were getting out of bounds. Among these complainants, we suspect, was Aye, who, although a priest of Amon, had other interests closer to the throne.

Nearly all the high-ranking government officials were nobly born. They held many ranks in the palace where their lives centered, and where each gave some special service to the king, and was in turn awarded with high honors, privileges, and titles.

But again, as in Aye's case, an ambitious and talented scribe, artist, artisan, or even merchant who could bring himself to the attention of the king might be given a government appointment and title and asked as a guest to the palace feasts.

The high-ranking military had always commanded respect. A noticeable lack of deference began to be shown them during Akhenaton's rise to power. Even less than his peaceful parents was Akhenaton interested in plans for war. Egypt was complete in itself, the perfect country. He saw no reason for increasing either its holdings or its military forces. The frontiers were well protected, the vassal countries well patrolled. Akhenaton's thoughts were reserved for more peaceful projects. He was never to don the polka-dotted blue leather crown of war.

Milling around the palace as part of its working life, without social recognition but not without honor, were vast armies of tradespeople and craftsmen. As in later and even modern civilizations, these would be permitted to lay public claim to the royal patronage by proclaiming from their tombs they had been "wig-maker of the queen," "sandal bearer to the king," "tender of the king's orchards," "caretaker of the geese."

There were the manufacturers of wigs, perfumes, sandals; textile workers, dyers, ropemakers, brewers of beer and distillers of wine; carpenters, stonemasons, furniture makers, jewelers, sculptors, metalworkers, artists; the fashion artists who set the rapidly changing styles by creating the royal wardrobes; the potters, shipbuilders, makers and repairers of chariots. Overseer of these and their works, reporting all they did to the king, was the court scribe. It was Aye and his aides who kept the tallies and accounts of the tradespeople and saw that they were justly paid.

Government, industry, commerce, and agriculture, were regulated by rules set by the state, and to insure their observance hundreds of thousands of civilians occupied clerical positions in the civil service, supervised by officials who were the choice of the high priest of Amon.

They were the fortunate. By birth, adaptability, or privilege they had been blessed by Amon. Beneath them, far down in the social scale, labored the vast human foundation made up of the serfs of Egypt.

These were the tenders of the flocks and fields, the rowers of

the river craft, the builders of the monuments, the attendants of
the dead.

The builders of the first pyramids had set the pattern of enforced labor battalions a thousand years before. Slave labor had
become accepted. Slaves had built the pyramids, dug the ditches
and canals that drained the marshes and irrigated the fields along
the Nile, built the temples and palaces and monuments and
tombs, made Thebes the most splendid of cities, and constructed
its stone wharfs and the ships that left those wharfs to return
with riches for the king's treasury and Amon's.

Near the valley of the tombs was a walled village the two children of the palace would never see. In it lived a large community
of people who attended to the necessary work of the adjoining
necropolis. They were the descendants of slaves captured long
before by ancestors of Akhenaton. Not actually slaves, they were
not free to come and go from their ghetto, or seek other work
or another way of life. Their lives were spent assisting the priests
in the mummification and burial of the dead people and their
dead animals and guarding the graves. They lived, reared their
pariah families, and died amongst the tombs.

Nefertiti and Akhenaton would have seen since childhood long
lines of manacled prisoners driven through the streets of Thebes
on their way to be slaves. And they saw bands of marching
draftees, equally captive, being marched off to be soldiers.

At times, when the labor supply dwindled, soldiers were put
to work at building the monuments, and their complaints must
have been bitter as those of soldiers are in any place or time.
Farm workers, too, could be drafted for the labor battalions during the seasons they were not needed on the land.

These were the true builders—these nameless millions, who
toiled and hungered through the dynasties without knowing that
on their thin bodies rested the economy of Egypt. No words on
stone record them. They lived and died in ghettos that reeked
with the sourness of centuries. Their bodies, wrapped in scraps
of coarse linen and perhaps partially mummified, were left under
thin layers of desert sand, far from the royal tombs, prey to
Anubis, the jackal god of the dead. A poor person might be
buried in a coffin of rough planks or in a large clay pot.

For the boy and girl in the palace thousands labored, tended their properties, built their monuments, rowed in their fleets, fought in their armies, until their bodies attenuated by lifetimes of malnutrition were absorbed into the desert.

This by the law of Maat, goddess of order.

Egypt was the most civilized country in the world.

Nefertiti would see these people as moving figures against a delightful colorful screen that was Thebes. She knew no more of them than the small bejeweled dog she petted knew of the hard-working hounds that turned the spits in the palace kitchen. But the strange thoughtful boy who was to inherit Egypt may have been aware of them, for his feverish young mind was crowded with thoughts that were new to mankind.

Those around Akhenaton recognized in him the potential of a brilliant, powerful Pharaoh such as Egypt had never before produced. In his years as boy co-regent he had shown himself worthy of the greatness of Egypt. King Amenhotep III, wearying of cares of state, was well pleased with his son.

He showed his faith in the boy when, in the year 1369 B.C., with formal coronation ceremonies in the great hall of the Temple of Amon, he placed the two crowns on the sixteen-year-old boy's head and named him full regent.

In the same year, in the same hall at Karnak, there was another impressive ceremony. Aye had made one more triumphant move on the chessboard of Egypt. He took full credit when Nefertiti was married to the boy who was now King Amenhotep IV.

She was fifteen years old when she married and became Queen Nefertiti, Empress of the Two Egypts.

CHAPTER SIX

Bride of the Sun

North Thebes, 1369 B.C.

No building on earth was as large as the Temple of Karnak.

The "gigantic wonder" at North Thebes was compounded of many temples, courts, halls, chapels, pylons, obelisks, and tombs. The largest and most splendid temple was that of Amon.

Before its enormous central door, which was of bronze centered with a gold image of the god, towered the cedar staves which by a triumph of transportation had been floated up the Nile from Lebanon. From these hung the banners of the chief god.

Champollion, who created Egyptology, was to write of the builders of Karnak: "they thought in terms of men one hundred feet tall."

Akhenaton and Nefertiti were small in stature. Standing in the great central hall of the temple they were dwarfed to doll size by the 134 pillars, some of which were almost 80 feet tall.

This splendid hall had been built by Akhenaton's "conqueror" ancestor, the mighty Thutmose III, when he had added to his other impressive deeds by enlarging the temple. It was a cavernous golden tabernacle of sanctity, incantation, and mystery. Dimly lighted and heavily scented with incense, it was designed to inspire awe and fear.

Far up on the ceiling was the map of the stars, which were known by names that are not used today.

Everywhere through the dimness shone the incalculable wealth of Amon.

The burning focal point of this incredible magnificence stood on the altar, which was a portable throne supported by eleven sacred carrying staves. It was the gold man-image of Amon. It wore splendid clothing, which was changed often by the priests in charge of bathing and dressing the statue, and many jewels.

A king or high priest could converse with Amon. One of these might speak to the idol, and its head nodded.

The floor of this glittering temple was earth. This was symbolical. It was the center of the country, and from it spread a religious network that controlled the life of every person living in Egypt.

The average Egyptian was never permitted to enter Amon's shrine. It was sacred to the royal, the noble, the highly placed politically and economically, and the thousands of priests in the service of Amon who lived in the temple.

In this hall were celebrated the rituals, festivals, celebrations, and every event of importance in the lives of the royal family. Here Akhenaton was crowned king of Egypt, and here, shortly after the coronation, he and Nefertiti were married.

We know a great deal about the coronation ceremony in early Egypt. The entire country took part in the jubilee that lasted for days. There were rites, secret and public, but the final ceremony took place in the temple in the presence of the social and spiritual elect. The actual crowning of the new king was attended by ritual preparation. Night and day, the rites continued.

At all ceremonies the priests were massed under the columns, while the image of the god, carried by eleven high-ranking priests, proceeded slowly around the great hall to the pounding of gongs and chanting of hundreds of voices, male and female.

Restored to its altar, the cold golden face of Amon looked down on advancing lines of hundreds of young priests in festal procession, led by the chief priest, shaking the sacred sistrum which was a tambourine-shaped musical instrument hung with wire disks that rang "with a pleasing sound" when shaken by its handle that was usually shaped like a god.

Advancing slowly, dancing and singing to music, came the procession of white-robed women priestesses, all daughters of noble Theban families. Step by step they followed the ancient intricate patterns of the sacred dances before the altar, while offerings were made to the god of honey, oils, fruits, flowers, baked meats, and trussed animals; but the climax of the sacrifice was the offering of the incense loved by all the gods but most in demand by Amon.

Hung by wands waving in rhythm under the idol were red pottery bowls smoking with fragrant burning myrrh. (The bowls once used were never used again and their shards fill the rubbish pits behind the temples.)

The rapt voices of women and men soared in a high oriental keening:

"The incense comes. The incense comes.
"Its perfume is over us.
"The perfume of the eye of Horus. . . .
"It washes us, it anoints us, it makes fragrant our hands.
"Hail, O incense."

Akhenaton offered incense, lifting the sacred bowl in his hands and chanting the verses requesting the recognition of Amon. Thick clouds filled the cavernous space with the scent of myrrh.

At the conclusion of the coronation rites the aging King Amenhotep placed on his son's head the white and red double crown of the Two Lands and pronounced him king of Egypt.

Under the image of Amon the new king took his place on the golden throne. The royal footstool was placed under his sandaled feet. The chanting continued, the incense deepened, while the priests were explaining the new king's many new titles and divine credentials to Amon.

So King Amenhotep IV of the Eighteenth Dynasty took the throne.

Now it was written after his name: "He who brings the world to Amon, who has placed it in his hands."

(Did Aye, watching from his place close to the throne, know what was going on in the mind of the young king? Had Akhenaton already resolved his doubts against Amon? Certainly in this august ceremony he paid full devotion to the god and gave fulsome credit to Amon for having placed him on the throne.

(And Nefertiti, watching proud-eyed amongst her women, did she know? She had his confidence. Her loyalty through all that was to follow leads to the suspicion that she knew.)

Now the new king led the procession of hundreds around the hall, holding the sacred emblems of power, the crook and flail, while the great dim cavernous place resounded like a drum to the chanting: "Let the whole land rejoice. Happy times have come to Egypt. A new king is risen!" This was the ceremony called "going around the wall."

The chant grew to a roar. It was heard outside the temple, where other voices took it up and a cry echoed over Thebes from both sides of the Nile:

"Long live the king! Long live King Amenhotep IV! May he live a million million years!"

This was jubilee. Thirty years later, if he lived, the king would be permitted to hold another—but what Egyptian king reigned thirty years?

Before the temple four wild geese were released and soared upward into the unclouded Egyptian sky to the chanted orders:

"Go to the four corners of the sky.

"Tell the gods of the North, South, East and West that King Amenhotep IV wears the Double Crown!"

So a bird flew to each corner of the world.

It was known that the earth was flat and square and on each corner stood a pillar that held up the sky. And each corner had its god that ruled, "unto the rim of the world"—beyond that, the winds began.

Under the shadows of the speeding birds the chariots raced over the land, carrying the news to every part of the empire, from the deep South into Asia, that a new king ruled over Egypt. And back from the known lands came other couriers, and ambassadors, and consuls, bringing congratulatory messages and priceless gifts.

In the temple, all the gods rejoiced with Amon that under the auspices of the chief god a new reign had begun that would add to the greatness of Egypt's history. And "on their bellies and breasts" the dignitaries of the land pledged loyalty to the new king. "Smelling the earth, crawling on the earth," they paid homage to Amenhotep IV, "exalting his beauty."

Egypt burst into festival. Soldiers distributed bread and barley beer to the people, and there was music and dancing in the streets and market places. Up and down the Nile the shouts echoed for many nights and days; "Long live the king!" A new era had begun in Egypt.

The girl Nefertiti stood close to the golden throne and regarded with wide and innocent eyes the terrifying majestic person of the king.

The boy with whom she had played childish games, exchanged childish kisses, and fished on the river, had become the personification of temporal and spiritual power.

No longer a boy, he was man and monarch and a god. He had always been divine. The gods had recognized his divinity when Akhenaton was born, for the god Amon had occupied King Amenhotep's body when the boy was conceived. Every Pharaoh, as the representative on earth and co-spirit of the sun god Amon-Ra, held in his body the presence of the sun.

"Nowhere else," Julian Huxley has written, "was the sacred priest-king magnified to such an extent as in the person of the Pharaoh."

No human has ever presented a more fearsome image of majesty than an Eighteenth Dynasty Pharaoh.

Tied to Akhenaton's long boyish chin was the false gold beard worn by kings, which was in itself a god. The crown he wore possessed a supernatural force of its own.

Now he could choose among many crowns, each with its special significance for differing occasions. He would never again be pictured without a crown, and always with the royal symbols of Upper and Lower Egypt, the vulture and asp.

He owned many scepters, wands, symbols of power. All were of jewel-studded gold. The Ankh was the symbol of life. The flail and the crook, symbols of punishment and guidance, represented his supreme authority over the two Egypts.

For his coronation Akhenaton probably wore a kilt of gold cloth and a gold shirt with one sleeve that left the right arm and shoulder bare. Around his slender waist was tied a brilliantly colored sash with long ends hanging, and over his shoulders was a short, brightly striped cape fastened at the throat with a heavy jewel. He looked preternaturally tall.

He was lightly clad but wore many jewels in his pierced ears and on his hands and fore- and upper arms. His towering crown fitted over a wig not unlike the one Nefertiti may have worn. And like Nefertiti's, his eyelids were painted green or blue and the air around him was heavy with perfume. Now he was king, wherever he walked courtiers would go before him waving enormous ostrich-feather fans, and others would chant praise of him.

He was terrifyingly regal and male.

Sun begotten, flashing with gold, it was impossible to regard the Pharaoh and not consider him miraculously born. "The fear he inspires terrifies . . ."

His eyes flashed. It was believed a Pharaoh could look upon a trembling human and read him to the depths. His look must have sought the girl's where she stood amongst his hundreds of worshipers.

Akhenaton's years as co-regent had given him the authority born only of unlimited power. In the dark, slender hands of this boy was the future of Egypt. Its harmony, the perpetuation of its greatness depended upon him.

His was the right to control wisely or by evil, to keep peace or wage war and send thousands to their deaths. He could sit in judgment, forgive, reward, or condemn.

Akhenaton was only sixteen, but no man or woman could deny him, and no god could stand in his way. Who could dispute the will of the sun?

They were married shortly after the coronation.

Once more Egypt went into festival, with dancing and cheering in the streets. The marriage was hailed as a promise of the continuation of the great Eighteenth Dynasty that had brought Egypt to its fullest glory.

Once more, in the great hall of the Temple of Amon, the glittering figure of the young king stood under the eleven sacred standards offering bowls of smoking incense to the image of Amon. Once more the elite of Egypt were together, the priesthood attended, the long processions came and went, and the young girls danced their antique steps of homage.

In her full-flowing white robe, flower-decked, jeweled, fragrant with the costliest perfumes, Nefertiti went forward to meet her destiny under the standards where the commanding figure of the king waited beside two golden thrones.

As at the coronation, the jubilation would be in public domain, but much of the lengthy ritual was carried out in the dim mysterious depths of the temple. Complicated legal procedures had been arranged in advance of the ceremony. They were attendant upon any marriage. Even an ordinary Egyptian assigned two thirds of his wordly goods to his bride. In time this would be turned over to their children. We cannot imagine the vast fortune Akhenaton assigned to Nefertiti at this time along with the same rights of monarchy his father had invested with Tiy when they married. The premarriage arrangements must have required much thought on the part of the royal attorneys and grand vizier, and much careful scanning of agreements by Aye.

But the ceremony itself was based upon love, for married love and family devotion were all-important to the Egyptians, and had been since earliest times.

Like all other Egyptian girls in those days, Nefertiti had prayed to the goddess Hathor for a husband and a home. That wish had been granted on the most extravagant terms. She was marrying a king. Her duties as queen were carefully outlined for her, and her duties as wife were made as clear. An Egyptian wife, she was told, as all brides were told then by their priests, must earn praise for her amiable nature, her capacity to accept affection, the care she provided for her husband and children, and beyond all else for her ability "to make herself loved."

That Egyptian brides listened to these rules and did their best to follow them is proven by the affectionate tribute given by their tombs. As a woman, Nefertiti listened, and her success is part of the testimony of Aye's tomb.

As a queen, Nefertiti's responsibilities were greater than those of the average bride. A queen must have all the womanly virtues intensified. The rules for her regal behavior were exact. She must be feminine "to a divine degree." She was to be "charming, adorned with plumes, filling the palace with the waves of her perfume, pleasant of disposition, affectionate, with a voice that delights all who hear."

The priestly advice given the young groom was equally explicit. The rules for a successful marriage were alike for commoner and king. In this life and the next, even a king might have but one woman who was truly his wife. She was to be his companion, his love and his equal, in the present life and throughout all the future.

So King Akhenaton, like all other young men of Egypt who

married, was solemnly advised by the Amon priests: "seek always to please your wife, as long as you live."

(So much out of early Egypt is hauntingly familiar. "As long as you both shall live!")

But of the actual marriage rites of Nefertiti's time little is known. The private ceremony in the temple must have been mysterious and prolonged, in this case, doubtless, lasting a week or more. We can only guess at the purification rites and the oath-taking and offerings and promises made to Amon.

There is one early Egyptian painting of a marriage. Priest, bride and groom are seated, facing one another, with their hands raised in what is evidently a solemn oath-taking. They wear curious headdresses, the symbolism of which is forgotten. Glimpsed in an adjoining corridor are the parents, dancing for joy.

The parents present at Nefertiti's marriage may have danced for joy under the towering columns of Amon. Certainly the abdicated king father, Amenhotep III, was there, a tired but noble figure, with lines of pain making his face that of a prematurely old man, for all the physicians of Egypt had failed to ease the fire in his abscessed gums. He had lived lustily, delighted in prowess and in pleasure. Now upon his sagging frame there was evidence of a great weariness and he had gratefully released the scepter to the sure grasp of his son.

From the time Akhenaton was crowned we hear little of his father.

Hovering beside the old king was Queen Tiy, a stalwart middle-aged wife showing unflagging devotion. Now she lived with him in his retirement, but she would remain close to her son and to Nefertiti. Nefertiti assumed the queenly duties from this day on; she had been well trained.

Queen Tiy was an emotional woman. She must have been open in her pride on this day for the slim figure of the young king waiting for his bride under the altar of Amon.

All the great of Egypt were present, as at the coronation.

Among the noble maidens was Princess Beketaton, sister of Akhenaton, and Princess Nezemmut, who at this time was about eleven. And with the family group would have been half brothers of King Akhenaton whose mothers, although honorable wives, had not had Queen Tiy's good fortune of being named the "great wife."

Standing close to the throne was Ptahmose, in his flowing white vizier's robe. He held the staff of vizier, for when Amenhotep III had left the throne, he had not been asked to lay it down. The new reign had only increased his power. Two kings utilized his valuable knowledge of law and his passion for honesty. He had been the last vizier of Amenhotep III, now he was the first vizier under Akhenaton.

(Ptahmose was building a splendid tomb for himself at Thebes. Aye was not planning a tomb; did he have far-reaching knowledge of Amarna even then?)

Leading his own group of priests was Queen Tiy's brother Anen, who, although humbly born, had been elevated to priestly rank by his royal brother-in-law. He was second in rank to the high priest. His statues show him as a stern and solemn man, with none of his sister's gaiety.

Also among the priests, wearing the sash of Amon, was Aye. Hawk-eyed and triumphant, he watched the girl approaching the throne where the boy-king waited. He had guided them both to this supreme moment. He had never been far from them during their brief lives. This was his triumph.

Sharing it with him was his wife, Tiy the nurse, following her charge, Nefertiti, to the altar as she had followed the girl through her fifteen years.

As for the girl, she looked through the clouds of incense and met the burning gaze of the new king who was also a god. Under the trappings of power was her brother and playmate. She did not dread receiving the love of the sun. This was Akhenaton, and she knew him well.

The small head was held high as Nefertiti entered under the eleven staves and took her place on the golden throne beside Akhenaton. It bent only to receive the close-fitting double crown that bore the emblems of Upper and Lower Egypt. She would never again be pictured without these symbols. The crown she was to adopt as her own would be more like a headdress, but it was always decorated with the vulture and asp. Even in moments of intimacy she would be pictured wearing that crown, and there are portraits where she wears it and very little else. It is probable that at this time her head was shaven to insure its perfect fit.

The cheers and cries of the elect followed the newly married pair out of the dim depths of the temple and into the sunlight. For a moment we see them, small as dolls before the bronze entrance, facing the gardens where bloomed the descendants of trees and plants brought from strange lands by Akhenaton's ancestors. Curious animals, wandering free under the trees, lifted their heads in wonder as the bridal procession left the temple, listening to the musical roar coming from every side out of the streets of Thebes, bidding long life to the new king and queen and to their marriage, that it might last like all good things "for a million million years."

Let them stand for one moment before the temple, in the clear light of the vanished centuries. We see them radiant and touchingly young. Akhenaton was the most powerful king ever to assume the throne of Egypt. Nefertiti was its most beautiful queen.

They were possessed of the power of gods, but they were not large people. The trappings of power magnified their personalities. A keen observer such as Aye would have noted that Nefertiti's body was still childlike as glimpsed through the transparent white draperies. The proud lift of her head made her seem tall. Actually she was not likely to have been more than four feet and a half tall, as few Egyptian women of her day grew beyond that size.

Every line of her small body spoke of authority. By the mysterious alchemy peculiar to royal Egyptian marriages Nefertiti was now not only royal but divine. As Tiy had been named before her, so Nefertiti was now the "great royal wife." With that title she assumed Akhenaton's birthright of divinity. Marriage had transformed the scribe's daughter. She was now a goddess of Thebes.

As Queen Nefertiti, Empress of the Two Lands, she was equal in power to Akhenaton. Her name would follow his in important places. With him she controlled the destinies of five million Egyptian subjects and no one knew how many more subject millions in the vassal countries ruled by Egypt. She had her choice of many crowns and many titles.

But her proudest title was one Nefertiti shared with all Egyptian women, rich or poor. Without it the others were worthless. It was that of "mistress of the house." This, to an Egyptian woman, meant that her husband had chosen her beyond all other women to share his home and bear his legal children. To Nefertiti, it was the guarantee that only Akhenaton's children born to her could expect to inherit Egypt's golden throne.

So the future of the Eighteenth Dynasty and of Egypt rested on this pair glittering in the sunlight.

Their greatest responsibility was to share and to represent the glory of Egypt, present and past. It was Nefertiti's supreme duty to personify her name's meaning, "the beautiful." To all Egyptian women she was to emblematize the perfect woman. It was a feminine ideal she would achieve, and uphold through the ages.

As for Akhenaton, whose presence awed all save his bride, and who was so often portrayed as colossal, he could not have been much over five feet tall. But his majesty reached to the sun, and it is doubtful if any observing him then noticed the physical imperfections his Amarna artists were to ruthlessly portray.

A gigantic head of Akhenaton found at Karnak is considered one of the finest pieces of portraiture of the antique world. It reveals him as narrow of face and skull, with the deep, hooded eyes that so often mark the super-intelligent (or the fanatic). Straight, thick brows are pressed down by the weight of the crown. The mouth with its full, finely cut lips, is voluptuous. The chin is narrow and long, the nose straight. Yes, one would say, a good face.

Other portraiture shows him large in stomach and hips and with such bad posture than centuries later one archaeologist would hazard a guess that the "heretic king" had been a woman, and had in fact been Nefertiti! This canard was soon dispelled.

The appearance he gave was of supreme authority. That was his principal duty as king. He portrayed to his people the male ideal; the perfect being that served as the sublime ideal to every Egyptian.

His next responsibility would demand much of his strength and character. As king, it was his duty to maintain the harmony in Egypt that had been achieved by his illustrious ancestors with the help of the gods. To conserve that harmony Akhenaton must earn the continued protection of the gods, particularly Amon. If necessary, he would enforce it with the tremendous might of his armies and navies and police force.

These were heavy responsibilities to rest on the shoulders of a stripling. Nefertiti's duties were simpler. She need only to be herself, beloved and beautiful.

We see them clearly, two teen-agers who had inherited the world. And that world was Egypt.

Why did the triumphant young Akhenaton risk the loss of that world when, shortly after his coronation and marriage, he began his controversy with the powerful Amon priesthood by precipitating a quarrel between two rival Theban gods?

In the first flush of their married happiness Akhenaton and Nefertiti were the ideal lovers of Egyptian legend.

It is a curious fact that no scarabs have been found commemorating their union, such as Akhenaton's father had issued in such quantities upon his marriage to Tiy. But Aye's tomb has retained for us Akhenaton's own words testifying to his having made Nefertiti his co-regent over the two Egypts.

"The heiress," so Akhenaton named his bride, "great in favor, lady of grace, sweet of love, Mistress of the North and South, beloved of the living Aton, the Chief Wife of the King, whom he loves, lady of the Two Lands, great of love, Nefertiti, living forever." Elsewhere he named her his "lady of happiness," a title that became her well.

In the words is concealed the beginning of rebellion. "Beloved of the living Aton," Akhenaton named himself. What had become of the vaunted loyalty to Amon, chief god of Thebes?

In this year of his coronation and his marriage Akhenaton showed his first defiance of Amon. He began by reviving an ancient argument.

Two sun gods disputed authority in Egypt. The city of Heliopolis in the north worshiped Ra-Harakhty, while Karnak's chief god, Amon, had combined with the sun as Amon-Ra.

Shortly after Akhenaton became king he took upon himself the prerogative of his architecture-loving ancestors and began building. He raised statues of himself larger than life at Karnak. He began the construction of a large temple near the Amon temple to the Heliopolis sun god, under its shortened name, Aton.

Aton had the concentrated meaning of "disk of the sun." Its emblem was a circle with many arms ending in hands.

This honor, paid to the hitherto obscure Aton in the sacred compound of the chief god of Thebes was regarded as a decided affront by the powerful entrenched priesthood of Amon.

The young king and queen paid no attention to the first mutterings of the priests of Amon. They had many responsibilities to church and state. They could take part in fascinating adult pleasures. All these they shared.

Still they were well aware of their august places as king and queen. Court life at Thebes was relaxed but dignified, and there was a large amount of protocol to be observed.

Nefertiti had been well prepared for her new status. Thebes had known her as a sweet-tempered, playful girl. Now she assumed in public the manner befitting a goddess and a queen. She had the strong support of Queen Tiy, and of Aye and his wife.

There was no change in Akhenaton. He had been born a god and served as co-regent. As a boy he had been dignified, given to poetry and mysticism. These traits were only accentuated by the assumption of absolute authority. In Akhenaton the mystic warred with the man. He still wrote love poems to Nefertiti, but there was burgeoning in him a greater poem that was to help change the history of Egypt.

There were occasions when the two were obliged to present an awe-inspiring unity. Rigid as statues, they sat through affairs of state, interviews with the grand vizier, members of the nobility and judiciary and the services, and ambassadors from foreign lands. They stood through the "public appearances" when endless homage was paid them. They memorized conventional speeches designed to match the importance of those who came before them, literally "crawling on the ground," for they were hosts to the world. They accepted fortunes in tribute as their divine right.

They knew litanies, rituals, procedure and prayers, for much of their responsibility had a religious base and was shared with priests of Amon.

Then, freed from affairs of state, the two played together like happy children. All Egyptians prolonged childhood if they could. This pair midway between adolescence and maturity were light-hearted companions as well as husband and wife.

The kingdom they had inherited was a land of pleasure, entertainment, holidays, festivals and deep religious feeling. "Hundred-gated Thebes," as it would be named by Homer, was known as the city of a thousand delights. As a married pair they could enjoy together its endless festivals and banquets. Games, music, dancing, and feasting were part of the pattern of life. They had been intensified during the reign of Akhenaton's father, whose reign had been so luxurious and pleasure-filled that Breasted refers to him as "Amenhotep the Magnificent."

The young regents assumed the leadership of a court that in luxury, richness and gaiety can be compared only to those of France under the Bourbons and Rome under the Medici.

Nowhere else did the fortunate live in such comfort and elegance as in Thebes. Even a moderately well-to-do home held more luxury and beauty than most homes do today. The families of the rich, noble, or highly placed lived like sybarites.

They entertained in immense columned salons which opened into other living rooms, and dining rooms, and lustration rooms, and bedrooms, all beautifully furnished and equipped with ventilation and lavatory systems. Every house was surrounded by gardens.

Did they sleep better, these wealthy ones who rested on costly beds under fine linen, with crescent-shaped headrests of wood or stone or glass, than the poor who huddled by night on their dirt floors in low-ceilinged mud rooms in the slums of Thebes? Within the tenants cooked and kept warm over camel-dung fires in pottery braziers, but the outer walls were hidden by forests of bloom and even the meanest flat roof had its pavilion where the poor could spread their mats and sleep under the stars, without dread of dew or rain. And wherever one walked in Thebes, night or day, it was always to the high oriental keening of the street musicians.

The delights of Thebes centered in and around the palace, and the two children of Thebes, now grown, led a court suddenly revived in a ceaseless round of amusement and pleasure.

They displayed their personal happiness with a frankness that had never before been revealed by Egyptian monarchs.

Every previous Pharaoh had shown a forbidding façade to his people. He was traditionally the granite monarch, a hundred feet tall and impervious to human passion. Akhenaton turned his back on tradition. He was not yet living in another world. He was not a laughing man, but he loved the laughter of others, and the gaiety of Nefertiti, "lady of happiness," entranced him.

Portraits show them, young faces alight with ecstasy, sitting close together as couples must when in love.

The court banquets were frequent and extravagant as scenes from what would later be the Arabian Nights. There were more than a hundred holy days and days commemorating important events in Egyptian history. The gay young members of the court celebrated them with the excitement of children. Even regents could forget their exalted positions and relax into playfulness at the palace banquets.

The hosts and their guests lay on bolstered divans, or sat, if they preferred, on low, cushioned stools or chairs. The palace guests were the favored of the court, or artisans or artists worthy of honor, or distinguished guests from foreign lands. All were lightly clad but decked with jewels and flowers.

Flowers were massed along the long table in magnificent vases. Bouquets of flowers filled larger vases on the floor and hung from the ceiling and walls.

Small black slaves from Nubia stirred the air over the diners' heads with ostrich-feather fans. Naked slave girls holding carafes bent over the guests to fill goblets with wine. Other slave girls stood watch in strategic positions against the walls with basins, ewers of scented water, vials of unguents and linen towels, lest a diner sicken from a surfeit of rich food and sweet wine. Cow-headed Hathor was the goddess in charge of music, dancing, banquets, and all these festive affairs, and since drunkenness came under the heading of pleasure, it was not considered a disgraceful state, even on the part of a great lady.

Under each lady's chair was her make-up box, without which no beautiful woman could be expected to survive the damage done by hours of feasting. And many of the ladies, for comfort's sake, dined without their wigs, and atop their shaven heads were cone-shaped cakes of tallow scented with a strong fragrance such as myrrh. The tallow melted in the heat of conviviality and dripped perfume over shoulders and arms.

The table was long and low and glittered with silver and gold. Each dish had engraved on it designs of flowers, fruits, or beasts, or a representation of some epic event in Egyptian mythology or history. Each was the work of a great artist, as were the goblets, and wine bottles, and even the handles of the spoons, which were cunningly designed as gods, people, animals, birds, or fish.

There were dishes of faïence or pottery, bordered in *repoussé* or decorated in blue or gray, and exquisitely colored glassware.

The basic foods of the land were simple. The Egyptian chefs, always men, took pride in their cuisine and could develop every staple into a variety of dishes. They were skilled at confections made of cornmeal, wheat, and barley flour, eggs, milk, and honey. There was no sugar cane and honey was the only sweetening.

The staple loaf for rich and poor was a thick-crusted loaf baked in a brick oven, but there were forty different recipes for bread and cake. Meat was usually roasted on a spit and seasoned with garlic and spices brought from lands beyond the Red Sea. Wild game was always popular, particularly the wild geese and ducks that lived in the marshes, and there was always fish from the Nile.

There were special chefs for soufflés.

Salads were favored. The perpetually renewed banks along the river were ribboned with vegetable gardens, and a good dinner always featured bowls of leeks, onions, olives, and lettuce, dressed with olive oil. Lettuce was a favorite vegetable. It was supposed to be an aphrodisiac, and Min, the god of sensuality, was known as the "lettuce eater." This reasoning seems odd because a few centuries later, in England, lettuce was being recommended by doctors as a non-stimulant and prescribed for priests and nuns "to prevent obnoxious dreams and lewd thoughts."

Desserts were rich sweetmeats made of honey and fruits— pomegranates, apples, figs, and dates. Date palms grew all along the Nile and the fruit clusters could be had for the climbing. Rich or poor, the Egyptians ate dates at every meal and considered them as needful as bread.

The staples of the poor were dates, bread, and barley beer. The beer was made by a roundabout method. Loaves of barley flour were baked, then soaked in water. The liquid was allowed to ferment, and the result was known as "the beer that ignores awakening." It was popular on the tables of rich and poor and was left in earthenware jugs in tombs as gifts to the dead.

The sweet wine served at every festive meal was made of grapes or pomegranates.

Dining and drinking through long leisurely hours, the wealthy and their guests were entertained by relays of performers. The palace and all great houses had their own troupes of musicians and entertainers, but celebrated guest artists were invited. We know little more about early Egyptian music than that much of it was in minor key, of oriental flavor, and was played on a variety of instruments, lyres, lutes, flutes, oddly shaped guitars, trumpets, tambourines, pipes, cymbals, ivory castenets, and, it is believed, drums. Probably the best-loved musician was the harpist, who might be man or woman and was often famous. Some harps were as tall as the player and had sounding boards as large as those of modern harps. Musicians and singers as a rule were women.

At the palace banquets troupes of dancing girls performed, who lived and had been trained there. Many were Semitic slaves captured during forays into Asia. They danced naked the languid, rhythmic dances of the Orient, while the musicians played and sang or clapped hands to the staccato beat of bare feet on the painted floor.

There were acrobatic dancers. A sketch shows an Eighteenth Dynasty performer bending backward. Her long hair almost sweeps the floor. She wears a tight kilt and a bandeau crossing her breast leaves the stomach exposed.

There were women acrobats and tumblers, but many professional artists were men. There were celebrated blind harpists. When one of these was led into the banquet hall as guest artist and, seated on the stool placed for him, struck the opening chord, the noisiest celebrant paid him the honor of silence.

The Egyptians delighted in many kinds of songs. There were comic songs, "occupational" songs, and songs about love. There were many about animals and birds. One popular favorite was supposedly sung by a swallow.

The "occupational" songs were originated by Eighteenth Dynasty workmen to lighten their labors. Some were humorous. One was based on a jest: cattle were used for threshing, but in this song a band of sheep are milling around the threshing area stamping out the grain. To explain the absurdity, the farmer sings:

"The herdsman is in the water with the fish.
"He talks to the shad . . ."

Another "Thresher's Song" was serious and supposedly sung by a farmer who was driving his herd of cattle around the circle:

"Thresh for yourselves, thresh for yourselves,
"Oh, cattle!
"Make the straw you will eat, and barley for your masters . . ."

The "Ploughman's Song" concerned a farmer whose team was dragging the wooden blade through rich black earth:

"A good day! It is cool.
"The oxen are pulling the plough.
"The sky does as we desire. [The day was clear.]
"Let us work for the noble!"

Another was supposedly sung by the reapers as they swung their copper-edged blades through the grain:

"This good day has come to the land.
"The north wind has come.
"And the sky does as we desire."

Most of the recitationists were male. They told stories, or recited hymns and poems, some of their own making. The poet was popular. And when the professional storyteller appeared and, seated cross-legged before his host, began the spinning of his wondrous tales, all listened and never tired of their telling, although many of the stories like the songs were as old as Egypt.

And all the time the beautiful naked slave girls poured wine into goblets now treasured in museums, and the air was heavy with the scent of perfume, flowers, and wine. A great lady might slide from her divan and be promptly hidden behind helpful slave girls. Some of the older couples called for taborets and game boxes, and with these beside their chairs played such gambling games as Senet, which resembled checkers, and knucklebones used as dice, and throw sticks shaken from a box. And while no money existed, a fortune in jewels could be gambled away.

Other couples, after feasting, slipped away into the outer gardens, to the pavilions and summerhouses.

The same stories were told in the palace and in the homes of the poor. The Egyptians never tired of them and heard them over and over with the absorption of children. But it is unjust to regard them as children. The world was in its infancy; story and song were new. The Egyptians were the sophisticates of the world, but their intelligence was not jaded. Akhenaton and Nefertiti had heard as children the songs sung and stories told them by Tiy the nurse; they would listen again to the same songs and stories with their own children at Amarna.

Literature was to soar during Akhenaton's reign. Little was written down. A few of the poems, hymns, and folk tales are all that remain to us. Many are based on an earthy humor.

The Egyptians delighted in puns, and play on words, and syllables that matched, and words that when placed together formed others. They liked stories of reality and fable and the supernatural. They doted on satire, for any man could be made to seem ridiculous, even a priest or a king. They loved stories about love, vengeance, adventures, serpents that attacked ships, men without heads, sorcerers, evil monsters, men, women, and gods. There were fairy stories for men and women and children, and stories expressly for women, and morality stories. There were stories for children and stories that were definitely not for children.

And all could be heard over and over without tiring, as they had been told for centuries in Egypt, and some of the stories to which Akhenaton and Nefertiti listened would appear centuries later in other languages and other lands, for fairy stories are universal and can be recited in all countries forever.

Of these the best-known is the story of Sinuhe, which Rudyard Kipling considered one of the world's great literary masterpieces.

As a student Aye would have copied the story of Sinuhe many times, for it was one of the country's classics and always given as the perfect literary example to those learning to write. Sinuhe was a courtier in early Egypt who fled the land during a political upheaval. He made his way across the Isthmus of Suez and became a wanderer in the desert. Eventually he made a new life for himself, but he was homesick for Egypt and began a journey back that would last through many years and adventures. He was shipwrecked; he had a romance with a serpent queen. But he survived and came back to Egypt and was awarded wealth and honor. This was the sort of story with a happy ending that delighted Egyptians young and old. It has pleased young and old in many lands since Nefertiti's time, for Sinuhe was the original of Sindbad the Sailor.

Another tale may have given rise to that of "Ali Baba and the Forty Thieves." The hero was real, and the story based on actual happenings, although they may have been greatly exaggerated. It told of General Thutiy, who was a favorite officer of the great Pharaoh Thutmose III, known as the Conqueror and Akhenaton's most illustrious ancestor.

The general, wishing to take the seemingly impregnable fortress of Joppa, sent a donkey train into the town led by officers disguised as merchants. Each donkey carried two large leather panniers; in each sack was one of Thutiy's finest soldiers. Once inside the walls, the warriors burst their sacks and by night threw open the city gates to the army. Joppa was captured and Thutiy "richly rewarded." True or not, in the Louvre in Paris is a gold dish inscribed with "affectionate tribute from King Thutmose III to his favorite, Thutiy, prince, priest, scribe, commander, and governor of the North countries."

Among the best-liked fairy tales was one of a girl who lost her malachite hair ornament while rowing on the Nile. A magician parted the waters and the girl recovered her treasure.

The Amarna Letters have preserved several popular Eighteenth Dynasty fables. One, found in the archives, with a faïence label reading FROM THE LIBRARY OF AMENHOTEP III, is a papyrus on which is written in Egyptian script, "The Tale of the Sycamore and the Date Palm."

Another was a mythological treatise. In it a goddess, Irishkigal, had lost her husband, Mergal, to death. She sued the other gods, who agreed to let her pass through the other world to the place where she would find her husband. She passed bravely through the twelve gates of death, but after she found her husband, the two quarreled. He was about to kill her, but words came to her and she pleaded her love for him. He lowered his hand and burst into tears. In an effecting reconciliation, the two agreed to rule together over all the world, and whatever she might wish for would be done "from that time until now."

It was an ending to please women—the women who lived in Nefertiti's time.

Another popular story was "The Eloquent Peasant."

A peasant who had broken the law was brought into court and argued his own case so masterfully that he was brought into the august presence of the Pharaoh that the great one might enjoy his eloquence.

There were stories in discussion form. One was between a cat, a donkey and a hippopotamus. Another was a debate between a man and his soul: did the man have the right to commit suicide?

There was one narrative that never failed to silence those who listened. This was the prophecy made by the prophet Ipuwer who had lived back in the Twelfth Dynasty, half a century before. In the presence of the Pharaoh he foretold the coming ruin of Egypt, of social and political organizations overthrown, and then the coming of a Messiah, one with no evil in his heart, who would be as a shepherd to his people, and whose presence would be "cooling to the flame."

And this was recited in meter, sonorous as the rhythm of drums, in a cadence that would later be known as Biblical. Breasted would write of such ancient Egyptian recitations: "It remained for the Hebrew to give this old form a higher ethical and religious significance."

The final words of the prophecy were like thunder: "Verily he shall smite evil . . . Where is he this day? Does he sleep among you?"

The boy-king Akhenaton may have heard these words with a sense of summons or of doom.

The Egyptians knew a man's heart controlled his body and

being. Akhenaton's heart was active with many emotions, including a religious conviction still held secret and poetry that would not be denied.

Much of their life centered on the Nile.

The deep valley cut by the river bisected Egypt. On either side lay the Libyan and the Arabian deserts. The country's existence depended on the river, and its wealth was concentrated in this narrow ribbon of living green studded by yellow cliffs and lined with clusters of palm, sycamore, tamarisk, acacia, and papyrus.

No Egyptian knew the actual source of the Nile. But each summer the river was swollen with floodwaters rushing down from the melting snows of Abyssinia. The waters were the tears of Isis, weeping for her dead love, Osiris.

This happened around mid-June, at the time of summer solstice. Then the city filled with pilgrims, and festival and feasting celebrated the feast of Isis, who was the goddess of life and love. In the sky shone Sirius, the star of Isis and the brightest of all stars, its arrival in the heavens marking the beginning of the New Year. From the palace to the lowliest hovel there was feasting and exchanging of gifts. Young and old were remembered, nor were the dead forgotten. The king opened his treasury and presented gifts to his nobles, who in turn brought their most valuable treasures to lay at his feet, so that the throne room of the palace was heaped with treasure being exchanged—gold and silver chariots, portraits of the king, shields, quivers, bows and arrows, swords, daggers, sunshades (carried by slaves over men and women), chairs, vases, goblets, and the endless exquisite little pieces of bric-a-brac which all Egyptians loved.

This was the season of the mystery plays, with young actors playing the roles of gods in ceremonial dramas like passion plays. The people delighted in these performances and wept in anguish at each staged death of Osiris.

The god was dead, but all knew his death was temporary, as was all death; without this brief tragedy there would be no tears from his goddess-wife Isis, and the water would remain low in the Nile. A summer when the river ran low foretold famine, which the Egyptians feared as greatly as they did the plague that at intervals devastated Egypt. Too great flooding was equally feared.

In the fall the Nile gave further cause for rejoicing. The Pleiades vanished behind the night rim of the desert, the month was November, the time of Athyr. The waters sank, and the rich, dark fields appeared that were the Nile's gift to Egypt, and to this earth seeds were offered. The seeds sprouted, and Osiris was reborn, it was the annual symbol of life everlasting. The people made images of the god of wet mud mixed with seeds, and these fertility symbols sprouted as additional proof that life was eternal.

During the fourth month of the year all Egypt awaited the resurrection of Osiris. The halls of the temples were closed and rites were held within in dimness and secrecy. This was a time of meditation and prayer and the searching of one's soul. At last the doors of the temples reopened. The priests came forth and announced to the jubilant people the mystical message that the god had been reborn.

Harvest time was in the spring. Again there was festival, beginning in cries of lamentation and gestures of mourning as the first seed of Osiris fell under the copper-edged scythes. But Isis was watching; Isis approved the scything of the corn, or the wheat or the barley, and the harvesting began in earnest with general rejoicing.

The river gave so much that the Egyptians considered the country itself a gift from the Nile. It was their source of life, hence a god. The spirit of the Nile was Hapy (or Hapinou). Each year a special celebration was held in his honor. A beautifully dressed virgin was dropped into the water to serve as Hapy's bride. A special prayer was said to the river every day: "Keep Egypt alive!"

The Nile was the playground for all Egypt. Akhenaton and Nefertiti had played on its banks as children and fished and hunted in reed coracles not unlike those the people of the Stone Age had sailed on thousands of years before. As far back as man could remember there had been boats on the river. The young king and queen had their own pleasure and sports craft and their royal barge, bannered and cushioned and rowed by tiers of sailors, that carried them to and from eastern and western

Thebes. And theirs were the great royal fleets. Some of their ships
were 70 feet wide and 200 feet long and manned by 100 men.
These ships traveled under both oar and sail.

Traffic was heavy on the Nile. The king's ships came and
went on the river. The wide, square sails carried them rapidly
northward, but on their return to Thebes, heavily burdened and
fighting both current and wind, the sailors were obliged to take
to the oars. They had been to strange places and returned with
much treasure, for the Nile was the thoroughfare of world trade,
commerce, and adventure, and through it and into the royal
treasuries of Akhenaton and Nefertiti were channeled the riches
of Asia.

As soon as the returning galleys were sighted an impressive
figure appeared on the long stone wharf at Thebes. His white
robe flowed about his still figure and his hand gripped the staff
of the vizier. It was Ptahmose, one of whose duties was to meet
all foreign and domestic vessels bringing tribute to the king.

The wealth of the world was in the returning ships.

The ships came from strange and far-off places. Some had been
"up river," to the south, into Abyssinia. Others had sailed "down"
to the delta, into the Mediterranean, and up the eastern coast
beyond Jerusalem and Tyre and to Byblos in Syria. Others,
reaching the delta, had turned south again, crossing down to
the Red Sea. There was a natural waterway joining the Nile to
the Red Sea. The Egyptians tried to cut it through from the Red
to the Mediterranean, and one attempt had taken the lives of
120,000 men, but the sands kept refilling the man-cut channel.
Centuries later Ferdinand de Lesseps achieved the permanent
Suez Canal.

The vizier waited on the wharfs with all Thebes that did not
have work to do massed behind him watching the heavily burdened ships move against the stone piles. The wide gangplanks
were laid down and the unlading of the treasure began. Tur-
quoise and copper from Sinai. Rafts made of fragrant cedar logs
from Lebanon lashed together. From Asia Minor and Tyre came
fortunes in beautifully shaped vases and vessels of silver and
gold, and from Cyprus, Crete, and the Aegean fine ivory furniture
and chariots of silver and gold. The finest produce from the
fields of Asia was stacked on the wharves, and magnificent

blooded horses were led ashore, and the fine dogs favored by the
Egyptians. From all the lands came gold rings and bracelets and
necklaces that were paid instead of currency to Egypt. From Asia
also came the thousands of newly captured slaves, most of these
of Semitic origin, who were highly prized for providing the
finest of dancers. Led with bound arms past the wondering Egyptians, who were lightly clad in thinnest white, and smooth of
face and even skull, they presented a curious contrast in their
clothing of thick, bright wool and with their long matted beards
and hair.

From Punt (the Somali Coast, down the Nile at the southern
end of the Red Sea), which was the original home of the gods,
came rare spices and attars and gums and perfume, fragrant cin-
namon wood, nard, myrrh, and frankincense, skins of rare animals, and living beasts in cages, such as baboons and panthers.

Slaves carried the treasure from the ships to the stone wharves,
and the air over the Theban waterfront was filled with the rich
aromas of spices and materials and aromatic woods breathing of
the mystery of Asia.

Now the vizier, in his splendid robes, watched over the guards
who marshaled the slaves bringing the endless treasure in solemn
procession from the waterfront to the Temple of Amon.

In the dim, cavernous hall, under the altar of the god, Akhenaton and Nefertiti sat on their golden thrones, as Amenhotep and
Tiy had before them, while Ptahmose, the vizier, saw placed before them the glittering tribute until treasure was heaped around
them throne-high. Rigid as the gold statue of Amon over their
heads, watching the glittering treasure flood rise about them,
they accepted the tribute and homage of their world.

And of all this treasure, it was the duty of Ptahmose to declare
how much belonged to the king, and how much must be given
to Amon.

The Nile was the waterway, but other treasure routes led into
Egypt.

Over tracks as old as time crossing the desert marched the
emissaries of the Pharaoh, leading the long caravans of donkeys
burdened with tribute from every Egyptian city and hamlet and
farm. Thebes was the center of world and domestic trade, and

all that was given to Thebes belonged to the young king and queen—all save the share reserved for Amon.

That share grew with Egypt's good fortune. Amon was the richest god in the world.

But Akhenaton the king was also Amon the god.

The boyish king on the throne had always been a questioner. In his mind he was pondering questions to be asked of Amon, whose name he bore. He had shared them with Nefertiti.

Their plans were made. The new temple would soon be completed. He would not long be known as Amenhotep IV.

CHAPTER SEVEN

In the Temple—Heritage

North Thebes, 1369 B.C.

Behind the great hall of the Temple at Karnak were a hundred other rooms and halls, including a mortuary sanctuary on which were recorded the names, lives, and achievements of the brilliant ancestors of Akhenaton. Their statues lined the walls; they still exist.

The ruins of the sanctuary hold the ghosts of the young Akhenaton and Nefertiti, reading on the high walls the inspiring history of the country they now ruled. The walls spoke to the married teen-agers of the heavy responsibility of Egypt.

What drama the sanctuary walls recorded! It was told in cuneiform and illustrated with statues and relief drawings of the gods and of kings and queens who were also gods.

While it was true that Egypt had no historians, its leaders had never been reluctant to record their achievements on stone. The history of the Eighteenth Dynasty as lived by Akhenaton's people was clearly recorded not only by peak achievements but with fascinating glimpses of ancient family feuds and jealousies.

It has rightly been said that Egypt is history. We know of it first thousands of years before Christ as the oldest and most advanced civilization. By 4241 B.C., when the calendar was introduced, it was already well developed, with large agricultural settlements, cultivated lands, and herds of domesticated cattle. The Egyptians used tools of wood, stone, and copper, wove linen from the flax they raised, wrote in pictographs, painted, and paid allegiance to many gods.

It was a self-supporting country, with one weakness, for it was a land divided into two sections, Upper and Lower Egypt. These were the Two Lands, and they wasted centuries in a state of enmity.

Menes (also known as Narmer), a rather legendary figure,

welded the two countries together around 2900 B.C. and made Egypt a nation. He donned the red crown of Sais and named himself Lord of the Two Lands, one of the many titles inherited by Akhenaton. Menes laid down the country's first laws and as the first of the Pharaoh conquerors founded the First Dynasty.

The series of strong dynasties that followed brought Egypt to the Eighteenth, which was Akhenaton's and Nefertiti's.

The first Eighteenth Dynasty king was the "great liberator" Ahmose I (Amosis, also Kamose), who ruled Egypt from 1570 to 1545 B.C. He was famed for having founded the dynasty, and for driving the Hyksos out of Egypt.

"Like mice in the wheat," Egyptian historians described the Hyksos. No one knew who they were, or where they had come from. Some time in the eighteenth century B.C. they had swept down, perhaps from somewhere in the Caucasus, and in an avalanche of conquering hordes invaded the Fertile Crescent. Egypt was a self-supporting, peaceful, pastoral country with no "foreigners" in its midst when the Hyksos disrupted their pastoral lives. The invaders came by thousands, in unbroken lines, led by horses and chariots, which the Egyptians had never seen—these at least they gave to Egypt.

Josephus, the historian, writing many centuries later, described the Hyksos as being an unknown nomadic people who swarmed down into Egypt from "someplace in the East," and overtook the peaceful Egyptians with such surprise that "not an arrow was fired in defense."

Once in, the "shepherd kings" did not integrate. They built their own walled and fortified cities from which they sent out armed forces thousands strong to destroy the Egyptian temples and levy tribute on the people. Even the leading city, Thebes, had to accept rule from the foreign overlords.

The helpless Egyptians hated them and referred to them as "the enemy," "the barbarians," "the Asiatics," or even more contemptuously, "the rulers of foreign countries." The Hyksos continued to rule, mysteriously arrogant and contemptuous of the Egyptians. So for three hundred years Egypt lay helpless under the Hyksos, and this period was known in history as the time of "the great humiliation."

Little is known of this period, for the Egyptians were a cheerful people and more given to recording their triumphs than their failures. There were attempts at long intervals to drive out the invaders which were severely punished. The mummy of King Senkenre, who lived before Ahmose, shows deep wounds made by battle weapons, which probably caused his death and are supposed to have been suffered while he was leading a futile rebellion against the Hyksos.

Other Egyptian kings made attempts at protest, but for three hundred years prayers continued for a Pharaoh to be born who would serve as the liberator of his people.

The Pharaoh who had been all-powerful and divine was subject even to the whims of the foreign rulers. There is a legend of an insulting note sent by a Hyksos overlord from his palace on the delta to the Pharaoh in his palace at Thebes, complaining that the bellowing of the hippopotamuses in the royal pool at Thebes was so loud it was annoying him on the delta, four hundred miles away!

The priesthood at Thebes fought the invaders with prayers and curses. The Pharaohs aided the priests by pronouncing certain royal curses which were supposed to be a sure means of destruction. One of the most effective ways of destroying an enemy was to write his name, surrounded by curses, on a red pottery jar and smash the jar. Many an anti-Hyksos jar must have been smashed with due incantation under the image of Amon in the great temple at Thebes. But these cursing ceremonies that had never failed before, perhaps because those cursed believed in them, had no effect on the Hyksos. It was said they worshiped Set, the god of evil, and they continued to demand increasing tribute from the priests and kings.

By the time Ahmose became king the Hyksos had been living inside Egypt for three centuries "on the fat of the land." They dominated from the delta and had made Nubia in the south an ally; Egypt was helpless between two entrenched enemies.

The records do not state how Akhenaton's first known ancestor achieved the tremendous feat of combining the two Egypts and leading them in a concerted drive against the enemy. North and South Egypt were resentful of one another. Somehow Ahmose linked them in a common bond of hatred of the Hyksos and the hope of driving them out of Egypt. The entire plan must have been executed in secrecy. His only means of establishing communication between the two sections was by couriers who raced their chariots through territory guarded by Hyksos troops and spies. Somehow he brought understanding between the two Egypts and made as one a country that had been bewailing its helplessness for three centuries.

A people who had nursed resentment for centuries were reunited and recharged with hope and hatred. There was no more talk of North or South; it was "our country" to be delivered from evil. It was no longer "the king's forces," but "our army." Before the Hyksos knew what was happening, all Egypt was on the march. It was said the humblest citizen found some means of contributing to the crusade for freedom.

The war raged on for years. One by one, the fortified towns of the Hyksos fell under the fury of the Egyptians. Slowly the enemy were driven back, out of the delta, out of Egypt, into Asia. The Egyptians had suffered too long to consider mercy. They pursued the fleeing Hyksos. This was no longer retribution. It was vengeance.

One town in Palestine was besieged for three years by Ahmose's soldiers before the barricaded Hyksos were forced to yield.

After many years the last of the Hyksos were gone from Egypt, but they were not forgiven, nor forgotten.

Egypt was free, and for the first time it was a united nation. King Ahmose had achieved lasting fame as the deliverer of Egypt from bondage, as the unifier of his country, as the founder of the Eighteenth Dynasty and the father of its heroic kings.

He was the direct ancestor of Akhenaton.

The boy-king had other illustrious forefathers. Following Ahmose into the Eighteenth Dynasty was a series of aggressive and constructive rulers who had culminated in the dreamy, thoughtful boy who had married Nefertiti.

They were:

Amenhotep I	1545–1525
Thutmose I	1525–1495
Thutmose II	1495–1490
Thutmose III	1490–1486
Hatshepsut	1486–1468

But Ahmose was not Egypt's leading hero. The greatest of the conqueror kings was Akhenaton's great-great grandfather Thutmose III, who has been described by Breasted as having had "more color and personality than any king of Egypt save Akhenaton."

The name and deeds of Thutmose were written large on Egypt's history. They blazoned the walls of the sanctuary at Karnak where Akhenaton and Nefertiti read and rejoiced for the heritage he had left them. Much of the conquered territories, the wealth, the security of the Eighteenth Dynasty were owed to Thutmose III. It was to him the young regents owed a supreme kingdom that had known only peace and prosperity for one hundred and fifty years.

The ancient records had only praise for Thutmose III. "The Great Conqueror" was written after his name as a matter of course. He was also "The founder of the Egyptian Empire," "conqueror of foreign lands," "conqueror of three hundred and sixty-seven cities," "hero of seventeen campaigns," "conqueror of Aleppo," "punisher of Nubia, of Mitanni, of Syria," and in final, crowning praise, "hero of the battle of Megiddo."

Modern historians are even more laudatory. He is considered "the Napoleon of Ancient Egypt," and "perhaps the greatest military genius that ever lived."

Like his descendant, Akhenaton, Thutmose III was a thoughtful, serious, and ambitious king. Like Akhenaton, he inherited a united nation that had long been at peace. Three hundred years had passed since Ahmose had driven out the last of the Hyksos. Thutmose III had no more need to conquer than had Akhenaton. But in both was the will to power, to create and to conquer.

Thutmose III determined upon a greater Egypt.

There was only one way to rouse a contented, prosperous country. He revived a hatred that had smoldered for three centuries.

Behind the Metropolitan Museum in New York's Central Park stands an obelisk Thutmose III raised to his own memory in Thebes. On it he described himself as "the smiter of the rulers of foreign countries who had attacked him." As is often the case in the claims of kings, this was untrue. No Hyksos had dared drive his chariot into Egyptian territory for three hundred years.

But the disgrace of their having tyrannized Egypt still rankled, and the memory of the "great humiliation" was still green. Thutmose III had a ready made whetstone for the blade of his military genius.

He rallied Egypt to vengeance. Armies gathered such as never had been massed together before in any land, and led by Thutmose, under the protection of the little before recognized Theban god Amon, set forth in final pursuit of the scattered "rulers of foreign countries." If, as Thutmose III claimed, the pursued ones were the aggressors, he was not the first, nor the last, leader to demand vengeance on such grounds. As "Thutmose the defender" he carried the pursuit into foreign lands. If during the pursuing the countries into which the Hyksos fled were conquered and annexed to Egypt, it was by the will of Amon.

Thutmose III campaigned year after year, by the seasons, setting out from Thebes with his armies directly after the spring rains were over, leading the way in his "light and glittering" chariot of electrum (silver and gold). Wherever he went, he sent his marshal on ahead to commandeer the palace of the local ruler and see that every luxury and comfort was provided for his stay.

Seventeen times he led the way into Syria and beyond. A new empire, the Hittites, had come to power in Asia Minor and was pressing into Syria. In pursuing the Hyksos Thutmose III invaded the fastnesses of the Hittites and a new and lasting enmity began.

He had brought his army, war chariots, horses, and troops to northern Phoenicia by sea, in galleys. This country was so rich in vineyards and in grain that he was able to report his soldiers "drank wine and were anointed with unguents every day," as was only possible on special feast days in Egypt. When his troops left Phoenicia much of the country's wealth went with them.

He led them on to Kadesh, the Hittite stronghold between the two Lebanons, on the Orontes River. The most formidable fortress in Syria, it commanded the harvest-ripe valley with its only road, but Thutmose's soldiers harvested the grain and cut down the trees, and with the lumber built scaling ladders they placed against the walls of the besieged city. So Kadesh fell to the Egyptians.

1. This unfinished head of King Akhenaton (also known as Amenhotep IV and Amenophosis IV) is that of a poet, priest, and dreamer who inherited the world's greatest kingdom and whose ideas were centuries ahead of his time. The profile indicates the fanatic personality that would risk the throne and even life rather than yield up his faith in the one god.

2. Nefertiti was fifteen when she married King Akhenaton and became empress of Egypt. This head by an Amarna sculptor, showing her in her mid-twenties, is representative of the great school of art sponsored by her husband. Lost for centuries, it has been named the best-known bust in the world.

3. The damaged head of King Amenhotep III, the father of Akhenaton, shows the serene qualities of a man so deeply in love with beauty and luxury that he was known as Amenhotep the Magnificent.

4. This provocative mouth is believed to be that of the fun-loving and glamorous Queen Tiy, mother of the serious-minded Akhenaton. This bust in yellow jasper does not show Tiy's coloring. Paintings show her to have been a blue-eyed blonde; like Nefertiti, she was evidently part Aryan.

5. When this head was made of Queen Tiy, the youthful pertness that had won for a girl of humble birth the love of the world's most powerful king, had been lost under the pressure of great responsibilities and many sorrows. This bust, probably made at Amarna, shows her as a widowed queen mother and grandmother, deeply troubled by the problems being brought upon Egypt by her brilliant, headstrong son.

6. Amarna art as sponsored by Akhenaton became so free in expression i
verged often upon caricature. This statue of the king is illustrative of the liber
ties taken. His features and chin are elongated to an absurd degree, and mad
to appear longer by the false gold beard of royalty. Evidently he placed n
restraint on this public ridiculing of his person, nor on the number of picture
and statues made of himself and Nefertiti. Previous Pharaohs and their queen
had permitted sculptures made of themselves not more than once or twice i
their lives.

7. This head of Akhenaton typifies the revolutionary new art expression. For the first time the royal personages were permitted to be shown not as **giant** blocklike figures but as they were.

8.   Two statues of Amenhotep III, the father-in-law of Nefertiti.

He crossed the Euphrates River and conquered the Mitanni. But his greatest victory was Megiddo.

Thutmose III, who wrote his name wherever possible, raised a gigantic leather "death scroll" in the Temple at Karnak on which he listed those he had captured and slain and all his victories, and on this he claims title as "the hero of Megiddo." Akhenaton and Nefertiti read from that scroll which has long since vanished.

On this campaign Thutmose marched an army of 20,000 men into Palestine, leading the way at its head in his glittering chariot "like a flame."

"By his own footsteps," so he claimed, he led his endless columns through the narrow pass that Allenby's army would thread centuries later in A.D. 1916. It was a dangerous defile where a misstep would send a man flying down hundreds of feet onto rocky shale. But he brought his men out safely onto the rich level plains of Esdraelon near the Canaanite stronghold, the city of Megiddo, where miles of ripened grain shone in the sun, and fat herds were grazing, and there, lined up by thousands, were the formidable armed soldiers of Asia, commanded by the king of Kadesh and many allied princes in chariots of gleaming gold.

When the battle of the plain was over, dead enemy soldiers were stretched out on the land "like fishes," and all the princes in their gold chariots were taken captive save the king of Kadesh, who somehow in the heat of battle had escaped but left his golden scepter on the field. The surviving soldiers fled and took refuge in Megiddo. Thutmose followed and laid siege to the city.

Megiddo fell to him, and he marched on through Lebanon, conquering everywhere. When he returned to Thebes he had with him thousands of prisoners, hundreds of horses and chariots, 426 pounds of silver and gold, many hands cut from the bodies of the dead in proof that they had been slain, and the scepter of the defeated king of Kadesh.

Among his captives were the princely leaders of the enemy forces, and the sons of the north Syrian kings. So formidable a conqueror might have been expected to execute these defeated ones in formal ceremony under priestly sanction. Akhenaton's other ancestors were often pictured cutting off royal heads with sickles. Thutmose had proven his ferocity; now he demonstrated a compassion that was fairly new in war. The scroll reported: "The princes of the foreign country came on their bellies to kiss the ground to the glory of his majesty."

And Thutmose III "by the breath of their nostrils," granted them the gift of life. He prudently permitted the conquered regents to return to their kingdoms on donkeys and retained their horses and chariots.

But the captive sons of the "barbarian" kings he did not set free. He who had ruthlessly slain hundreds of thousands of men built special palaces for these princes in Thebes and gave them the best educations Egypt could provide. In fact they were given such noble and joyous treatment "as befitted their nobility," that they lost all interest in returning to their less luxurious homes, but sent reports back to their fathers praising their fortunate state, and the kindness of Thutmose III and his people. As a result the kings and people of the alien countries lost all fear of Egypt and came to regard it as protector and friend. Leaders of Lebanon and Cyprus and Mitanni and many other lands gladly paid tribute from this time on to the kings of Egypt.

This was the consolidation by Thutmose the Conqueror of the vast Egyptian Empire inherited by Akhenaton and Nefertiti.

Like his great-great grandson, Thutmose III was a mystic. A vision had placed him on his many-jeweled throne.

As did many of the powerful Eighteenth Dynasty figures, Thutmose III forced his way to power out of humble beginnings. He was not of royal birth. The walls of the great temple recorded his "miraculous accession" to the throne.

His father was royal. He was Thutmose II, a son of Thutmose I, who was king when the third Thutmose was a lad. But the boy's mother was an obscure concubine in the Theban palace named Isis, and since her humble origin barred the boy from all rights of succession he was placed at an early age in the Temple of Amon. He might have been lost there as one of the many thousands of young priests in the service of the god.

But there burned in him an awareness of the rights of kings, and he was not surprised when the god Amon appeared to him in person in the great hall and informed him, "You are to rule Egypt!"

The message came at a crucial time. The temple was always

in touch with the gossip of the palace, and even a young priest would have known of the vicious quarreling that had risen in the royal family. Thutmose I had been a great king. He was the first of the conquerors of the New Kingdom. But he was old and weak and clinging to the throne. Thutmose II was claiming the right to rule. He had taken over the throne and was threatening to have his father dethroned on grounds of incompetency. The family scandal must have shaken the palace and the temple to their foundations, and it was during this time of upheaval that the young priest saw his golden opportunity—and the vision of Amon.

He evidently confided his experience to the high priest and other leading members of the priestly circle, who saw the advantage of having a member of their brotherhood made king. The hour and place for revealing the god's message to the public were carefully chosen. It was in fact staged in the presence of the leading members of the royal and priestly hierarchy.

It took place during a ceremonial ritual in the temple. The gold idol of Amon on his altar was being conveyed around the great hall by priests. Thutmose II, the self-appointed regent, was innocently offering incense to the god. He stood in a spot designated as sacred, holding the smoking bowl. The procession would halt before him that the god might grant ceremonial recognition to the king.

But the procession did not stop. It moved on to a place under the columns where the young priest was standing in semi-shadow, surrounded by his fellow priests. A moan of religious awe went around the cavernous hall as the heavy idol on its eleven silver carrying poles tilted, slowly, as if in obeisance to the young priest. Then a shout was raised, for at this unmistakable sign of preference on the part of Amon, Thutmose II was overthrown and his half-royal son, an obscure young priest, became King Thutmose III of Egypt.

He gave full credit to Amon: "I am his son, who came forth out of him, perfect at birth . . ." It would never be known how this "sanctified revolution" was carried out. Some hinted it was the work of the boy's mother, Isis, with the connivance of the old king. Others suspected the entire coup had been staged by the priests of Amon. It may possibly have been aided by Queen

Hatshepsut, who was the daughter of old Thutmose I and had
made Thutmose II eligible to the throne by marrying him. He
was her half brother, a son of Thutmose I by a concubine. She
was the aunt of Thutmose III and may have recognized his
capacity for leadership. They may even have married.

However Thutmose III achieved the throne, he continued to
be grateful to Amon for his exalted position and his success as a
conqueror. All his victories were credited to the god, and the
bounty shared. In turn Amon continued their friendship, and
when Thutmose, to display his gratitude, began the work of
enlarging the temple, the god was gracious enough to appear on
the site in person, in the shape of a handsome man, and give
advice as to the laying of the foundations. He even lent his
divine hand to the stretching of the plumb line.

The god again appeared in person when the Temple was completed and rededicated in his name, making his appearance
during the ceremonies beside the king and accepting the honor
in the most amiable manner.

All this and much else was duly recorded on the temple walls,
and in the sanctuary, and all over Egypt, and in far-off countries,
and even beyond the Euphrates River, the name and prowess of
Thutmose III was recorded on lasting stone, on monuments, obelisks, steles, and cliffs.

Thutmose III was said to be fearless. He led his soldiers into
the thick of battle and was not afraid to meet savage animals
face to face. Once he battled an enraged elephant, which was
getting the best of the contest when one of the king's generals
rushed between them and slashed off the creature's trunk. He
conquered many kings and countries and captured and slew
hundreds of thousands of humans, but there was one he could
not subdue.

The "Great Conqueror" met with one defeat. She was his Aunt
Hatshepsut and a thorn in his flesh for almost eighteen years.

Nefertiti may have been awed and amused by the history of
this irrepressible ancestress of Akhenaton's, but she would never
have been tempted to imitate her. Hatshepsut was the most agres-
sive of a long line of strong-minded Eighteenth Dynasty
queens. She is acclaimed as "the first great woman of history,"

"the world's first feminist," "Egypt's only female Pharaoh," and, "the woman who was king."

When Thutmose III, after the visitation from Amon, took the throne away from his father Thutmose II, who had achieved the throne by marrying his fully royal half sister Hatshepsut, he robbed this determined woman of her role as queen. Hatshepsut was reduced to the role of queen emeritus. It was an honorable position, and Thutmose saw that full deference and tribute was paid her, but Hatshepsut was not the sort to play a minor role.

A hero must be away from home for long intervals. Thutmose III spent much of his reign fighting with his armies in foreign lands and extending Egypt's frontiers.

Hatshepsut saw her opportunity. Her nephew had been placed on the throne by a vision. She too had a vision. In the hall of the temple where Amon had appeared to Thutmose III, the god appeared to Hatshepsut.

Taking advantage of the vision and the king's absence, Hatshepsut calmly usurped the throne and announced herself king of Egypt.

Not queen, but king!

The priests of Amon might have stopped her. They might have argued that no Egyptian queen had ever seen a vision and that such was the divine prerogative of kings. But Hatshepsut, while very feminine—in fact, she is declared to have been "more beautiful than anything"—was no ordinary woman. And also, she was intensely devoted to Amon.

Amon's priests kept silent, perhaps out of sheer curiosity to see what would happen.

A great deal happened. A feud began that was to enrich Egypt—and Amon. While Thutmose was away enlarging Egypt, Hatshepsut built from within. Following divine orders from Amon, she sent expeditions down into the Red Sea to bring back fabulous treasure from Punt, including the rare myrrh trees which were planted in terraces before the magnificent funerary palace she built for herself at Deir el-Bahari, carved out of the face of the mountain near the Valley of the Kings.

For she was building endlessly, monuments and temples and obelisks, in the tradition of the Pharaohs. In her own mind, she was a king. She wore men's clothing, which in that hot climate

was not very different from the feminine, and a king's crown.
As a final male touch she wore the exclusively male false gold
beard that was the symbol of a king's power.

Of the still existing statues Hatshepsut raised to herself, some
show her with large eyes raised coquettishly and the gold beard
tied demurely to her chin.

Thutmose III returned from his hundreds of campaigns that
had made Egypt the greatest world empire, to find that during
his absence his Aunt Hatshepsut had conquered Egypt. He had
the admiration of the Egyptians; she had their love. The greatest
warrior that ever lived had no weapons that could defeat a
small, determined woman. Hatshepsut refused to move from the
throne. And there she sat, doing good deeds and boasting about
them, for eighteen years.

In the colonnaded hall of the temple, Hatshepsut raised two
obelisks attesting to her greatness. The granite shafts were 97½
feet high, the tallest in Egypt. Under the direction of the woman-
Pharaoh's favorite architect, Senmut, they were sculpted and
brought down the Nile on its fullest tide of inundation on a
mammoth barge towed by thirty galleys, requiring almost a thousand oarsmen. It defies the imagination to guess how these pillars,
dragged up from the wharf and into the temple, were ever raised
upright.

One can see Hatshepsut, tiny and indomitable in the vast hall,
standing before her pillars amongst reed-woven baskets filled
with shining heaps of electrum and watching the precious metal
being measured out like wheat, to coat the obelisks with silver
and gold.

Not all was vanity building. Uninterrupted by war, Hatshepsut
had time and means to implement the peace. She restored temples destroyed by the Hyksos. She examined the workings of the
government, always likely to slacken during a ruler's absence.
She saw to it that the existing laws were enforced and that order
was kept in the land. Among other improvements she developed
the civil service into a smoothly running, competent machine.

And in all she built and accomplished, Hatshepsut gave full
credit to Amon.

Thutmose III was building in desperate competition. He, too,
gave credit to Amon. A feud began that was to enrich and

beautify Thebes and make a little-known god into the chief god of Egypt.

Thutmose III, between campaigning and constructing his own monuments, found time to tour Egypt and study its needs as no king had before. He was a volcano of energy, and when in Egypt he watched over every department of the government and punished corruption. He, too, restored temples destroyed by the Hyksos. His enlargement of the Temple of Amon and the increasing wealth and power of Amon's priests led to his making new laws and regulations for the tabernacle—all of benefit to Amon.

There was in this ferocious warrior, as in all the Eighteenth Dynasty ancestors, the same passion for line and beauty that was to distinguish Akhenaton. The boy-king could read on the Theban walls how Thutmose III had with his own hands drawn designs for vases and other exquisite objects which were later carried to completion in the state or temple workshops.

The great king had one weakness—his hatred for Hatshepsut. It came boldly into the open when she died.

It is not known if the woman who was king died of natural causes or if, as has been suspected, Thutmose III finally succeeded in having her poisoned. Being poisoned was an occupational hazard among the ruling classes of Egypt.

No sooner was she dead than Thutmose III launched upon an orgy of destruction. All Hatshepsut had built to her own glory was doomed. Her statues were broken down, her name chiseled from monuments, the monuments themselves were shattered. Even her myrrh trees from Punt were uprooted from their terraces before her funeral temple near the Valley of the Kings.

For some reason Thutmose III did not destroy this temple. Was this because, like its builder Hatshepsut, it was "more beautiful than anything?" (It remains the most beautiful monument in ruined Thebes.)

The two towering obelisks in the temple defied the kings most skillful demolition squadrons. No mason or architect could find a way of bringing them down. It infuriated Thutmose that they stood in the great hall of the temple where he held his tremendous "Feasts of Victory" that became annual affairs. It ruined his pleasure while feasting to be confronted by the obelisks of Hatshepsut.

He finally ordered the twin pillars sealed behind a solid wall of masonry; the first "spite fence" in history.

Akhenaton and Nefertiti, celebrating in their time the continuation of these annual feasts, may have known the secret hidden behind that blank wall. Thutmose III had ordered the fame of Hatshepsut removed from the earth, which in Egyptian was a means of murder after death, but enough remained of her history to carry down to our present time, and certainly in Nefertiti's day her fame was still fresh in the minds of men.

Nefertiti may have pondered the fate of Hatshepsut and determined never to be an aggressive woman. Not even Hatshepsut had possessed greater power than the girl who was now queen of Egypt, whose strength ran in secret ways and would not be apparent for many hundreds of years. Nefertiti was the daughter-in-law and foster daughter of Queen Tiy, who knew so well the ways of love. Like Tiy, she had achieved supremacy through the adoration of a king. There was no hour of Hatshepsut's life Nefertiti envied.

She was Nefertiti, the beautiful and beloved, and, as with Hatshepsut, hers would be the final word. Thousands of years after Hatshepsut's death archaeologists broke through the sealed wall of the temple and Hatshepsut's obelisks tower again over ruined Thebes.

Thutmose III had also raised obelisks recording his triumphs; a few remain. They stand in Rome, London, and Constantinople, and one in an America that was unknown in his time.

The obelisk of Thutmose III in Central Park is the monument to a frustrated man whose glorious reign of half a century was disrupted for eighteen years by a woman. It was his one defeat.

Several hundreds of years after the death of Thutmose III, his funerary temple in the Valley of the Kings was the scene of the world's first sit-down strike. Money was still nonexistent and the tomb workers of that time were paid in clothing and food. In 1165 B.C. the attendants of the dead settled themselves in the shade of King Thutmose's tomb and chanted through the hours, "We have not been paid!"

The necropolis workers were social outcasts, but their work

was of utmost importance to the death-conscious Egyptians. The first strike in history was won in a matter of hours.

That tomb remains in the Valley of the Kings. The mummy of Thutmose III is in the Cairo Museum. It shows no resemblance to statues and pictures of Akhenaton.

Thutmose III was of stocky, determined build, with none of the long-boned elegance that distinguished his descendants. But the iron of the conqueror Thutmose was in Akhenaton, and the example of Thutmose was before the young king wherever he turned in Thebes.

His life was painted in glowing colors on the Theban walls. His praise was cited everywhere in cuneiform. The account of the victory of Megiddo was blazoned on leather on the wall of the temple. In another place of honor on the walls were illustrated lists of the rare plants and animals the conqueror king had brought back to Thebes for the glory of Amon. The descendants of those plants and beasts flourished in the gardens outside the temple where Nefertiti and Akhenaton spent many of their idle hours.

The presence of the "Great Conqueror" was felt most strongly in the Temple of Amon where the rich and grateful priests who had benefited so greatly by the long-dead Pharaoh who had once been a member of their ranks, still sang a hymn supposedly composed by Thutmose III: "I bound the Nubian Bedouin in ten thousands and thousands, and the northern people in hundred thousands."

Thutmose III had founded the empire and fathered other mighty kings who had kept the kingdom intact up to Akhenaton's time.

Born of the seed of Thutmose, worthy of his greatness, were first his son, King Amenhotep II, who reigned from 1439 B.C. to 1406. He was the great-grandfather of Akhenaton and a king to be remembered. After his powerful father's death certain vassal kings threatened insubordination. The new king stopped the resistance before it began by setting out with an army and returning to Thebes in triumph with seven of the rebel kings hung upside down from the prow of his royal barge. These he personally and piously sacrificed to Amon in the temple and hung their bodies to dry in the sun on the walls of Thebes. The seventh he slew and sent to be hung on the walls of the city of Napata, to subdue any threat of uprising that might be brewing amongst the Nubians.

He was a man of violence, of prowess in war and the chase, and his favorite inscriptions boasted that "no man could draw his bow."

But like the other Eighteenth Dynasty ancestors, he was a builder. He contributed greatly to the architectural beauty of Thebes. An impressive pylon he had constructed before the Temple of Amon contained twelve thousand pounds of malachite, set in inlay, as well as silver and gold and lapis lazuli.

Amenhotep III, son of Thutmose IV, assumed charge of the empire in 1398 B.C. and turned it over, unimpaired and architecturally and economically improved, to his son Akhenaton.

The ancestors had handed down to Akhenaton and Nefertiti a kingdom larger than any in the world, which extended from northern Syria to the upper Euphrates, and down across Africa into Nubia, to the Fourth Cataract of the Nile. In faraway lands dark-skinned strangers bowed down to the hawk-headed, cat-headed, and ram-headed gods of Egypt, and chanted in alien tongues of the illustrious rulers Akhenaton and Nefertiti.

The young regents ruled all the known world. Lesser monarchs of that world paid them tribute. Akhenaton was truly "king of kings."

Did he ever wonder, this sixteen-year-old Akhenaton, how he could be worthy of Thutmose III and all the other warrior ancestors who had conquered and held Egypt?

Akhenaton was a thoughtful but positive king.

He may have considered his ancestor's statues in the temple sanctuary and known that he would rank as the greatest of them all.

Nefertiti, small as a doll under the statues, could regard their stern features with equanimity. History had placed as heavy a burden upon her as upon Akhenaton. It was a great responsibility for a girl of fifteen.

Being a woman, Nefertiti was without conflict. She was content and fulfilled. They had been married only a few months when she knew that she carried their first child. Now she was part of the illustrious ancestry; part of the history of the Eighteenth Dynasty. Her childish perfumed body held in custody the future of Egypt.

CHAPTER EIGHT

Revelation

Thebes, 1369 B.C.

They were the brilliant stars of the religious feasts and festivals that crowded the Egyptian calendar. The greatest celebrations in this festive land were those of the gods. Many of them were for Amon, but the days of hundreds of other gods were duly celebrated and all required the attendance of the young king and queen.

At such times thousands of pilgrims came from every part of Egypt to share in the public feasting and watch the sacred processions for dazzling glimpses of Akhenaton and Nefertiti. The royal pair rode on thrones carried by priests high over the heads of men—the living images of the gods. Crowds ran before them, shouting praises, and their jeweled ears heard only words of adulation.

Many of the great celebrations were held in the hall of the Temple of Amon, where Thutmose III's tremendous "Feasts of Victory" had become annual events.

One feast honoring Amon called for eleven continuous days each year of dining, drinking, and entertainment.

The dead were never forgotten. On festival nights long processions of Amon priests, masked and carrying torches, went to the tombs to hold services.

The happiest of the festivals was the Day of the Dead. On that day all Thebes flowed to the necropolis carrying food, flowers, and written messages for the departed.

But the finest part of the festival started at sundown, when the city, usually darkened then, blazed with light. Oil-burning lamps fastened outside every door burned the night through, for on this happy occasion the dead were permitted to return home to feast with the living and the lanterns were to light them back to their graves when the annual visit ended.

(Were these lamps the origin of the lighted pumpkins of our Hallowe'en which was first recognized in A.D. 998 as the Christian feast of All Souls, the Day of the Dead?)

There were smaller feasts for the dead all year long, when families trooped, picnic fashion, to the necropolis carrying food and flowers and other gifts to the tombs. But those were private celebrations, and not national holidays.

Akhenaton and Nefertiti would have paid many family visits with the retired King Amenhotep and Queen Tiy to the family funerary temple near the Valley of the Kings which was one of the most splendid in Thebes. Feasts were held there in anticipation of the happy future life this devoted family would eventually share. Other celebrations were held in the splendid funerary palaces of other ancestors. These funeral banquets were festive. The guests wore flower leis and feasted on roast geese, meats, and wine.

But the greater festival of the year at which Akhenaton and Nefertiti made their most dramatic appearance was the sacred feast of Opet.

Opet was the most popular goddess of Thebes and the ugliest. She had the face and figure of a hippopotamus. But she was the divinity of the Nile Valley revered for her goodness and influence.

Her feast lasted a month, and it was during this time that the god Amon left his Theban temple and made his annual processional visit to Luxor.

The public took part in the procession of Amon to southern Thebes. Thebans flocked to the banks of the river to watch as eleven sturdy priests gripping the silver carrying poles brought the holy image of Amon from the dim recesses of his temple into the sunlight and carried it with chanting and incantation through the gardens and down to the river's edge where Amon's own sacred barge was waiting, as it had waited all year for this single journey. The barge was brave with banners, and when the king and queen came aboard, and took their places under the platform upholding the image of Amon, the craft glittered under the hot sun of Egypt like the mystical boat of the sun it represented. Amon was the sun; Akhenaton, seated under the image on his golden sun, was also the sun, and it was not for

Nefertiti, smiling her happiness upon the people of Thebes cheering on the shores, to question this, for her life was made up of such miracles.

The sacred barge filled with chanting priests of highest rank, and the sailors took up their oars. The heavy barge turned "upstream," south, toward the southern section of Thebes. It was a brief but dramatic journey, for the procession on the water stretched almost the full length of the city. Scores of decorated boats followed in the wake of the Amon barge, and along the shore marched the musicians and singers, and thousands of other Amon priests, for this was Amon's greatest festival and all who served him must take part in the procession escorting the god to Luxor.

Priests, clapping their hands and singing, kept pace with the slow progress of the barge and set the pace of the marchers.

After the priests came the women of the temple, dancing the sacred dances, shaking the sacred sistrums, chanting the sacred hymns to the gold image of the god.

After the women came the members of the king's armies. Led by the flashing lines of charioteers came the archers, spearsmen, and foot soldiers, and among them were troops of dark-skinned, shining soldiers recruited in Nubia who could not restrain their pride in their god and king but broke ranks with jubilant dancing.

And after these trooped thousands of exulting men and women and children who were the citizenry of Thebes and who were starting off the great holiday by marching in the triumphant procession of their god of gods and their youthful king of kings.

Along the river bank at intervals were open-air booths where barley beer and grape wine awaited the dry throats of the rowers of the heavy barge of Amon and the soldiers who marched as honor guards on shore, and when they neared these places the sailors rowed more lustily to a song of their own:

"A drinking place has been built for the sailors
"Who row in the ship of ships . . .
"Carrying the beauty of the god,
"Amenhotep, beloved of Amon . . . favored lord of the Gods . . .
"Nefertiti, beautiful of Amon."

The king's soldiers roared back from the river banks through throats loosened with wine:

"Oh Amon, Lord of the Thrones of the Two Lands, live forever!
"King Amenhotep III is bringing Him who begot him.
"Happy is the king who brings Amon."

Which was the god in such moments, and which the king?

The young regents on the barge sat motionless as the gold idol over their heads. Who knew what they were thinking? Akhenaton would not serve again as the earthly representative of Amon.

The journey of a little over a mile took the better part of a day. The barge disgorged its sacred and royal passengers at Luxor, where Aye had rebuilt for Akhenaton's father the Amon temple known as "the Harem of the South." The image was carried into this temple and the public halted before the doors. What went on inside the temple was secret, to them, and to us.

By another of the peculiar transfigurations made possible by the Egyptian religion, the god Amon upon arriving in Luxor became his alter ego Min, the lettuce-eating god of sensuality. The four weeks of celebrating that took place in the southern temple was known as "the beautiful festival of the Harem." It was evidently based upon ancient fertility rites.

We do not know the exact nature of these rites in "the Harem of the South," but we know they were prolonged and earthy and the feasting and festival continued by night and day. Certain ceremonies were presided over by Aye, miraculously changed from a priest of Amon into a priest of Min. Sometime during the celebration young priestesses from the Theban temple danced the sacred dance known as the Muu, which had been created by religious dance instructors centuries before in honor of the beloved hippopotamus goddess Opet. The girls wore very short kilts and tall crowns of woven reeds on their heads. The dance began slowly, as arms and hips began moving slightly to the clapping of hands and the jingle of tambourines. The movements became more rapid until all the slender bodies were in rhythmic motion, and the dancers swept forward in a choreographic pattern that was evidently like a ballet.

One month later, satiated with many delights, the celebrants

returned Amon to his temple at Karnak, escorted again by all of
Thebes that had recovered from the less intimate scenes of festival.

The feast of Opet was over.

It was back in the great temple, standing under the towering
stone columns of the tremendous hall, that Akhenaton dared
question the god Amon. Other kings had queried the golden
image. Some reported the god made answer. Others declared
the head of the idol had nodded.

Akhenaton was one who struggled after truth. He was an idealist, tutored by Aye in both myth and logic. He could not accept
trickery. No gold image bowed its head before him; no carved
lips spoke his name. He saw no visions as had certain of his
ancestors. When the great revelation came to Akhenaton it did
not take the form of a vision. It burst over him as a conviction
out of his youthful years of doubt and questioning. It was to
win him the hatred of generations, and deathless fame.

What need was there for this boy-king to query the will of the
gods? All had been laid down for him centuries before by priests
from the Book of Thoth.

"How does one know?" he had asked.

The priests frowned at such questions. Their thoughts ran in
deeply incised channels worn by centuries of acceptance. Because Osiris decrees . . . because this is the will of Amon . . .
These were the answers, and sacrifice must be made and prayers
said that had always been said, and the fragrance of incense
and flowers and fruits and roasted meats continue to waft upward into the grateful nostrils of the gods.

All one was, owned, suffered, or triumphed was by the will
of a god.

This Akhenaton could accept. But between the amusements
and festivities that filled his life, and the blandishments of his
beloved, the question intruded like a wasp's buzzing: "Which
god?"

He was Amenhotep IV, king of kings. All his life he had been
assured of his greatness as a man and a divinity. In temples his
image was worshiped. Wherever he walked, sat, rested, groups of
musicians walked with him, and choristers chanted: "You are

designed for eternity, King Amenhotep. All is done according to your will. Whatever you order is obeyed."

It is no light matter to be born divine. Akhenaton took seriously his dual role of god and king. He and Nefertiti played leading roles in rites celebrated since religion began. Egypt's gods had proven their value.

The country had prospered under them. It had become an empire under Amon.

And still the new and youthful king dared lift his deep-set, fanatic eyes to the cold metallic gaze of the idol Amon and question his authority. A brilliant sixteen-year-old boy pitted his intelligence against the blind will of a god.

By what right, he asked, was Amon god of gods?

The questions Akhenaton asked had never been asked before. Since the beginning man had accepted the presence of the many gods. They were part of all life, in all that grew, in the water and earth and air. No one but Akhenaton wanted proof of their reality. Only a king who was himself a god would dare confront the cold image of Amon and ask, Do you exist? Are you only an idol, shaped by the artisan's mallet, burning with jewels brought from every part of my domain?

Mine, Amon! Not thine.

Burning-eyed, with his fanatic vision, the young king demanded explanation. And the god did not answer.

He challenged all the other Egyptian gods.

There were many gods and goddesses in Egypt. Over two thousand were listed in the holy writings handed down by Thoth. Only a brain as great as Aye's could be expected to memorize them all. But all had their individual prayers and services and ceremonies and sacrifices, their temples and priests. What havoc might such a divinity as the Nile god wreak, for example, if prayers were not said to him every day?

The two children of the Theban palace had been brought up in awe of ancient and terrible deities.

The intricate Egyptian religion was simple enough to the uninitiated. The average unlettered Egyptian need only know that the earth was his mother, the sun his father, and that every living creature, rock and tree held the spirit of a god. Polytheism was an ancient and natural belief.

This was an uncomplicated and comfortable point of view.

But Akhenaton had been tutored by a master of sophistry, and Aye had encouraged him to probe the intricacies of the Egyptian faith. From childhood, the rapt attention of Akhenaton had been held by the religious teachings of Aye.

Aye had taught him the faith of Amon, the chief god, according to the Book of Thoth.

"In the beginning," so ran the haunting gospel of pre-Christian Egypt, "there was only the darkness of a watery abyss."

(Other legends from man's prehistoric past hold the primordial ooze to be the birth material of all life.)

"There was only the darkness of the waters," the sacred book continued, "and darkness lay over the waters, and there was no sign of life.

"Then out of the darkness of the waters oozed a mound of mud. It heaved, bubbled, struggled, and shaped itself into the first god, Amon.

"And Amon tore off his limbs and arms and all parts of himself, and from these he made men, and all animal life, and all creatures of the cosmos, and all things that exist . . ."

The meaning of Amon was "the hidden one." He was creation and all that existed in everything everywhere for ever and ever.

So Aye had instructed the boy-prince placed in his charge, and Aye was the wisest man in Egypt.

Now the boy was a king and a searcher of the meaning of the gods, for if each of the cults held the true answer, who had asked the first questions, and who then had answered?

Before the rise of Amon, Osiris had been chief of the gods. Amon and Osiris were often confused. Each was the male member of a trinity, possessed of a wife and son, and each claimed as his "animal" the ram with the twisted horn. Every god had an animal that was his symbol on earth.

The trio is persistent in world mythology and in Egypt it had been worshiped longer than man could remember. The original trinity had been Osiris the father, Isis the mother, and Horus the son.

The origin of Osiris is unknown. He may have arrived in early

Egypt as one of the corn gods from Syria. He may have begun in the delta as the Libyan god Anzety, who was shown carrying the flail and wearing a headdress shaped like the vulva of a goat, which was a symbol of authority. (The original, perhaps, of the cocked hat?) One legend claims him to have been a wise king who introduced agriculture and arts and crafts into Egypt and was first to make it into a leading country.

Osiris began in northern Egypt as a king. He was one of the four divine children born to Geb, the earth god, and Nut the sky goddess.

Osiris was the personification of good. His brother Set (Seth) represented evil. Set was always shown as a tall, lean, and elegant man with pointed animal ears and a forked tail—an early representation of the devil.

Osiris was happily married to his sister, Isis. Set, his jealous brother, murdered Osiris and took the throne. To hide the evidence of his crime he cut the body of Osiris into many pieces and scattered them throughout Egypt. But the weeping Isis gathered up the parts and, aided by Anubis (the jackal-headed god in charge of embalming), joined them together and restored Osiris to life.

So Osiris became immortal, but he did not return to the upper world. He remained in the underworld as its king and became its god of the dead and presided over the weighing of their souls. Images show him mummified, grasping in his cloth-bound arms the crook and flail that were the emblems of royal power.

Isis joined Osiris in the underworld and bore their son, falcon-headed Horus, who avenged his father's murder by meeting Set in battle and killing him and taking Set's place as king.

The immortal Osiris became the symbol of the sun that never dies but is always born again, and in some mysterious way he also became identified with the river Nile, which was also a god and immortal in that its waters ebbed to lowest level each year but rose again miraculously. So all Egypt worshiped Osiris, and in time the dead were worshiped because they were part of Osiris.

One fine point may have troubled Akhenaton: when a king died, he became Amon, but in the Osiris faith the lowliest man to die became Osiris!

As for Isis, this wife-sister-mother image was the goddess of fertility, maternity, love, mirth and "social joy." She wept each year for the death of Osiris, and it was her tears that flooded the Nile and brought abundance to the land. Isis was sometimes represented as cow-headed, and as a result was often confused with Hathor, goddess of love, whose cow-faced masks were popular on Egyptian columns. Hathor was sometimes surprisingly shown in the form of a snake. The Greeks were to identify her with Aphrodite.

These were the original members of the godly trinity. They reappeared in Thebes as Amon the father, Mut the mother, and Khons the son. And even after worship of the Theban trio spread throughout Egypt, it was typical of the country's religion that the original trio continued to be worshiped, along with the several thousand other gods.

It was a situation that apparently troubled only Akhenaton.

Amon was usually shown as a handsome human being, often resembling the current Pharaoh, although at times he had the head of his animal, the ram.

Mut's animal was the vulture, a bird greatly esteemed in Egypt as a scavenger and cleanser of the land. Among Mut's duties was that of protecting the deserts around Thebes.

Khons, her son, was usually shown with the head of his animal the falcon surrounded by a lunar disk since he was one of the moon gods. Later he appeared as a child. Khons was greatly loved by the Thebans for his kind nature and his ability to drive away evil spirits. His temple still stands at Thebes.

One by one Akhenaton assayed the values of the ancient gods and their creatures on earth. What right had they, he asked himself, to worship and sacrifice?

Both he and Nefertiti had and would retain a special respect for Maat and would never deny her, for she was the goddess of law and order and ethics and above all, what this pair most respected, truth.

Maat was always pictured as a small and elegant woman wearing an ostrich feather almost as tall as herself in her hair. The feather was the emblem of justice and was displayed in the courts of law. Witnesses, both men and women, testifying in the courts did so "in the name of Maat." Even the grand vizier when taking his sacred oath "spoke according to Maat."

Maat took part in that awesome ceremony after death known as the weighing of the dead. She was shown standing beside her scales upon which Osiris placed the heart of the dead person being judged. It was Maat's duty to balance the scales. Sometimes she sat opposite the heart. At times she merely placed her feather on the scale. The future of the dead rested with the feather of Maat.

In one way only, Maat was terrifying. She had no face.

Another respected god was Aye's patron, Thoth, a male Minerva, god of scribes, creator of reading and writing. One of his animals, the jackal, was worshiped in the futile hope of keeping him from ravaging the graves. Other animals of Thoth were the ibis and the ape.

Any Egyptian who met a jackal skulking through the necropolis, or an ibis wading in the Nile, or glimpsed an ape's silly grin through the arched plumes of a palm, knew he was meeting the great god in one of his earthly shapes. The average Egyptian need not wonder why these animals had been chosen to represent the god of wisdom. The priests knew; that was enough. The ibis, poking its bill into river mud, may have symbolized intellectual curiosity. The ape, screaming his morning salute to the rising sun, may have travestied man in his reverent moods. The jackal may have impressed with his howled challenge to the moon.

But who can interpret the beliefs of the Egyptian of thirty centuries ago? We do not think as they did then. We cannot know how strong a hold their religion had on their imaginations.

Their every thought and act depended in some way on the will of a god.

Bes, for example, was in charge of fun, luxury, and fashion. He was a squat, jolly little man-shape who would be confused with the Greek god Bacchus and the Semitic god Baal.

Ernutet was the guardian goddess of childbirth.

Shu watched over the wind, Hapy the Nile; Nepri was god of the corn fields and Shai controlled human destinies.

The monstrous, bloated old beast-woman-demon, Babi, "the death eater," who waited crouched before the gates of the underworld, was privileged to devour the souls of the condemned dead.

There were animal gods and sacred animals that represented gods, and all expected to be remembered and placated in some fashion. The greatest respect was given the hippopotamus goddess, Opet. Sobek, the crocodile god, was in charge of the Nile, and in some towns along the Nile certain of the chosen reptiles were regarded as his avatars. These favored creatures had their own temples where daily hymns were sung to them, and they wore rings in their reptilian ears, and jeweled bracelets on their scaly legs. They even had their own cemetery.

Rome would be amused by the report of a furious battle between two Egyptian river towns when the citizens of one killed a crocodile that was worshiped by the other. Two other Nile towns went to war when a fish one had deified was eaten.

The holy animals were capable of harm unless placated. An Egyptian had to know which animal met with during his day was sacred and would take vengeance unless proper respect was shown, and which was merely of the stuff of gods and not a divinity in its own right.

Certain animals were divine, such as the jackal, the ape, and the cat.

Certain birds were divine, among them the ibis, the hawk, and the crane.

There were imaginary holy beasts, such as the phoenix, and the sphinx.

These were gods, but not all animals that represented gods were divine.

Only a ram born with twisted horns was Amon.

Not every bull was Apis, the sacred bull-god of Memphis, later identified with the Greek Zeus. Only a bull calf with a white triangle on its forehead was recognized as holy by the priests.

And still, in some curious fashion, all the sacred animals were divine. Everyone knew that the scarab was not actually the sun; but it was of the nature of the sun, and therefore sacred.

Akhenaton may have had early religious misgivings concerning the divine rights of the scarab. This may be why none has been found commemorating his marriage to Nefertiti.

The small black beetle had been a symbol of protection and

good fortune in Egypt for centuries. It was worn in the form of amulets or jewelry. It was stamped on seals and wrapped in the grave bandagings of the mummies to ward off violators of the dead. Mummies of the bugs are found in the tombs. On the New Year, scarab emblems engraved like cards, with the message A GOOD YEAR TO YOU, were exchanged by friends. Larger models of gold, silver, or precious stones were used as commemorative tablets. Akhenaton's father, Amenhotep III, had issued the famous series of scarabs upon his marriage to Queen Tiy, and other scarabs marked other glorious events in his life. (Replicas of these are sold as paperweights.)

Akhenaton may have pointed out to Nefertiti a scarab making its minute hieroglyphic tracks over the sand, rolling in its tiny forelegs a small ball of camel dung. "Dung beetle" is another name for the insect.

To all the rest of Egypt, the scarab was divine because the round pellet he was rolling before him was a miniature model of the sun. Centuries before some priest had marked this resemblance and impressed it into the already complicated religious matrix. Now only Akhenaton questioned the insect's authority. He may have asked Nefertiti: "Can a dung-eating bug be a god?"

And perhaps, for his was a curious mind, the sandaled foot of King Akhenaton came down on the shining wings and back of the sacred scarab and the insect lay crushed in the sand. And Nefertiti watched beside Akhenaton, breathless, as this was done.

And no skies fell.

Turning his thoughts from the animal gods, Akhenaton considered the lists of the demons. There were hundreds of them. Like the gods, they were always present, crowding into the everyday life of every Egyptian. At the family dinner table, in the bath or in bed, all were there. And like the gods, these genii were quick to take offense and to take vengeance unless one remembered to give them perpetual praise and frequent gifts and never speak or think words that might rouse their anger.

The Egyptian walked cautiously between two worlds.

The priests skillfully kept him aware of his dangers. Much of the priestly revenue came from the sale of indulgences, charms,

amulets, curses, and prayers. The priests dealt in oracles, prophecies, and the meaning of dreams.

They sold indulgence that insured happiness for the dead or
bliss to those about to be married. The priests of Amon were
trained in rites and special prayers for legal and family affairs,
birth, death, and marriage, while offering incense and sacrifice
to attract the attention of Amon. They had prayers to be spoken
in the necropolis while offering food and beer to the dead. There
were gifted priests in the temple who made prophecies and inter-
preted oracles and knew the meaning of dreams and of days.
Luck was determined by the calendar. There were good days
and bad days that only these special priests knew. There were
good dreams and bad dreams only these priests could interpret.

To dream of eating was a fine dream; it foretold a rich harvest.
To dream of the moon meant your mistakes were forgiven. These
were among the good dreams.

It was bad to dream of looking down a well. That might land
the dreamer in prison. And to dream of looking into a mirror and
seeing one's own face was almost as ominous as seeing one's own
ka, for it meant one had caught a glimpse of his other self and
the results might be painful, such as marrying someone heartily
disliked.

There were terrifying curses, to be solemnly pronounced to
the crashing of vases under Amon or some other powerful god.

These curses inculcated such mystic terror that some pronounced in the names of the ancient Egyptian gods are still
believed by many, as, for example, the "curse" of the Tutankhaton tomb.

For all these attentions the Egyptians paid heavily to the
priests of Egypt. Every oath and prayer and amulet added to
the wealth of the temples scattered over the land.

Protest grew in Akhenaton against the priests and their gods,
who were amassing so great a share of the country's wealth.

He and Nefertiti were king and queen, god and goddess, rulers
of the Two Egypts, regents of the upper and under worlds.

There were times when he could not suppress his thoughts. In
the night watches he summoned Aye and had him write down
the poetry and the questions that rose like lava in his mind.

Nights are long in the desert. Alone with Nefertiti on the

cushioned balcony of the palace, the poet and dreamer watched the progress of the stars. Admittedly they were lamps lighted by the gods. Even on a starless, moonless night, one knew the sky was there, firmly held in place by the four celestial pillars set at the four corners of the earth. Why then doubt the existence of two thousand gods who stirred and spoke everywhere in the night?

From the necropolis in the western desert came the quavering howl of Anubis, god of death. The black jackal was grubbing for the bodies of the poor hidden under thin layers of sand.

Akhenaton may have questioned the night: What manner of god lived by such infamy?

A monstrous roaring came from the river. A hippopotamus was bellowing to its mammoth mate. That clumsy animal a god? To believers the sound was the true voice of the goddess Opet.

A shrew squeaked on the balcony. A tiny mouselike creature, no larger than Nefertiti's thumb, it was still divine. Mummies of shrews were piously interred in tombs.

What sort of god was the shrew, that Miw, the household cat-goddess, could pounce on and shake as a toy?

Nefertiti evidently did not protest the rebellious questions troubling Akhenaton. He was her god and regent as well as her love and father of the new life stirring in her body. A contented woman does not question. She may have been bewildered at first, for what other queen had been married to a king who dared doubt the ancient and terrible gods? In the beginning she may have clung to her faith in the goddess Bastet, for even an empress might find it difficult to deny the divinity of cat.

Apart from her role of goddess, the cat-goddess, Bastet (Bubastis), was the most loved of all the divine animals. Her Egyptian name, Miw, was given as a pet name to girls. Female cats received special veneration.

Bastet was one of the oldest of the deities. She represented the face of the sun. In one antique painting she is shown crouched under the Tree of Life tearing into shreds the slimy lengths of the Serpent of Evil.

Her statues portray her as smiling and sleek, the friendliest sort of cat. Some show her gleaming with jewels, seated on a small but elegant throne.

Bastet was also the divine patroness of many matters of particular interest to women, such as love and fashion. Despite her cheerful appearance, she also served as the messenger of death.

Unlike other goddesses, Bastet had no god consort. She was truly "the cat that walks alone."

As Miw, she was the most pampered of pets. Her divinity was respected; her skill at mouse-catching praised. And with dignity ruffled, Miw could strike with violence worthy of a god.

On velvet feet, Miw walked proudly through the palace, the temples, the homes and streets of Thebes. In or out of doors she was a favored companion of young and old. Collared and leashed, she went bird-hunting with her masters. Many a loved Miw had her ears pierced like her mistress, and wore tiny gold rings in her ears. She wore beautiful little jeweled collars, and necklaces, and even belts.

Nearly every cat that died was given the honor of mummification. Thousands of the tightly wound bundles have been found in the graves of Egypt.

Our own domestic tabbies are descended from these ancient Egyptian cats.

And Nefertiti, being woman, may have found it difficult to look into eyes that could widen like water lilies and hold in their jeweled depths all the mysteries and say sadly, You are not Bastet and a sun goddess, but Miw, catcher of mice in our royal bins!

Akhenaton was through with qualms. One by one, he had disqualified the thousands of gods until only Amon remained to defy him, and Amon was the most powerful of all the gods.

He contemplated the greatness of his ancestors. They had led armies and conquered nations. How could he crown their triumphs? A thousand years after Akhenaton, Alexander would weep because his father had left him no worlds to conquer. Akhenaton's forefathers had made him heir to still another world —greater and far more mysterious than Egypt.

Several of his ancestors had glimpsed that world. They had been merciless warriors and conquerors, but they saw visions.

Even Hatshepsut, the woman who named herself queen, had met face to face with the living Amon.

Thutmose III, Akhenaton's mightiest ancestor, had been made

Pharaoh after a personal meeting with the god. His son, Amenhotep II, Akhenaton's great-grandfather, owed his own crown to a dream he had when, on a visit to Gizeh, he fell asleep in the shadow of the Sphinx, and the Sphinx spoke, and told Amenhotep that if he would have the sand cleared from its base, he would become king of Egypt.

Revelation may have come to Akhenaton on a morning when with Nefertiti he saw the sky reddening over the eastern cliffs, and watched the elevation of the disk that was the fiery face of the sun. The desert warmed, the city wakened, and men, birds and beasts, each in his own tongue, sang anthems to the daily miracle of the dawn.

The king lifted his face to the sun and knew.

This was the answer given: The one god, the true god, creator of all life, of plants and trees and animals and man, the eternal flame and the source—was the sun.

In that blinding moment, fourteen centuries before the birth of Christ, the doctrine of monotheism was born. Its first converts were Akhenaton, ruler of the greatest empire on earth, and Nefertiti, the most beautiful woman in the world.

It is impossible for modern minds to follow the convolutions of religious thought in early Egypt. Amon-Ra represented the sun, but in Thebes the sun's fiery face was Aton, and he was a minor god virtually unknown to the rest of Egypt. It was Aton Akhenaton proceeded to elevate over Amon and all the other gods. According to Freud, this new faith was ". . . the first and perhaps the purest case of monotheistic religion in the history of humanity."

The young king began building in the tradition of his fathers and forefathers. His was the right, the vision, and unlimited materials, means, and slave labor. As his ancestors had built to the glory of Amon, he would build to the glory of Aton the one god.

The Amon priests watched, horrified, the invasion of Aton on realms hitherto sacred to Amon. Akhenaton's new temple was completed. It stood in the sacred garden between the two Amon temples at Karnak and Luxor. This was the property of Amon, and the temple was thrust amongst temples dedicated to Amon, and a large share of the income of Amon had been diverted to its building.

There were angry prayers and incantations in the Amon temples as Akhenaton and his growing ranks of Aton priests with solemn ceremony rededicated this parklike area that for more than a century had been owned by Amon, and decreed that henceforth it should be known as "The Brightness of Aton, the Great."

The elevation of a new god was a long and costly matter, and as Akhenaton increased Aton worship, the hatred of the Amon priests increased.

The completed Temple of Aton was large, magnificent, and brilliantly colored. Its interior may have disappointed those accustomed to the gaudy, flashing images and paintings that brightened the temples of the other gods. It was puritan, austere. Akhenaton's new religion had no mythological base. It was pure faith. His temple contained no idols of gods or their sacred animals. Aton had no image and no animal. Aton was shown over its altar as it was—the many-rayed disk of the sun.

The rays, stretching down over the heads of the worshipers, ended in hands. One of these grasped the Ankh that was the symbol of life.

(Centuries later, science would corroborate Akhenaton's belief that life began with and depended upon the sun.)

With massive celebration, Akhenaton dedicated the new temple to his chosen god under the new designation: "Ra-Harakhty, who rejoices in the horizon in his name of the Sun-Light, that appears in the Sun-Disk."

In shortened form, this was Aton.

Akhenaton placed thirty statues of himself in the new temple. They were unlike any sculptured before.

These were the first statues to portray a king as the sculptor saw him. They are not flattering. They show a stern, ascetic young man, with a long, narrow face and strange eyes leveled under the royal headdress. The pierced ears are frankly large and the pendulous chin made longer by the false gold beard of power.

Egypt's artists had their orders from the young king. They were to portray life as it was. Maat was truth, and art must follow the law of Maat.

This was one of the first of the iconoclastic decisions made by Akhenaton.

It was the beginning of the "revolution of Amarna."

Akhenaton named himself high priest of Aton and Nefertiti high priestess. They presided together over the dedication services and all following rites held in the new temple. Their court followed and the royalists worshiped no longer in the Temple of Amon.

Before the rayed disk of the sun, Nefertiti led the long processions of white-robed Theban girls in the sacred dances, chanting the prayers that were no longer said to Amon, but to Aton. Her slender arms shook the jingling sistrum, her clear young voice rose in the hymns, and Akhanaton the priest and lover, offering incense at the altar, watched her ritual movements with pride. In his heart rose words he ordered carved on stone to preserve her loveliness forever, praising the grace of Nefertiti's hands and sweetness of her voice.

And watching them both, as he had watched over all their lives, was Aye, now a high priest of Aton.

Akhenaton had his disciples. Nefertiti was the first and most faithful. King Amenhotep was still living. One of his statues carries the words: THE GOD ATON SHEDS HIS RAYS ON KING AMENHOTEP III.

This is the only hint that the old king may have known his son would attempt to change the faith of Egypt.

Portraits made at this time show Amenhotep enfeebled. Queen Tiy is beside him, comforting him in his old age as she had in their lusty youth.

There is no indication that Queen Tiy turned to her son's religion. She was too much the pragmatist, and she was wise in the ways of Egyptian politics. It is believed that she saw early the danger threatening the new faith and from the palace in Thebes exuded an aura of traditional authority that did much to stem the resentment that was beginning to rise against the young king and his one god. Tiy evidently served as co-regent in trying periods to assist her son.

In other ways Akhenaton broke with the past. His father had turned against oriental tradition when he shared his power with the woman he loved. Akhenaton shared his with two women—

his mother and Nefertiti. In these last of the Theban years he is
shown with Nefertiti and Queen Tiy, and often, in the background, one glimpses the presence of Aye. So the king's counse-
lors and confidantes were an ambitious scribe and two beautiful,
brilliant women.

The most surprising of the converts to the new faith was Aye,
and still, it is not surprising when one considers his relationship
to Nefertiti. As a priest of Amon he had been a powerful leader
in the temple at Karnak. But Aye was an opportunist skilled in
reefing his sails to the wind. He was obviously pleased to see the
Amon authority cut down in favor of Aton. Now more wealth
would go to the crown, and less to the temple. Aye threw his
invaluable support to the new god.

Ptahmose, formerly grand vizier to Amenhotep, had turned
his allegiance over to Akhenaton. He was an early Aton convert.
His beautifully decorated tomb at Thebes is one of the art treasures of the ruined city, and in it is one of the first paintings ever
made of Akhenaton and Aton.

The priests of Amon were infuriated by the new temple and
the elevation of the rival god. The authority established by
Thutmose III was being disputed for the first time. The Temple
of Amon was not only the largest building in the world, it was
the wealthiest institution in Egypt. It was the center of the
country's spiritual and temporal power.

Its high priest ruled over the thousands of priests who lived
in the temple and over the hundreds of smaller temples to Amon
scattered over Egypt, each a palace with its own army of priests.
The Amon priesthood was a network of power stretching to the
farthest realms of Akhenaton's kingdom. The largest share of
the lands of Asia conquered by Akhenaton's ancestors had been
assigned to Amon. Since the time of Thutmose III much of all
tribute and taxes had been paid to the god.

All Amon's temples were treasure houses. The priests presided
over vast areas of cultivated and pasture lands, and thousands
of sheep, goats, and cattle, tended by laborers and slaves in
Amon's name. The poorest serf in Egypt gave what he could to
Amon, whose priestly tax collectors could invade the meanest
hovel and find a partial bushel of wheat or a scrap of cotton that
might be owed to the god.

And because wealth breeds power, the Amon priesthood was assuming an increasingly strong pressure in government affairs. Administrative rights were being taken over by the priests. Appointments were made or support withheld by the authorities in the temple.

The priesthood had become the best-paid profession in Egypt, and a young man who could attain the sash of Amon was assured of lifetime luxury.

Would even a Pharaoh offer contest to such a god?

Akhenaton dared.

He announced he was no longer the living representative on earth of Amon, the god whose name he bore. He was Aton, the sun.

From this time on, so he decreed, he would no longer be known as King Amenhotep IV. He would be King Akhenaton IV, in honor of the sun, meaning either "brightness of the disk" or "the sun is satisfied." He decreed that Thebes, then known as No-Amon the City of Amon, should henceforth be known as No-Aton the City of Aton.

And he asked all disciples of the new faith to discard names that stemmed from the old deities, unless they were sun gods, and take such names as honored Aton or Horus or Ra. It was now that his Grand Vizier Ptahmose changed his name to Ramose, for Ra, to please the newly named King Akhenaton IV.

The great temple at Karnak hummed like a shaken hive. To the priests of Amon, this change was heresy.

These events took place in the year 1369 B.C. in which Akhenaton and Nefertiti had married. A great deal had happened to the youthful regents in this year. They had founded a new religion and given new values to Egypt.

Also, in this year, Nefertiti gave birth to her first child.

CHAPTER NINE

The Building of Amarna

Tell el-Amarna, 1369–1368 B.C.

A queen's body rocked in the rhythm of anguish, and the court physician and other priestly doctors came and went in Nefertiti's harem in the painted palace on the Nile. On her golden bed Nefertiti lay under the protection of Mut, who was still to be trusted, since one of her special duties was protection of women in childbirth. Over the queen's bed was Mut's emblem, the vulture, the bird symbol of birth, as the stork is today.

The rooms were crowded as always with Nefertiti's people, under the watchful eye of Tiy the nurse.

The doctors conferred, the ladies in waiting wailed their sympathy, and the girlish body wrenched until a reddish, squalling, stringlike creature appeared who was the first-born of Nefertiti and Akhenaton and who was named Meritaton, "Beloved of Aton," in honor of their only god. After her name was written, "Daughter of the Great Royal Wife Nefertiti." This child would grow to be beautiful, like her mother.

Nefertiti's portraits reveal her content and her deepening beauty. Apparently childbearing enhanced her happiness and Akhenaton's love. One artist would be permitted to show her in the tender act of offering her breast to her child.

In the seventeen-year-old Akhenaton the miracle of fatherhood demanded the release of words. It was not enough to hover over the newly born Meritaton, holding the emblem of the Ankh that was the symbol of life, and offer the conventional wish of "one million million years of living." Song ripened and burst in his heart, Aye was summoned, and the young father put into words his awe of the miracle wrought by Aton:

"Creator of germ within woman, maker of seed in man,
"You who give life to the child in the womb of its mother . . .
"When he comes forth from the womb on the day of his borning
"You open his mouth to its widest; you supply him with all he shall
  need . . ."

This was among the poems by Akhenaton Aye would preserve
by having them engraved in his own tomb.

Mother and child throve, but the long-robed physicians continued to visit the palace. Their concern now was the old king,
for Akhenaton's father was gradually losing his hold on life and
his interest in the kingdom.

The doctors were impressive but helpless. Each medico arrived
with his own staff of male interne-nurses, with a slave or two to
carry the handsome faïence cases filled with fine metal instruments and vials of powerful medicine that could do so much to
alleviate suffering and sometimes prevent or hasten death.

This was hundreds of years before a religious Europe decreed
the human body was sacred and outlawed the study of anatomy.
Egyptian medicine was not limited by such scruples. The processes of mummification opened unlimited opportunities for medical study, since a certain amount of mutilation was necessary to
the process of embalming. A body taken apart could be put together again, wrapped snugly in its burial wrappings and fitted
neatly into its body-shaped mummy case. Since a doctor was
inevitably a priest, and priests presided over the burials, the
Egyptian physician knew a great deal about the human body.

His scientific knowledge was infiltrated with religion and
magic. Medical wisdom extended into the next world. All attempts at cures were administered with incantations and charms.
These formed a large share of the equipment of any well-stocked
medical case. Since all illness was inspired in some way by evil
spirits the physician brought to the bedside of the patient an impressive collection of magical cures calculated to placate any
offended demon or god. There were small statuettes and insignia
of the gods, images of the sacred animals, amulets and charms,
and incantations, prayers and spells written on papyrus.

Only a medical authority could determine which god or demon
was responsible for an illness, and offer the correct emblems, and
mutter the right prayers.

And still, the Egyptian physicians in those days were surprisingly advanced in their knowledge of medicine and anatomy. They knew all the bones in the body, and the uses of many of the organs.

They knew that the heart was the source of life. Since, if it died, its owner died, they considered it the seat of all thought, will, and emotion. Doctors checked the pulses of various parts of the body "to see how the heart speaks."

Research in the embalming pavilion had taught them much of the workings of the brain. It and the bowels were the containers of wisdom. Did a brain go wrong, perhaps with a tumor implanted by Set, the god of evil, a skillful surgeon could saw through the skull with a fine copper toothed saw, trim out part of the brain and replace the skull section and its flap of flesh. The mummies of patients who underwent trepanning thousands of years ago are proof that a certain percentage survived.

Broken bones required little magic. The Egyptians were energetic in games and in war and their mummies reveal many breaks. These were treated much as they are today; set with knowing hands, perhaps lightly wrapped in linen bandagings, with a moderate amount of incantations spoken and medicine administered to ease the pain. The doctor departed, leaving advice that cannot be bettered today. "Rest until the bone has a chance to heal."

The medicines were largely based on a knowledge of plants. Many are still used in various parts of the world. Modern Greek peasants take some of the prescriptions made up by the ancient Egyptian doctors.

Among the medicines best known to us were castor oil, sulphur, anise, niter, and sodium carbonate—this last in great demand in a land and age where heavy drinking was regarded as one of the social arts. The Egyptians specialized in purgatives, emetics, enemas, aphrodisiacs, antidotes for poisons, and poisons. The deaths of many notable ancients are held suspect.

Some of the medical prescriptions puzzle modern science. What healing qualities could possibly exist in a mixture made of the contents of an owl's stomach, the milk of mother mice, the milk of a woman who has just borne a son, or the excrement of flies? One cure calls for the mincing and salting in brine of seven slugs, seven flies, and seven earthworms.

The Theban doctors must have exhausted their resources in their efforts to restore Amenhotep III to health. They were priests of Amon, and knew that as long as he was alive, no matter how feeble, a certain amount of protection for Amon was assured. The old king's brilliant young son was openly giving more and more rights and privileges to his Aton.

So they fought to save Amenhotep, aided by the devoted Queen Tiy.

The sybaritic life of a potentate may have contributed to the deterioration of the old king. Portraits show him now as an old man, sagging of belly, lined of face, obviously ill. Queen Tiy sits beside him, erect as in her youth, but her face is lined and sad. It was rare for Egyptians to be portrayed as ill and old; they wished to be remembered as forever young. These portraits show the new realism determined by Akhenaton.

Among the complaints of Amenhotep was that of abscessed teeth. For these and for sore eyes, the Egyptian physicians had no remedy, only the relief of applying live, freshly shelled mussels. Many of the cooling mollusks must have been applied to Amenhotep's tormented gums.

And still, during the years of the old king's illness, the personal life of Akhenaton's father continued in a way we might never have known if it were not for certain gossipy revelations in the Amarna Letters. He was ill, he was old, but there were signs of recurrent activity that were to have future historical results. Due to the skill of his physicians or a final resurgence of his once lusty nature, Amenhotep rallied to the extent of accepting at least one more "extra" royal wife for his harem.

This was the Princess Gilukhipa, a daughter of Prince Shuttarna of Mitanni. Evidently the customary return gifts were sent and revived the greed of the wealthy King Tushratta of Mitanni, whose daughter, Princess Tadukhipa, had arrived in Thebes with the impressive dowry.

Tushratta had carried on a persistent correspondence with Amenhotep ever since the Egyptian king accepted the first daughter sent by the Mitanni king. Tushratta was the most dedicated letter-writing in-law in history. His letters were written in

red ink and in them this devoted father never failed to send
"greetings to my daughter, the wife of Amenhotep III."

But the underlying message of the letters was always the same:
"Send gold. Send more gold."

Word evidently crossed the Euphrates that the old king of
Egypt was failing, and Tushratta panicked at the thought of losing so valued (and wealthy) a relative and one who had been
unfailingly generous. Evidently he placed little faith in any future generosity on the part of Akhenaton, who as far as is known
had shown no interest in acquiring an "extra" wife from Tushratta or any other king.

Tushratta hastily sent Amenhotep his chief religious treasure.

The dominion of Mitanni included Ninua (Nineveh, the capital of Assyria), which placed King Tushratta under the protection, and gave him authority over, the powerful goddess Ishtar
of Assur.

It was her sacred image that came with a letter written by King
Tushratta to the failing King Amenhotep in Thebes.

"The words of Ishtar of Nineveh, Mistress of all Lands:

"To Egypt, to the land I love will I go, and there I will
sojourn. Now I send her and she goes. Let my brother worship
her and then let her go in gladness that she may return. May
Ishtar protect my brother and me for a hundred thousand years."

Evidently the return news from Thebes was not good, for one
last anxious letter is found in the Amarna archives from Tushratta
in which he begs Amenhotep to increase the worship of Ishtar
in Egypt "that my brother's life may be preserved."

Akhenaton was not in Thebes during this exchange. Shortly
after the infant Meritaton was born, he and Nefertiti deserted
the ancient capital and began the building of Amarna.

Akhenaton had not turned his back completely on Amon. He
had not refused the old god his right to exist. He had offered
the world a new religion, starting at Thebes. And Thebes, even
under its new name of No-Aton, Aton's city, continued to worship Amon. The Amon priests kept their hold on the people. Offerings continued to pour into the Amon temples.

The Amon priests had ways of stirring the suspicions of the
people. The young king and queen had been carried over the

heads of the crowds like gods while the city roared its adulation.
Now, where they rode by sedan chair or chariot, they must have
noticed that the shouts had lessened and that frightened faces
turned their way. The Egyptians had been ruled too long by the
terrible gods. They feared for themselves and for the gay young
couple on the throne who were daring the vengeance of the
ancient deities.

Akhenaton was not the man to defend his principles. He was
not a warrior. He had never known the need to conquer; his
world had been given him. He offered his people a faith based
on love. With that faith, they could rid themselves of the ancient
terrors that haunted every moment of their lives, and free themselves from the corrupt reign of the priests. He would learn that
some feel more secure in chains.

If he had chosen to fight, he could have disbanded the Amon
priesthood then, leveled their temples and wiped out the Amon
cult. At his command were the armies, the fleets, the police
forces, and all the civic and legal departments. He had the
support of other cults that had long resented Amon, among them
the strong priesthood of Ra at Heliopolis.

It is not known why he did not try at this time to make Aton
the sole god.

He did not, perhaps for many reasons. His religion may have
handicapped him, for it was based on peace.

He may have felt some lingering trace of loyalty toward the
Amon cult that had worked the "miracle" of placing on the
throne the member of their cult who became his ancestor
Thutmose III.

Also, the old king was still living. Amenhotep had not changed
his name nor his loyalty to Amon. His son may have hesitated
to strike against his father's god as long as Amenhotep lived.

Nefertiti and Queen Tiy may have tempered his wrath against
the Amon priests. Perhaps Aye, in his wisdom, advised caution.

Akhenaton and Nefertiti reached a decision. Thebes had rejected their religion; they would reject Thebes. They would turn
their backs on Amon and all the other monstrous animal-headed,
bird-headed gods and their demons and animals that kept the
capital of Egypt hag-ridden with superstition. As Akhenaton's
fathers had built, they too would build.

Akhenaton's ancestors had been mighty builders of monuments and temples.

He would build a new life and a new city for Aton—a city of the sun.

The first important move was the locating of a site. It had to be virgin land never before dedicated to any god, and on the Nile, since water was the lifeblood of any settlement.

The ideal site when found was a lonely plain in central Egypt. It was a secluded crescent area of tawny sand protected on three sides by desert cliffs, approximately halfway between Memphis and Thebes.

On either side of the river a seventeen-mile area was marked out for the homesite of the god and named Akhetaton, "the City of the Horizon of the Sun."

On steep rock cliffs at the four corners of the site large handsome steles were carved, one twenty-six feet tall, to mark the boundaries of the holy city. On these the royal family are shown in adoring attitudes under the many-rayed disk of the sun. By the number of Nefertiti's children shown on the Amarna monuments we know the city's growth. It was founded in the year 1368 B.C., when Meritaton was less than a year old, and Akhenaton and Nefertiti were seventeen and sixteen.

One of these boundary stele, broken but extremely beautiful, is in the Cairo Museum, flanked by two colossi of Akhenaton found at Karnak. Akhenaton is shown kneeling in adoration before the solar disk, and the inscription reads that when he founded the city, he toured in his chariot of silver and gold the area where the future capital was to be.

The stele testifies: "His majesty raised his hand to heaven, to him who made him, even to Aton, saying, 'This is my testimony forever . . . I have made Akhetaton [the city] for my father as a dwelling . . . He has made the circuit for his own, he has made his altar in its midst, whereupon I make offering to him.'"

And with the dedication of the land the king also dedicated "all that should stand upon it, the cliffs and waters, mountains and fields, cities or towns, people and cattle and trees . . . I have made it for Aton, my father, forever and ever."

In his dedication Akhenaton named the new capital of Egypt

with these words: "The whole land shall come hither . . . whoever has purpose with the King must come to Aton's city."

The priests of Amon in Thebes made bitter use of this pronouncement. The Thebans were a proud people. Their hearts hardened toward their young king when they learned their "city of kings" was no longer the capital of Egypt.

The city's resentment may have been responsible for a curious clause in Amarna's dedication. In it Akhenaton promised never to extend Aton's city beyond the seventeen-mile-area fixed by the steles. This restriction may have been a last feeble effort on the part of Amenhotep III to limit his son's unpopular experiment. Or it may have been Aye, whose ear would remain close to affairs in the Amon temple, who urged the restriction of a project that was causing so much consternation in Thebes.

Akhenaton would build two other "sun cities," in Asia and Nubia, but Amarna was the holy city of Aton.

On that day when he drove his chariot from cliff to cliff, holding his whip "like a scepter," dedicating the sacred area, he knew what the city was to be. Its plans were already on papyrus, down to the smallest home.

Amarna was the world's first city to be built to a master plan.

There had been tremendous construction projects in Egypt ever since the use of stone began. But no other Pharaoh had ever built on as vast a scale as Akhenaton who only a few years before had been a dreamy-eyed student in Thebes.

Other cities had grown carelessly. Amarna burst complete and perfect from Akhenaton's agile brain. Egypt's finest architects had been consulted to insure the practicability of his vision.

The king's choice as chief architect was Bek, whose fame would be lost for centuries, until the excavation of Amarna.

Bek was among the pilgrims in the great expedition that set out from Thebes in the year 1368 B.C. It was the sixth year of Akhenaton's reign and the second of his marriage. The move was probably made in summer to give the burdened ships the advantage of the flooded currents running north. Akhenaton and Nefertiti doubtless led the long procession of barges and ships on their own brightly colored royal barge, seated in their golden chairs on the deck under the blue and white flags of the Two Egypts. Over their heads was the new gold symbol of Aton.

Other craft equally gay carried the members of the court. All were young and light of heart and delighted to leave the gloom of a resentful Thebes for a new life in the sun.

A merry pilgrimage that must have been, and how mad it must have seemed to sober Egyptians who flocked to the river banks to watch their king and queen sail past at the head of their fleet to the rhythm of oars and song. On the crowded barges were all the pilgrims of the sun might need to insure their happiness. The children of the nobles played on the decks; the beloved pets were along. With them were the court musicians and their instruments, the dancing women, the storytellers and poets—all the delight-makers from the old palace at Thebes.

After the court barges came more barges and ships of the royal fleet, heavy with household furnishings and treasures and tools of every kind. There were saplings and rare plants and shrubs ravaged from the sacred gardens of Amon. There were sacks and baskets of seeds.

Marching apace with the fleet on the shore came the endless processions of servants and slaves, horses and chariots, donkeys drawing burdened carts and sledges, herds of cattle, goats and sheep. General Mai in his chariot led the way, for he was head of King Akhenaton's army, and many divisions of warriors marched after him to guard the royal cavalcade, singing lustily as they came. Among them rode the queen's cavalry, for even Nefertiti, gentlest of women, had her own squadron.

To the glum Egyptians left behind in Thebes it must have seemed that all Egypt had left on the pilgrimage, for with the king and queen went the chief heads of the government and the military high command, and all the ministers and officials of the court, nobles and courtiers and their families, hundreds of ladies in waiting, armies of secretaries and scribes and accountants and the great chefs and their kitchen staffs, and Aton priests, and servants and workmen of every kind. With them went the royal archives that would form the nucleus of the Amarna Letters.

It took perhaps a week for this joyous expedition to travel the 240 water miles to the consecrated site.

At Thebes the long stone wharf was deserted of the busy craft that had come and gone there for hundreds of years. The empty barge of Amon rocked, neglected, on the water. In the Temple

of Amon the deserted god glowered over gatherings of mutter-
ing priests.

The Amon priesthood had reason for their anger. A massive
amount of the city's wealth and power had vanished down the
Nile with the willful king. Akhenaton had answered their protests
against Aton by leaving Thebes; now they realized the extent of
the damage his move had made to the city and to their hitherto
all powerful priesthood. A Thebes no longer the capital would
no longer be the trade center of the world. Taxes and tribute
collected would not be brought into Thebes, to be divided by
the grand vizier between the palace and the temple. Now that
Egypt's wealth would go to the new city, for the first time in
their pampered history the Amon priests faced the problem of
survival.

They exerted what pressure they could on the palace, where
Queen Tiy and her sick husband remained in token representa-
tion of the crown. Tiy may have been serving as co-regent dur-
ing this delicate period, for the complex administration of
Egypt had long been centered in Thebes and it would be years
before it was completely shifted from the old capital to the new.
Meantime the country would be run to a great extent from
Thebes.

Couriers kept her in close touch with King Akhenaton, 240
miles away, and her influence over her son remained strong.

The contact may have been maintained by Aye. Among the
many services credited to Aye in his tomb we find listed "superintendent to Queen Tiy, of her palace and her treasury." We
know he joined Akhenaton at Amarna, but during the initial
period of adjustment he may have stayed behind in Thebes
where with the aid of spies and secret police he could guard the
king's interests in the old capital and nip in the bud any anti-
Aton plots that might be brewing in the Temple of Amon.

The continued presence in Thebes of the aging Queen Tiy
acted as a deterrent to the resentment against the young king.
King Amenhotep III and his wife had won the love of the Egyptians. As regents they had maintained the peace and helped
develop prosperity in the land. They were an imperious pair,
but they had the gift of making themselves popular.

With Akhenaton love was deep but reserved for his intimate

circle, for his father and mother, Nefertiti, their children, and those close to him he referred to as "great favorites." To these he gave affection, honor, and extravagant gifts. In return he had the love and loyalty of his court.

Aye and his wife, Tiy the nurse, were always listed among those favored by Akhenaton. In the group that went with him to Amarna were his trusted favorites Bek, the new royal architect, General Mai, the chief commander of the Army, Merire (Ramery), a beloved priest of Aton, and Ramose, his grand vizier.

To these, and to the trusting court that went happily with him to Amarna, Akhenaton gave his strange, fanatic devotion. He evidently made no effort to hold the devotion of his people. What need had he for their humble love? He was King of Egypt. All Akhenaton valued went with him in this adventure of building a new and perfect city, in a newer and better world.

The sandy crescent over the river blossomed with tents and rang with excited voices. The pilgrims from Thebes encamped on the Amarna site lived a picnic existence while work began on the new city. For luxury and splendor the tent city would only be equalled many centuries later on the Field of the Cloth of Gold.

Life was as gay for the pioneers as it had been at Thebes. They dined out of doors in colorful pavilions, but the service was of silver and gold, the royal chefs worked miracles in the cook tents, and the kitchen dogs turned the spits as they had in the old palace.

The barges went back to Thebes and returned, bringing the finest of the country's stoneworkers, carpenters, sculptors, artisans, painters, gravediggers, embalmers, craftsmen of every kind. Barge after barge came to Amarna with fine materials chosen by Queen Tiy for the building of Amarna. Heavy bargeloads of sandstone came down from the First Cataract, Aswan, at the entrance of Nubia. Other ships went north to the Mediterranean and returned with rare woods. From the famous marble quarries of Hatnub, on the desert road leading eastward out of Amarna, sledges drawn by slaves brought tons of alabaster, for Akhenaton was determined the new city should gleam like the sun. Copper came from Sinai, and shipments of silver and gold, and lapis lazuli, and green and blue malachite.

Bek was a man of tremendous energy. He set gangs of men to work shaping millions of adobe bricks and setting them to dry in the hot sun. He watched the most skillful stonecutters of Egypt at their work of sawing the sandstone into exact blocks with their copper saws that could penetrate the hardest stone. He allotted to the sculptors the marble blocks to be shaped into building adornments and statuary, and he kept an eye on the coppersmiths and jewelers.

These may have been the happiest months Akhenaton and Nefertiti would ever know. Under the bright rays of their worshiped sun they saw its first city brought into existence. They saw with Bek the outlining of the streets by surveyors who worked with stakes and strings, duplicating on the sands the "blueprint" drawn first on papyrus. No modern city designers could offer more exact a plan. With King Akhenaton symmetry was of primary importance.

Thanks to the many great archaeologists who have made studies of Amarna, we can re-create in exact detail Akhenaton's long-vanished city.

We are not certain who drew the plan for Amarna. Bek, as chief architect, chiseled beside his own name that of King Akhenaton's as "he whom himself hath taught me." In turn, Aye has been credited as having tutored Akhenaton in his study of architecture. But the basic concept of Amarna was Akhenaton's, and it was built to a single plan.

We can still trace on the leveled sands the shadowy outlines of what was once the world's most splendid city.

The ancient camel track running parallel to the Nile became the fifty-foot-wide Sikket es-Sultan (King's Highway). Four chariots could drive abreast along this central boulevard crossed by fine wide streets that would be the pride of any modern metropolis. The holy city spread out on either side of the highway, as neatly as a modern subdivision.

Work began on the eastern bank, as it had at Thebes centuries before. It started with the construction of a great temple for Aton, "House of the Sun." In front of the temple was a square or plaza, and on the other side of that rose the royal estate and the palace.

The palace was the second largest building in Amarna, and when completed it was the largest non-religious building on earth. It was known as "the House of the Rejoicing of the Aton." It contained many departments, including the North and South Harem, the state apartments, and the private quarters of the king. It was surrounded by smaller buildings, and like all the great and small buildings in Amarna, in its gardened courtyards were the inevitable wells.

Within a few months a magnificent city stood beside the Nile. It was splendidly colored, many-gardened, flawless—a jewel of cities.

When completed Amarna was about two miles long and a half mile at its widest. Its preplanned symmetry gave the illusion of airiness and space. The King's Highway ran between the king's palace and the royal estate, which were connected by a bridge spanning the highway. To the north stood the temple of the Sun, and presently, the North Palace, Nefertiti's palace, and the elegant gardened villas of the nobles. As at Thebes, there were northern and southern suburbs. There were many temples scattered throughout the city as churches are in modern cities.

Some of the finest and largest buildings ever built in Egypt had risen, as if overnight, in Amarna.

There were a number of palaces. Wine jars found in the Amarna ruins with their mouths stuffed with palm fiber and sealed and marked with the date and locality of their vintage and the names of their owners have identified the royal and noble homes of Amarna.

One palace was built for the Princess Beketaton, Akhenaton's sister, and another, complete with treasury and granary, for Queen Tiy. Evidently Akhenaton hoped his mother would eventually move to Amarna. Palaces would be built for several of Nefertiti's daughters as they attained maturity.

By those silent witnesses, the wine jars, and other objects bearing her name, we know Nefertiti occupied in turn three palaces in Amarna.

Farming began with the birth of the city, and within a few months the west side of the Nile was under cultivation. Oxen pulled wooden plows through the rich virgin soil, grain was sown, and orchards were planted with seedlings brought from Thebes.

Gardens began everywhere, and the city was far more beautiful than Thebes or any other Egyptian city.

Akenaton rode through the new streets in his golden chariot, driving fiery horses that wore atop their tossing heads, in a fashion distinctly Amarnian, crests of ostrich plumes. Nefertiti rode beside him in queenly beauty, showing no hint of the inner strength this city would ask of her. Amarna was their faith and their kingdom, and wherever they went eyes lifted with theirs to the sun.

In Thebes, the priests of Amon read reports of the happiness of Akhenaton and Nefertiti in their new capital, and cursed Amarna, and bided their time.

The first building completed was the great temple "House of the Sun," raised by Akhenaton to Aton. Its exact site and measurements are known.

The temple was totally unlike any other place of worship built in Egypt. Nowhere else had such enormous halls been built, nor such forests of pillars. The shrine alone was two hundred feet long. The altars were stepped. Its enclosure was a half mile long.

Pictures of the ancient temples of Egypt always show them with tall staffs set before them flying pennants. The sockets of such staffs have been found only before the temple at Amarna.

Howard Carter, Dr. Frankfort, and Sir Leonard Woolley are among the great archaeologists who helped clear Akhenaton's temple. More than three thousand years after the destruction of Amarna, Sir Leonard, excavating the leveled cement foundations, found faint red lines where the king's workmen had stretched cords soaked in red paint along the newly laid floors, and by snapping them down had marked out the lines where the walls were laid, as straight as any ever built. Those walls had been completely demolished during the merciless destruction of the city, but scraps revealed decorations of a style never seen before.

Akhenaton conducted the first services in the new temple, officiating as high priest while Nefertiti as high priestess led the hymning "to propitiate the Aton with her sweet voice, and send him to his rest, with her two beautiful hands bearing the sistrums." (So Akhenaton praised her.)

Aye made dramatic appearances in the temple. Evidently he did not spend all his time at Thebes, for he appears listed as "a well-known general and courtier of Amarna," and as enthusiastic a supporter of Aton as he formerly had been to Amon.

Standing under the rayed emblem, Aye led the chanting of the men's choir:

"Hail, Oh living Sun's Disk, shining in the heaven!
"Who fills all hearts, and brings joy to the earth with his shining . . ."

Then, turning his priestly form to Akhenaton, Aye chanted:

"Aton rejoices in his son, the King.
He embraces him with his arms
And gives him eternal life."

Turning to his fellow priests of Aton, Aye carried on the chant in personal terms.

"I am one of the greatest of the nobles and friends of the king.
"I am the chief of the faithful followers of His Majesty
who has given me the knowledge of Truth.
"I hold evil in abomination, for I know that the Unique
One in the eyes of the Sun finds satisfaction in Truth . . ."

Aye, always the practical philosopher, may have reasoned that since Amon-Ra and Aton were simply different names for the sun, it would not matter too much to the solar god under which name it was worshiped. This sophistry is much more in line with modern reasoning than it was in Aye's time. He was always far ahead of his century.

So, in the great temple at Amarna, Aye sang lustily to Aton, as he had to Amon in the temple at Thebes, in the faith of Akhenaton his king and high priest.

What was it Akhenaton taught in his tabernacle that his world would so shortly condemn?

He has been compared to Jesus Christ. The comparison is unfair. Akhenaton had inherited a prosperous and peaceful kingdom but one ridden by superstitions impossible for modern minds to grasp. The Egyptian was threatened on every side by dangerous deities.

Akhenaton was trying to rid Egypt of superstitious terror. He offered a pure and sublime faith in the one god, Aton, the kind creator and all-giver. Aton demanded no sacrifice, made no threats, laid down no laws. Akhenaton, Aton's voice on earth, believed that love transcended law.

There were forty-two laws in the Egyptian code of ethics. Ten are familiar. "Thou shalt not lie . . . thou shalt not kill . . . thou shalt not bear false witness . . ." These had been made by wise men before Akhenaton, and man was able to enforce them. Akhenaton's god was above threats.

Aton was life. He was love. He was to be praised and exalted and by his shining example man could live in earthly and future happiness.

Akhenaton did not preach. In an age of violence and terrifying ideology he praised the simple theory of peace. Surrounded by the threats of gods and demons in Thebes he had envisioned the need of man to see things as they were. He spoke of honesty and love and gentleness, and these in a land ridden by demons were not easy to understand.

In Thebes, the Amon priests had a new and terrible name for Akhenaton. They whispered it in secret to the people. "The heretic king."

But in Amarna, Akhenaton wrote after his name the proud words, "living in truth."

Akhenaton did not serve long as high priest. A day came when he summoned Merire to the palace "in solemn purpose." Merire (or Ramery, Beloved of Ra), was the revered priest who had bravely served the Aton at Thebes.

On the River Palace, as on the palace at Thebes, was the many-columned balcony known as the "window of appearances" where the Pharaoh showed himself to those he wished to honor. On this day, when Merire appeared with his friends under the marble balustrade, King Akhenaton announced his own retirement as high priest and named Merire "Great Seer . . . High Priest of Aton in the Temple of Aton in the City of Aton."

There are records of other honors paid Merire. In one illustration the "Great Seer" is shown standing in the entrance of a temple. Akhenaton, Nefertiti, and two little daughters are handing him gifts, and the king is saying: "Hang gold at his neck before and behind, and gold on his legs, because of his hearing the teachings of Pharaoh concerning every saying in these beautiful seats which Pharaoh has made in the sanctuary of the Aton-table at Akhetaton."

Evidently Merire had been a reverent listener to the teachings of Akhenaton. His piety was richly rewarded and his was one of the finest homes in Amarna.

Among other "favorites" honored at the "window of appearances" was General Mai. Aye was frequently honored.

At the honoring of Merire two little daughters are shown. Nefertiti had given birth to a second daughter, the first of the little princesses to be born at Amarna. Like her sister, the little girl was given a "sun name," Meketaton.

Meketaton was born in 1367 B.C. Akhenaton put his love for his family into enduring words:

"Sweet love fills my heart for the Queen, for her young children. Grant a great age to the Queen Nefertiti, long years may she keep the hand of Pharaoh. Grant a great age to the royal daughter Meritaton and to the royal daughter Meketaton and to their children; may they keep the hand of the Queen their mother eternally and forever."

He was now eighteen. Nefertiti was seventeen. They had lived a great deal in the two years of their marriage.

Certainly no more beautiful royal house has ever graced the world than the North Palace, the second palace built at Amarna. (This was Nefertiti's last, her most distinctive home.) Illustrated books, paintings, photographs and colored post cards reproduce its magnificent painted walls and murals some of which by a miracle were buried under debris when the palace was destroyed.

There were many inner and outer courts, one with a great pool, and one with an altar for worship, and colonnades, and many rooms. One courtyard was solely for flowers, and one was planted with grapes.

In one large enclosure were kept many kinds of cattle. The

stalls were of stone, easily cleaned, and the stone mangers were carved with pictures of the animals whose stalls they were. One room was set aside for that marvelous bird, the hen, that provided daily delicacies for the royal table. Many of the ceilings of the palace rooms were as blue as Nefertiti's favorite headdress, to represent the sky, for the charm of this palace was its airiness and its resemblance to a garden.

The famous Green Room, the wall murals of which are so often reproduced, notably the famous mural painting copied by N. de Garis Davies and his wife which is in the Metropolitan Museum, contained an enormous window approximately twenty feet long—perhaps the world's first "picture window." It looked into a garden so that the room itself seemed an extension of the garden. The remaining three walls were painted to represent the blue waters of a river, and above were the richest greens of reeds and lotus. Among the feathered papyrus fronds were the most exquisitely painted birds—kingfishers and wild doves and a shrike. The black dado merged into the black bank of the pool. Floor and ceiling were white.

It was certainly the most beautiful room in the world then, and in that hot climate an oasis of coolness.

Other rooms were more ornate. The capitals of the columns were floral or inlaid with colored glaze made by Amarna jewelers exactly as they made their fine faïence vessels and jewelry. There were walls inlaid with ornamental stones where no plaster was used, the stones being tightly fitted together. A favorite ceiling decoration was a trellis covered with grapevines from which hung large clusters of purple faïence grapes.

The lavishness, the luxury, the beauty was such as had made beautiful the old palace at Thebes, but on a far more fantastic and cultured scale.

One of the most decorative rooms was the throne hall, where Nefertiti, seated beside Akhenaton, received the homage due her as Egypt's queen, while at their feet were heaped the treasures sent them by the vassal kings.

For Amarna had scarce begun, and long stone wharfs like those at Thebes been built, than the tribute from every part of Egypt, from Nubia and Canaan, that once had gone to Thebes, began pouring into the new capital. Now the king's fleets, heavy with bounty, making their way up the Nile no longer sailed on to Thebes but stopped their journey midway at Amarna.

A great event in the new city's history was the day the Temple of Aton received its first tribute. King Akhenaton is described as arriving before the temple in his chariot at the head of a "glittering procession" to be welcomed with shouts of jubilation at the temple gates. Entering, he found the high altar in the temple court and all the storerooms surrounding the court crammed with "rich oblations"—offerings newly made to the god Aton.

The Amon priesthood in Thebes, robbed of their best artists and craftsmen and now of the revenue that was the source of their power, fed the growing resentment of the deserted Thebans with a program of hatred launched against the young king and queen.

Akhenaton and Nefertiti were warned by Queen Tiy of the swelling venom of the Amon priests.

They were too happy in their new lives to be anxious. They had forgotten Amon and all the beast-headed gods. Theirs was a new and beautiful world—a true city of the sun.

They had no reason to fear the plottings of disgruntled Amonite priests. Amon was no longer the supreme god of Egypt. The beneficent Aton held its place above the throne.

Amarna was perfect, down to the last detail, as Akhenaton had foreseen.

The North Palace and the temple were departures from any architecture known, but the palace Akhenaton built for Nefertiti "against the wall" in the royal compound was not different. It was almost a replica of the painted palace his father had built for Queen Tiy on the west bank at Thebes. Fragments of the frescoed walls and painted ceilings and floors prove it was a setting of rare beauty. The roof was supported by carved columns, some imitative of palm trees. Again Nefertiti's love of pets, birds, and flowers is shown by decorated fragments.

High walls surrounding the palace gave it the harem seclusion loved by Egyptians, and there was a fine well.

All Amarna's carefully planned gardens were formal and magnificent and tended by armies of gardeners brought from Thebes. In those of the palaces and harems were the popular pavilions designed for dining and for dalliance. Amarna was for pleasure, but also it was a religious city, and stone shrines were in all the gardens, and in the gardens of the women's palaces were "Sunshade Houses," which were private chapels where the queen or other members of the royal family could offer special prayers to Aton, shielded from the fierce sun.

The Sunshades were small temples—small only in comparison with other temples—and they were built close to the larger temples. Every female member of the royal house had her garden chapel.

"The Sunshade of Queen Tiy," built for the queen mother by Akhenaton, is pictured in Aye's tomb at Amarna as a colonnaded court outside the Great Temple, with smaller courts and corridors.

One built for Nefertiti's first daughter, Meritaton, as she grew older, is identified by a fragment as having been "The Sunshade of the Princess Meritaton in the House of Rejoicing in the House of the Aton at Akhetaton."

Akhenaton built for Nefertiti as his father had for Tiy at Thebes. Before her palace was a vast parklike garden, with pools and a lake and a pavilion and a large "Sunshade" of which no description exists, although it is known that she worshiped there with her small daughters and ladies in waiting, that even Akhenaton joined her there, and that in it harpists played.

The royal lake duplicated the one Akhenaton's father had made for Queen Tiy before the palace at Thebes. It was filled with water resourcefully diverted from the Nile by a canal. Lotus plants floated on the water, and miniature barges, and Nefertiti's small royal galley.

Amarna's symmetrical appearance was emphasized by the curious fact that apart from the temples and palaces, all the buildings were identical. The larger homes were built to one plan, the smaller to another. They were of the flat-roofed bungalow type, and not crowded together, but set apart in gardens, so that the effect of the residential sections was that of suburbia.

The houses were of sun-baked bricks, but made splendid with stone pillars and paint.

The inner walls might be of Nile mud, but they were beautified with tinted plaster and paintings and fine woods. Floors were painted in designs. The householders gave free rein to their love of color; one painted his bedroom orange!

The windows were latticed, the rooms large and open to the sun, gardens in themselves, with walls foliaged with live and painted plants and flowers in garlands and rosettes. In them were paintings of birds—wild geese were the favorites—and animals. The asp was a popular motif. It was no longer a god but it was still the royal emblem of Lower Egypt.

Floral friezes were popular from the palaces to the smallest homes. Grapes, poppies, cornflowers, and the lotus were favored. Carved lotus petals were used as wall borders. Bunches of lotus and grapes made of faïence like those in the North Palace hung from the painted wooden rafters of the larger houses.

Even in the poorer section the houses were beautifully decorated with murals and the ceilings were often blue like those in the palace. The loving decorations the poorest Amarnian gave his home typified the lavish beauty of this strange new city.

The usual house had its large rectangular reception room or salon, a dining room, a bathroom—with stone bath and tank— a kitchen with a raised hearth, bedrooms where as a rule brick platforms were used for beds, and a servant's section with separate quarters for men and women. Rich draperies hung over the windows when the sirocco wind raced over the cliffs, and on the floors were fine, thick colored rugs and cushions the men sat upon; ladies preferred the handsome ebony chairs and stools. As in Thebes, but in more lavish profusion, there were many niches holding bits of rare treasure, vases, and costly bric-a-brac, hundreds of small decorative boxes lay scattered about the Amarna rooms, and there was fragrance everywhere. The rich had perfumes, but the poorest housekeeper could sweep her floors with a palm-leaf, sprinkle water on the floor for coolness, draw the blinds against the fierce African sun, and scent her home with herbs and flowers.

The entrances to the homes were charming. Every door was brightly painted in yellow or red. Those of the larger houses were framed in stone. All doors were low, measured to the height of the house's owner. Many had chiseled or painted upon them the emblem of Aton, and under it the householder's name.

A hanging basket of flowers hung beside nearly every door and on the lintel was placed each morning a basket of newly gathered grapes to refresh any strollers that might pass.

It was a city where all were known and all were friendly, but suspicion dies hard, and even as in Thebes porters armed with heavy wooden clubs stood guard beside the doors of the larger houses. This was an honorable office and such a guard was privileged to boast of his watchfulness in his tomb.

At night, young and old sought the flat roofs and watched the march of the stars against the cloudless sky and listened to the plaintive love songs so typical of Amarna that rose everywhere in the night. Against the wall of the palace stairs led up to a balcony where Akhenaton could sit with Nefertiti and contemplate his universe. Below them, black and silver, ran the eternal Nile.

Over Amarna, on cliffs too steep for chariots, the watchfires of the king's patrols winked in the clear Egyptian night.

One of the finest of the Amarna villas belonged to Ramose, the former Ptahmose, who had changed his name and his faith to follow Akhenaton. Ramose's fidelity had been richly rewarded. Now he was not only grand vizier but also "General of the King of Both Lands." He was in charge of all the armies remaining to Egypt, but the truth was his loyalties were stronger than his military knowledge. No victories are cited to his credit. Nevertheless, he was an important personage in the sun city and one of his rewards was the large, handsome house on what is now known in his memory as the Street of the General.

Its doors had elegantly carved stone frames. As in all these larger Amarna houses, the center of the house was a large salon with many windows looking out over the storerooms and the courtyards with their wells and beehive-shaped granaries in which were stored the household supplies of wheat and corn. Through these windows the "lady of the house," as a wife was known, was able to keep watch on domestic affairs.

But the general's household accounts contain no mention of a wife. A housekeeper is mentioned, by name J'net.

Merire's home resembled that of Ramose, and stood in what is known to students of Amarna as the Street of the High Priest.

Another favored house was the studio of Thutmes in the Street of the Sculptor, where so many of Amarna's citizens were immortalized in stone.

The appearance of Amarna was that of leisure and luxury, but it was the center of world commerce and active with business and production. There was a civic center where thousands of clerks attended to the governmental and foreign affairs. There was the records office, where the Amarna Letters would be hidden, and the House of Life, which was the school run by Aton priests similar to the Amonite Scribe's College Aye had attended in Thebes, and a religious library—the repository for sacred writings. There were the military barracks and the police headquarters where would be found stout leather collars (worn by the guardians of the law or their prisoners?) and bronze daggers and knives and a stylus for keeping records and seal rings stamped with the royal insignia of Akhenaton.

There was a large business section. There were offices and shops. There were three or four glass factories and factories where were made the ceramics, faïence, and pottery that became famed as Amarnian. There were mills where women sat at looms weaving linen and wool; and storehouses where grains and jars of wine would be found, many stamped with Nefertiti's name; and great sacks of wool that would be discovered thousands of years after Amarna had ceased to exist.

The most astonishing discovery at Amarna would be the uncovering of the ideal "workmen's village." It offers fascinating testimony to the social consciousness of Akhenaton. He was the greatest religious leader of his time but he was also a practical man, interested in every small building detail of the city.

In Egypt the workers had always been herded at sundown into their ghetto areas, like cattle being driven into pens. In a section where narrower streets stretched out from the King's Highway in the direction of the eastern cliffs, Amarna's workmen's village strangely resembles the low-cost housing subdivisions of our time. It was the first model village of its kind in history. Built like the main section of the city to a single plan, it was an attractive walled city in miniature. The foreman's cottage by the gate was fairly large.

The other houses were small, neat, and exactly alike. These

Amarna cottages have been praised as "the very pattern of mechanically devised industrial dwellings." Each had its combination living room and kitchen facing the street. In the rear were bedrooms and closets. The excavation of one of these rooms revealed a kitchen as it was left in working order thousands of years ago. Cooking pots stood in the fireplace, and utensils were in the bread oven and roasting place. On the raised hearth lay a poker laid down by some housewife whose domestic work was interrupted for some reason unknown.

Tools have been found in these houses, and among them, so close were these people to the stone age, were tools made of flint. Amulets were found, proving that even in Amarna superstition was slow to die.

Before one door hung a rope by which a donkey had been tethered by its master, three and a half thousand years ago.

Other mysteries have been found in Amarna. Trussed bodies of cattle were left ready for sacrifices never made. Under a stairway in one home were the dried remains of a horse. Perhaps the beast had been the family's most valuable possession and was kept there for safety. And sealed in one wall, and never explained, were the skeletons of a man and a woman—victims perhaps of an ancient never solved murder.

These houses of the model village were alike, but they were carefully planned as to simplicity and beauty of line, and, like all the homes in Amarna, they were set in gardens. In them lived the makers of the tombs and the skilled tenders of the dead brought by the king from Thebes.

In 1366 B.C. the workmen of this village began building under Akhenaton's direction a new Valley of the Kings, in a long, narrow slot of a valley running eastward into the desert between cliffs some of which were three hundred feet high. The valley was strangely similar to the one that held the graves of his ancestors at Thebes.

Only, like all else built by Akhenaton, this burial place was different from the old. It was built on the east side of the river, nearer the rising sun (that at Thebes was on the west), and the tombs, painfully carved into solid rock like the others, contained none of the fearful images that had crowded the old. In every tomb was the cheerful emblem of Aton and pictures of Akhenaton and his family worshiping the sun.

These were tombs created for the family of the Pharaoh.

Why then was the first to be started, even before that of the king and queen, the tomb of Aye? It was built on orders from Akhenaton, and this singular honor paid the humbly born Aye substantiates the belief that he was father-in-law of the king.

Aye's tomb was one of the finest in Egypt. It would never be occupied, but it holds some of the most valuable historical testimony. Akhenaton permitted his poems to be registered on its walls. Among the paintings is one showing Akhenaton and Nefertiti at "the window of appearances." With them are several of the little princesses and what appears to be a small prince. (Tutankhaton?) Below the balcony, looking up and smiling, are Aye and his wife, Tiy the nurse, while behind them their servants caper with delight.

The king, leaning over the marble balustrade, is showering down upon his "beloved favorites" gifts of gold collars, bracelets, and rings, and this honoring is explained: "The rejoicing is being made for Aye, the father of the god, and Tiy. . . . They are being made people of gold!"

Aye, giving a ceremonial bow, testifies as to the king's generosity: "He doubles for me favors in silver and gold."

And the royal response: "He is satisfied in seeing you without ceasing."

Evidently Akhenaton did not tire of his favorites.

Nefertiti, pictured in the act of tossing down two gold collars, is wearing her customary crown with the royal emblem. It does not detract from her queenly dignity that she is apparently wearing very little else. A wisp of chiffonlike material crosses her graceful nudity; a state in which a queen of her maturity would not be likely to appear save before the exceptionally trusted or the closely related. The picture gives an interesting sidelight on the devotion between a former scribe and his wife and the king and queen of Egypt.

Amarna was called "the city of flowers." Outside their private walls the Amarnians planted lavish outer gardens to delight all who walked in the wide, fragrant streets.

The fifty-foot-wide King's Highway was outlined with ornamental trees growing in square brick-lined pits as trees are set in the pavements of modern streets.

The coral bloom of pomegranates was everywhere, lotus grew in pools, and beautiful little summer houses stood between the trees like miniature palaces. Through all the green and fragrance gazelles and other pets wandered and shyly accepted tidbits from small, soft, brown hands.

The poorest could pluck their own blossoms, and in Amarna the professional florist came into his own.

Carefully arranged bouquets hung in the streets, at the doors, from the ceilings and walls of the houses and palaces. Striking arrangements of garlands and wreaths were made of combinations of fruit and flowers. A favorite table arrangement had a base made of the varying greens of celery, willow, olive, and papyrus. On it was laid a mat of deep-blue cornflowers and over that sprays of the lighter blue lotus. Women wore deep collars made of live flowers. Small corsages, the stems folded in an olive leaf, were carried or worn by women. Nefertiti carried such corsages; she wore flowers on her dress and in her hair; she exchanged flowers with her children and Akhenaton.

In these years she was queen of a city without a history and without shadows.

The lowliest slave could walk in Amarna and see on every side only magnificence and beauty. Akhenaton had created this city as he had his spiritual world, for all to share. Amarna contained no slum areas, no ugliness. Down to its last room it had been designed for happiness by its artist-king.

Amarna was unfinished, but Akhenaton's angriest enemies could not dispute those who praised it as the world's most beautiful city.

CHAPTER TEN

The Amarna Revolution

Tell el-Amarna, 1368–1361 B.C.

Now there began at Amarna a leap forward in time as out of place, it has frequently been said, as Akhenaton himself. The Amarna movement led by the rebel king was a complete break with the past. He had sacrificed his heritage, deserted Thebes, and cast aside all other gods to worship his one god in his own way. He shared that privilege with all who came to Amarna.

The results were new freedoms of expression in religion, politics, society, literature, architecture, and art. The oriental paradise of Akhenaton and Nefertiti became the exciting center of a new world.

The great poets and writers and artists and sculptors and architects and seers flocked to Amarna and the protection offered by the world's wealthiest king.

In return Akhenaton asked only that they express the truth.

Freed from the bonds of mysticism, there began the great creative movement known as "the Amarna revolution." The world's most beautiful city fostered not only a new religion but a new art.

Amarna was Nefertiti. It is impossible to separate the queen from the city. No other woman until our present time would be so publicized. Akhenaton's love for her was immortalized in an outpouring of advanced paintings, statuary, murals and bas relief.

"Amarna art," according to the Encyclopedia Brittanica, "is no more part of Egyptian traditional genus than the Aton doctrine: both were imposed by the will of a superman born out of his time."

The Pharaohs before Akhenaton had placed rigid restrictions on Egypt's artists. The human body had to be presented in certain prescribed poses; even the head had to be turned a certain way. Bodies were planklike, rigid, as if the ancients, like their statues, had been people of stone. To show the difference between the sexes men were painted red and women yellow. Women were usually shown as much smaller than men. Children were small adults.

These conventional rules had been followed by obedient artists since the First Dynasty. The Pharaoh was invariably a formalized majestic figure, sitting square as a block of wood on the throne or in full stride. Akhenaton's ancestors had been so portrayed, larger than life, fierce, and inhuman, and not more than once or twice in a lifetime.

Akhenaton "rebelled against the formalized flattery of traditional art."

At Amarna a freedom of expression began, a sense of relaxation and gracefulness, which was expressed in the dances, games, sports, social life, music, poetry, stories, and hymns, and above all in the works of the artists and sculptors. Even dress was freer. Long flowing robes were worn, distinctive to Amarna. The royal pair were the leading examples in the new freedom.

Egyptian art had always stressed love of nature. The paintings in the Theban palace had been beautiful. In Amarna the palace walls were masterpieces. Butterflies, birds, flies, and locusts flaunted their pleasure in being alive; calves gamboled with awkward charm. Such art had never before been seen in the world. Suddenly there sprang into existence the first true-life paintings of humans. Studies in relief and in the round began, flowing curves were shown, and flesh tints carefully imitated. Eyes were colored. Some of the art studies from Amarna were typical of the school that would later be known as "pure Greek."

The sculptors and artists worked together. Once a head was shaped in stone or plaster the artist took over; color completed the Amarna realism.

Amarna art specialized in the present active moment. Crowds, groups, working gangs, and marching soldiers were shown, not in the stiff poses that had served for centuries but in motion. Akhenaton's father and mother had departed from the conventional when they were portrayed of equal size, seated on thrones. Akhenaton and Nefertiti shared their married life with Amarna. In the city's houses were niches, like household shrines, which contained no idols but paintings of the king and queen and their little daughters, usually being blessed by the warm hands of Aton.

The terror inspired by the Eighteenth Dynasty kings was no longer a barrier between the palace and the people. Let the humblest slave share in a king's happiness. In every public appearance Akhenaton made, Nefertiti was shown with him. Each little princess was welcomed and added to the group pictures of the royal family that were to make an enduring Amarna album.

The intimacy of these scenes was new to Egypt and still touches the heart. Only the emblems on the king's and queen's brows betray their royalty.

There are many domestic scenes of Nefertiti and Akhenaton. They sit in affectionate closeness, they exchange flowers, he touches her breast, she leans her head against his.

They are shown together in the royal chariot, racing through the streets, leaning against the wind; they kiss, and the moment is immortalized on stone. In another chariot picture one of the little princesses, unnoticed by her parents, is shown tickling the rump of one of the horses with a stick.

In one picture Akhenaton lounges on the throne. He is the picture of indolence. Nefertiti sits on his knees. Her feet do not touch the floor. His are tiptoe. Obviously the great royal wife is being bounced on the knees of the king of the Two Egypts.

Beside them, two of the children are taking various kinds of fruit from an oval dish made with four compartments.

One fragment shows a woman's breast approached by the greedy mouth of a babe; it is labeled Nefertiti.

Petrie wrote of Akhenaton: "His domestic life was his ideal of the truth of life."

There had always been a certain amount of delightful irreverence in the Egyptian mentality. Art and literature poked fun at stodginess and pomposity. But ridicule had always before stopped short of the altar and the throne.

Egyptians were the first cartoonists. They drew pictures like comic strips, even to the "balloons" holding words spoken by the pictured characters, which might be human or animal. These cartoons delighted young and old. They were even placed in tombs to amuse the dead.

In their natural world, not far removed from the primitive, the Egyptians recognized certain animal characteristics as being similar to those of man and stressed such traits in their mythology. They were the first to humanize animals. Their gods had the heads of birds and animals. People were animal, animals were people, and all were of the stuff of gods. Artists and sculptors and poets helped develop the illusion.

The most revered animal, such as Miw, the cat, might be cartooned, and the ridicule was not considered offensive.

One often reproduced drawing shows a stern, determined cat standing erect and clutching a shepherd's crook. He is herding a flock of birds.

In another a hippopotamus is perched in a tree. A waiter climbs a ladder to serve him. The waiter is a crow.

Another portrays a small boy before the bar of justice. The policeman who has brought him into court, holds the policeman's staff—he is a cat. The judge, with the official staff in his paw, is a mouse.

In still another an army of mice are storming a fortress defended by obviously starving cats.

Some of these may have had political meanings. We cannot interpret now the significance of the drawing of a gigantic finger pressing a calf into what appears to be a cocked hat.

The Egyptians could laugh at those they loved and even worshiped. But the artists at Amarna took liberties that had never been dared before in Egypt, where majesty at least had always been portrayed as more than human—the perfect being, the ultimate godhead.

Akhenaton lessened his own terrifying authority when he adopted for his cognomen "living in truth" and urged realism on the Amarna artists. They responded with an enthusiasm that must have startled Egypt then and bewildered subsequent generations. Shorn of the traditional awe that glorified the Pharaoh and denied by his own edict of the divinity due a son born of Amon, Akhenaton appeared to the Amarna artists simply as a man among men—a man who ate, drank, and made love.

The artists, set free, became bolder in expression, until Akhenaton's portraits and statues approached caricature. Faithfully and without mercy certain bodily characteristics were not glossed over but emphasized. The artists missed no detail of the kingly physique—the strange, bulbous, elongated head, the slitted eyes, narrow chin, thick hips, and protruding stomach. One frank portrayal shows him bleary-eyed and badly in need of a shave.

The irreverent approach reached a climax in one sketch where Akhenaton and his children were cartooned as monkeys.

Nefertiti remained the darling of the ateliers. She was never subjected to ridicule. Now in her early twenties, she was probably at this time four times a mother, having given birth to two more daughters, Ankhesenaton and Neferneferuaton (1365 and 1363 B.C.).

Her second unfinished limestone head is even more beautiful, with a beauty that defies changes in taste throughout the ages. It was made later.

All that she was, all she was doing, was intimately and tenderly carved on stone, baked in faïence, penned in clay, and painted on pottery, pavements, walls, and papyrus scrolls. Poems and hymns and words of love were written down. Sealed in sand, they have lasted.

The artists and sculptors were not alone in developing Amarna into the greatest of creative centers. In the shops of the woodworkers furniture was being made that would disappear from the world for centuries and then be discovered, acclaimed for comfort and artistry, and copied. The cabinetmakers cut the rare woods with copper tools, and fitted the pieces together with dowling pins, as fine furniture is always made. They polished and made inlays. They ranked as artists, which they were.

There were craftsmen who made nothing but the exquisite small boxes that were the delight of every Amarna home.

The jewelers were fashioning jewels that would awe museumgoers after thousands of years and extending their art to faïence decorations or mosaic made of small stones to enhance the beauty of Amarna rooms. Faïence attained its highest level. The Amarna ware with its thin glass glaze developed in exquisite new shades—a deeper, more glorious blue than that attained in other dynasties, a chocolate shade, violets, yellows, and a sharp apple green.

Dishes for the lavish Amarna tables, spoons for unguents or eating, knives with carved handles—each was designed and fashioned by a master. They were of gold, silver, copper, pottery, and bronze. Discovered pieces of Amarna glassware are among the greatest treasures of antiquity. The jug shape originated there. Vases, bottles, goblets, and flasks were made in many colors. Pale blue and black were favored. Strips of color were skillfully fused. One magnificent bottle of variegated glass is shaped like a fish. Banquet tables were more beautifully appointed than ever before.

Small art reached perfection. The nearby marble quarries yielded the lucent alabaster from which the stone artists carved translucent vases and figurines and night lamps shaped like flowers.

We may be certain there was no object in Nefertiti's palace that would not give pleasure to museum visitors in another age and other lands. The ointment spoon her servant held would attract crowds to a Cartier window. Beauty was her heritage and her responsibility.

The love songs of Amarna became famous, but none of their music and few of the words have survived. A favorite of Nefertiti's describes a sycamore's wooing of a palm. "I am discreet. I shall not gossip." One chorus remains that was popular with the harpists entertaining at the banquets:

"Make holiday, and weary not therein!
"Behold, it is not given to a man to take his property with him!
"Behold, there is not one who departs who ever comes back again!"

(Eat, drink and be merry, or, in modern parlance, "you can't take it with you!")

Literature was soaring to heights never dreamed of before in Egypt. Akhenaton was among those who wrote. Certain portions of work by other writers was saved by the Amarna Letters. But it was Aye who saved the poetry Akhenaton was pouring out during these highly creative years. He was given permission to reproduce in his tomb in its entirety Akhenaton's great *Hymn to the Sun*. Other tombs contain parts of the ode.

Akhenaton's hymn was the world's first great religious poem. It is the finest piece of literature to come out of early Egypt.

Breasted placed "the most noticeable parallel passages" of the Psalms beside parts taken from the Aton hymn, showing them to be almost word for word alike. The words soar in the cadence that would become known as biblical:

> "Your dawning is beautiful in the horizon of heaven,
> Oh living Aton, Beginning of Life! . . .
> You fill every land with your beauty . . .
> Your footprints are the day."

Akhenaton sang of all he knew and gave credit to Aton for its creation. He praised the sun as implanter of the child in woman and the seed in man. In the palace was the hennery (the domestic fowl was new in Egypt), and he had observed that miracle, the hen, which "brings forth every day." For this he praised Aton:

> "When the chick cries out in its shell,
> You give him breath to sustain him,
> You empower him to break his way from the egg
> And come forth and chirp at his time . . ."

He sang of the Nile, not as a god, but as one more gift from Aton:

> "You have set a Nile in heaven that it may descend
> And make floods on the mountains like the sea. . . .
> The ships sail up-stream and down-stream. . . .
> And your rays are in the depths of the sea."

Akhenaton poured out his praise; the hymn is long:

> "No other knows you
> Save your son Akhenaton.
> You have made him wise in your purposes . . .
> The world is in your hand. . . ."

The poet-king climaxed his paean of adoration to the one god by identifying himself for the last time as the son of Aton, "living in truth, lord of diadems, Akhenaton, whose life is long."

Akhenaton's hymn ends in words for Nefertiti, his "Great Royal Wife, his beloved, Mistress of the Two Lands, living and flourishing forever and ever."

Amarna had been started in 1369 B.C. and made livable within a few months. For seven flawless years the youthful king and queen were happy in their perfect city. Their life was described as one continuous festival. The idyll was broken into in 1361 by news of the death of Akhenaton's father, King Amenhotep, at Thebes.

CHAPTER ELEVEN

The Rise of Enmity

Thebes, 1361 B.C.

Akhenaton may have returned to Thebes when his father was
near death. There is a portrait of him watching with a sad and
haggard Queen Tiy at the bedside of the obviously dying king.
Certainly he was in the old capital to oversee the burial, for it
was the duty of every Egyptian son to see his parent safely interred. It is unlikely that Nefertiti went with him; by this time
her fourth little daughter had been born.

Akhenaton, driving his chariot through Thebes to the palace
of his boyhood, where Queen Tiy was still living in token representation of the crown, must have noticed the silence in the
streets and perhaps credited it to the seventy days of national
mourning required by the death of a king. The former capital
grieved for the loss of the former king who had been one of
the truly great Egyptian Pharaohs. Amenhotep III had served his
country long and well. He had held a threatened Egypt, kept it
to its supremacy, handed it down unimpaired to his only son,
sired the continuation of the dynasty. If he had qualms at leaving Egypt in the hands of a young dreamy-eyed zealot, he did
not put them on record.

Thebes was a city of mourning. When word came from the
palace that the good king "had departed into the West," the
people wept, and black gloom descended on the priests in the
Temple of Amon for they must have suspected their survival had
rested with the old king, and now only a widowed ex-queen was
left to defend them. Could they count on Tiy, who, as all knew,
was close to her son? What other restraint remained to the
young king who had discredited Amon and built Amarna?

Never were more fervid prayers addressed to the ka of a
vanished king than were said in the Temple of Amon, begging

for the continued protection of King Amenhotep among the shades.

The seventy days or more of mourning was the time required for a body emptied of its softer parts to dry in the hot sun. During this time, while the thin shell of the king's body lay exposed and open in the Pavilion of Death at the necropolis, all Thebes grieved for him. Day and night mournful funeral dirges sounded in the streets and temples and homes. Twice each day the people formed crowds in public places and tore their clothing and heaped dust on their heads and wailed their grief in prolonged oriental keening. During this time no holidays were celebrated, no matter how holy, no feasts were held, and no persons, rich or poor, tasted meat or white bread or drank wine, to show their love for Amenhotep III.

Akhenaton's father died loved by his people and respected by the gods. None of the hatred rising against his son had touched him, although he must have known it existed.

In the palace the presence of her adored son solaced the grieving Tiy. She wore black, which was the color of resurrection (white was for happiness; red could be evil). She carried garlands made of poppy petals, cast dust on her head, and wept for the king who had been her youthful love.

The widow was assisted in her mourning by relays of hired professional mourners, women who, with streaming hair and high-pitched wailing, maintained lamentations for the dead. There was feasting in the magnificent funerary temple Amenhotep III had ordered built years before for himself and queen, by Aye, and there was dancing, for at funerals, as well as at the sacred feast of Opet, the balletlike ritual dance of the Muu was performed by the temple dancers.

Akhenaton probably grew a beard to show his sorrow. It would have been sparse. Egyptian men kept their faces hairless by plucking. He brought a princely retinue with him to the hostile city of his fathers. Ramose must have returned with him, for one of the duties of a grand vizier was to oversee the burial of kings. Aye would no doubt have accompanied the young king, knowing that to Thebes Akhenaton had come to represent a break with its secure and glorious past.

It may have seemed ironic to the Amon priests that they were placed in charge of all the royal funerary arrangements. The preparation of a king for his afterlife was among their duties. Queen Tiy would have insisted upon the traditional rituals. So the body of Amenhotep III, as his mummy testifies, was prepared for death under the protection of the god he had never deserted.

Mummification had once been the privilege of royalty or the nobly born. Now it had become general and a steady source of revenue for Amon. Only the very poor were piled up like cordwood in common tombs in the desert, or hastily hidden under thin layers of sand. The use of coffins had begun in the Thirteenth Dynasty and was now universal, so that some of Egypt's greatest artists were kept busy the year round, shaping and decorating with colors and gold overlay these costly works of art. In fact, a great share of Egyptian artistry and craftsmanship went into the furnishing of the tombs. There were studios that made only coffins and funerary furniture of the rarest woods and decorated the thousands of small objects that went into the graves. There were funerary jewelers who made the costly vials containing unguents and ointments to delight the interred in the other world, and their jeweled amulets, and the handsome death masks, often of gold, that protected mummified faces.

Other men were skilled at grave digging and concealing the graves they dug out of the stone cliffs, and still others were trained in embalmment, so that in Thebes entire armies of workers toiled under the jurisdiction of the Amon priests in behalf of the dead.

It was estimated that at this time an estimated 100,000 citizens lived in Thebes, and that one out of every four workmen had something to do with the burial and perpetual care of the dead.

From their crowded village at Deir el-Medina near the necropolis in the narrow valley leading to the Valley of the Kings, gangs of workmen went to work in the tombs and were relieved every ten days, as soldiers in action are. These were quarrymen, carpenters, painters, and laborers of every kind, whose hereditary duties were the shaping and decorating of the tombs, the building of funerary chapels and the final preparations for burial of the dead.

This began with solemn day and night rites in the Pavilion

of Death, where the emptied shell of the old king lay exposed through the seventy days of mourning. The surgeon-priests had been skillful and swift. The viscera had been removed, and the brain drawn out through the nostrils by means of fine hooked wires. The brain was the seat of a man's wisdom, and the heart and bowels, as all knew, were the seat of the emotions and mind. These were the essence of being (from this perhaps came the logos concept of the Greeks) and must be preserved, for who would wish to find himself in the underworld without the essence of his being? So the bowels and brains were saved in the four handsome canopic jars which were part of the funerary equipment of every tomb. Their tightly sealed lids were shaped like the heads of the four sons of Horus who helped guard the dead, human-headed Mesti, hawk-headed Qebhsneuf, jackal-headed Duanutef, and ape-headed Hapi.

Standing guard over the Pavilion of Death and the body of the old king was the image of Anubis, the black jackal-god who was the patron of embalmers as he was lord of the necropolis.

Wherever he went during the two months in Thebes, Akhenaton would have found himself in the presence of the gods he had denied and deserted. They were still dominant in Thebes. Anubis stalked among the graves; Bastet howled in the streets; Babi roared in the swamps; Amon brooded everywhere and plotted against the young king. The Egyptians apart from Amarna had not dared accept the one-god concept. Akhenaton must have been keenly aware of the horror and fear he inspired.

But he had death duties to observe. The emptied corpse dried. The preserved heart was replaced in the breast cavity, the "heart scarab" placed over the heart, and the process of embalming begun with chanting and incantations by the priests. Long winding strips of the finest linen, soaked in resins, gums, tars, bitumen, and scented with fragrant oils, rare spices, and floral perfumes, were tightly crisscrossed around the body. In the soaked linen bands were folded bits of priceless treasure—small images of the gods and the sacred animals, engraved scarabs, personal jewelry, and many amulets of gold, bronze, silver, precious stones, glass, and faïence. Each was engraved with the dead person's name, so that he would have no trouble establishing his identity when he entered the next world.

Contrary to popular belief, it was not the embalming process that kept the mummified body from decay. Centuries spent sealed in sand and the dry, equable Egyptian climate were the preservatives, so effective that mummies six thousand years old have been found with bodies, faces, teeth, and hair so well preserved in their yellowed linen bandagings that we are privileged to meet face to face with many of Egypt's ancient great in the museums and know them as they were. Their dignity and personalities remain.

The valley burial place was a secret cleft in the western desert, as strange and lonely as death itself. The forbidding façade gave no sign that the limestone cliffs were honeycombed with secret underground palaces in which were hidden the bodies of more than forty Theban kings. All Akhenaton's Eighteenth Dynasty ancestors were buried there, some in surroundings even more splendid than those they had occupied in life.

These were the actual burying places of the royal dead. The elaborate funerary temples were second homes where the king's other self might visit if he chose. The body was hidden away, far under stone rooms and halls and corridors, some of which were hundreds of feet long. It was of the utmost importance that a king's body be preserved, for without it he could not be expected to continue his reign after death.

Every Egyptian who could afford it tried to insure his eternal salvation by providing for his mummification and secure burial. For since the body accompanied the soul into the underworld, it was of the utmost importance that the body arrive on the far side of existence intact and with enough wealth to insure the continuation of a comfortable and luxurious existence in the next world.

The protection of a king's corpse and its accompanying riches had been a problem ever since the dynasties began. The great pyramids of the Fourth Dynasty originated as hiding places for the royal mummies. They had failed in their purpose. The royal bodies, and the possessions buried with them, were stolen from their secret hiding places under the man-made stone mountains.

Grave robbing had been big business in Egypt for more than a thousand years.

The incentive was great. With the bodies of the royal and the rich in the pyramids, masonry crypts, and graves had been buried incalculable treasure, of which little remains. For this reason the Eighteenth Dynasty had chosen for its royal burial ground the forbidding Valley of the Kings. In the subterranean palaces rooms opened upon rooms glittering with treasure, through doors carefully sealed and concealed, up to the last walled-in chamber where was hidden the body of the king.

Royal burials were held as secretly as if they were acts of shame. The small entrances to the great tombs were so artfully concealed with stones and sand the façade of the cliffs looked untouched. Every concealed door was hung over with protective amulets threatening curses against any who might break its sacred seals. Footprints were swept away with palm fronds.

Strict laws bolstered the threats of the incantations and amulets. The most severe penalties in the Egyptian legal code dealt with those caught robbing tombs.

But few were caught. The truth was they operated under powerful protection. They could never have found their way to certain hidden graves without information given by some bribed person who had been present at the burial.

The grave robbers were members of a large and well established guild. Their knowledge and affiliations were handed down from father to son and many an Egyptian family remained wealthy for generations with its share of loot taken from a single grave. It is more than suspected that certain sources of information led from the Temple of Amon. The robbers knew where every tomb entrance was concealed under its layer of sand and stones. Working by night, they could make their way through any door, rob the rooms by torchlight, and, upon leaving, cover the entryway so skillfully no one could know it had been touched. In some places they did not even go to the trouble of opening the door; they tunneled from the rear. All that was needed was a hole a man's arm could be thrust through, for the robbers knew exactly where the mummy lay and where each bit of treasure was placed. If, in their haste, they tore necklaces from royal throats, ripped apart and scattered beautifully set jewels, and broke off mummy fingers for their rings, no protest came from the despoiled dead. What curse followed the robber who tore off the braceleted arm of a queen?

Even mummies were stolen and sold as curios.

The descendants of the robbers who had found their way into the mysterious underground passages of the pyramids had no difficulty in penetrating the sealed fastnesses of the Valley of the Kings. Generations of Theban families grew rich in the ghoulish profession. Only one out of every hundred of the necropolis graves was unmolested and those unlooted graves remained intact because the robbers knew there was nothing in them worth the robbing. Long after Nefertiti's time, in the Twentieth Dynasty, a commission was appointed to investigate the robbing of the tombs in the Valley of the Kings.

By that time every royal grave, except one, had been systematically plundered.

The two months of mourning ended. Egypt had exhausted its grief for Amenhotep III. A night came when darkness lay heavily over the city of Thebes and the river and the cliffs beyond the river. Under cover of the dark a mournful procession made its way across the desert, past the funerary temples, and into the dark cleft that was the Valley of the Kings.

On a sledge drawn by oxen lay the sarcophagus that held the mummified body of Amenhotep. Following it over the sands came priests of Amon. They carried torches made of twisted linen twine sunk in oil; they chanted softly. The flickering reddish lights showed they were wearing the white robes and sandals of ceremony and masks and leopard-skin capes. They illumined the mourning figures of the closest of kin—King Akhenaton, his mother Tiy, his sister Beketaton. Ramose was certainly with them, and probably Aye, and a military guard stood watch as they entered the door in the side of the cliff that was so low the mourners had to stoop to enter.

There may have been other watchers on this night. Peering down on the torchlit scene from the upper rims of the cliffs were probably scouts of the robber clans, as furtive in their movements as the slinking jackals that had followed the death procession into the valley.

From that eminence, the robbers would have seen lights still burning in Thebes. The palace on the west side of the Nile, and the magnificent funerary temple of Amenhotep near it, were

9. Nefertiti's son-in-law, King Sakere (Smenkhkara), ruled briefly and under tragic circumstances. He was sensitive and beauty-loving and Akhenaton's choice as co-regent and heir. Little else is known of him. His loyalty to Akhenaton and to the religion of the one god cost him his throne and his life.

10.　Meritaton was the first of the "garland of princesses" born to Akhenaton and Nefertiti. The head forms the lid of a canopic jar intended for the tomb of her father at Amarna, but it was found instead in the so-called tomb of her grandmother, Queen Tiy.

11. Preceding Nefertiti as one of the strong-minded Eighteenth Dynasty queens was Hatshepsut, who was aunt to King Akhenaton, several genera-tions removed. She assumed certain masculine privileges and named herself not queen but king. She is shown wearing male clothing and the gold false beard intended to be worn only by kings.

12. This red granite head is believed to be that of Aye, the father of Nefertiti
and the tutor and mentor of Akhenaton. He was a humble scribe who became
the intellectual and political leader of Egypt.

13. Harmhab, raised to power by King Akhenaton, became his betrayer. He directed the destiny of the boy-king Tutankhaton who was little more than a puppet in Harmhab's crafty hands.

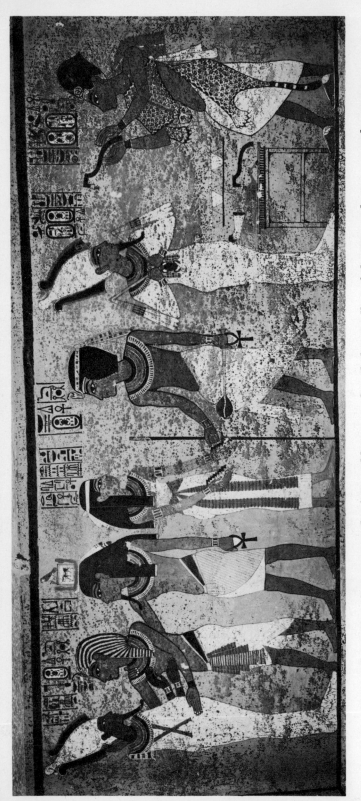

14. This wall painting from the tomb of Tutankhaton in the Theban Valley of the Kings shows events happening after death. In the left section the king embraces and is embraced by Osiris, the god of death. Behind him stand his ka, or duplicate self, with a protective hand on his shoulder. The center section shows the king appearing before the goddess Nut. The right section depicts King Aye performing the final after-death ceremony, the Opening of the Mouth, for Tutankhaton. The dead king wears the white of Osiris (the color of mourning) and the White Crown of Upper Egypt, and holds the ceremonial crook and flail. The newly crowned King Aye wears the white sandals, robe, leopard-skin cape of a priest of Amon, and the crown of the Two Egypts. This sacred rite was usually per-

15. This gold relief on the back of Tutankhaton's throne, found in his tomb, shows him in an affectionate pose with his young wife, Ankhesenpaaten, third daughter of Akhenaton and Nefertiti.

16. The gold mask of Tutankhaton, from his tomb. He was half brother to
Akhenaton and reared by Nefertiti as a son. The mask shows him at the time
of death.

brilliantly lighted. The temple of the king's ka would be ready to welcome his other self on this night, should it choose to enter. It was the safety of the king's body which was the concern of the mysterious pilgrims.

Those who could crowded into the palatial rooms shelled out of solid stone. Torches were set in sconces against the walls. The heavy sarcophagus was brought into the reception chamber and opened. The body of the king, stiffly wrapped in its embalming linens, was propped ceremoniously against the wall. The dead king could look about him and rejoice in the splendor of his surroundings.

Queen Tiy shared her dead husband's pleasure. She and Amenhotep had begun the building and furnishing of this underground palace when they had been a lusty young married pair. It took a lifetime to properly construct and prepare a tomb. Everything a king and queen might wish for in their future life —for Tiy would join him here when her time came to follow Amenhotep into the West—was to be found in these glittering rooms.

The ancient religion of Egypt, before Akhenaton, had its delightful as well as its terrifying side. One who respected all the gods and their animals, paid them tribute, and prayed to them was assured of a life of divine happiness in the hereafter, which was a continuation of life on earth, only better, happier, and permanent. Death itself was merely a brief interruption.

So every Egyptian, rich or poor, took with him in his tomb everything he had used in life and might need in the pleasant aftermath that was to last forever.

He took his furniture, household goods of every kind, clothing, and any jewelry he might possess. The musician took his musical instruments, the workman his tools, the wife her cooking pots and spindle, the beauty her mirror and cosmetics. Children were buried with their toys.

And all were permitted to attest on coffins or walls to their good deeds and virtues while living, and took with them into the grave copies of the Book of the Dead attesting to these things, that the gods who sat in judgment might read, and understand their worth.

The walls of the tombs were decorated with illustrated accounts of the greatness and the lineage of the dead, and the furnishings buried with them were beyond anything the modern mind can image.

The discovery in this century of Tutankhaton's tomb, the only unrobbed tomb in the Valley of the Kings, was the first revelation of the incredible riches placed in the royal crypts. It has often been pointed out that he was the least important of the Eighteenth Dynasty kings. By the splendor of his tomb we can guess at the wealth that must have been revealed in the light of the torches in King Amenhotep's.

Rich and beautiful treasures gathered during the lifetime of this beauty-loving king were stored in his underground palace. The rooms were packed ceiling-high with palatial furniture, beds, chairs, tables, gold chariots, chests of clothing and linens, images of many gods (including the emblem of the Aton), jewelry, vases, dishes, and pieces of art and bibelots that served no purpose beyond that of beauty. Vast quantities of gold was stored there, as is known by other tombs where treasure was overlooked. Amenhotep III was one of the richest and greatest kings of his dynasty. A king's ransom would have gone with him into his tomb.

(The Tutankhaton tomb would be found not far from Amenhotep's. It was prepared and furnished for the boy by Aye, who had built for Amenhotep and Tiy their great funerary temple on the Nile. Beyond doubt Aye assisted Akhenaton's father and mother in the preparation of their treasure-filled grave.)

Articles to insure comfortable everyday living crowded the tomb. Table and kitchen equipment and toilet articles were not forgotten. Food and drink of the finest was provided, for perpetual feasting with no ill effects was one of the advantages of the afterlife. Great jars of Egypt's choicest wines were sealed and stamped with the vintage and the king's name, and there were jars of olive oil, unguents, fats for cooking, honey, wild fowl salted and packed in jars, and other jars of meats, "pounded" and preserved. Perfumes, spices, incense, and live flowers sweetened the close air.

Laid tenderly close to the sarcophagus of the king were all the pets he had loved that had died during his lifetime, preserved for his eternal companionship by the same skilled embalmers who attended to the human mummifications and who used for them the same fine linen wrappings and preservatives. Dogs, cats, birds, even mice and bugs were mummified, for such creatures are required to make even a palace complete.

It is suspected that long before this time, in a more ancient Egypt, certain powerful Pharaohs went to their graves accompanied by complete retinues of palace servants. At least one king solved any future domestic problems by having his entire palace staff murdered and laid out neatly in his tomb. The sacrifice may not have been voluntary. Since then, wise priests had decreed it was not necessary to kill servants to insure service in the hereafter. Small images of carved wood did as well, for by the magic of the gods they were transformed in the other world into active full-sized workers. Therefore all the kingly graves were staffed by doll-sized figurines shown at their hereditary tasks in house and fields, and these charming puppets have contributed greatly to our knowledge of daily life in ancient Egypt.

It comforted the mourners in King Amenhotep's tomb that the good Pharaoh was surrounded by every luxury, as he had lived.

For the last time the son confronted the great father who, while living, had entrusted him with the foremost kingdom in the world. One final act remained to the somber-eyed stripling king. It was a son's sacred duty to perform the magic ritual which was the last kindness that could be given the dead—the Opening of the Mouth.

The mummy of the dead king leaned in dignity against the painted stone wall. The widow knelt weeping before the bandaged feet, pouring dust on her bowed head. A priest read prayers from the Book of the Dead. We do not know what incantations were spoken by King Akhenaton as he held the forked flint instrument to the dead lips. But when the mystic rite was over the mummified mouth of the dead king was considered restored to its former usefulness and Amenhotep III would be permitted to eat and enjoy food and drink as he had when young. For that was the beauty of life after death to the pious Egyptian—he woke restored to youth. Now King Amenhotep could live in the underworld as happily as he had in Thebes, and he had been a king who enjoyed the rich good things of life. Queen Tiy could take pleasure in the thought of his new happiness and in knowing that she was to join him in that joyful existence. Still she wept; the years of waiting would be long.

As for Akhenaton, no one knew what he was thinking. He had committed his father to Amon. But in his simple new faith he knew—his father had gone back to join the one—the all—the sun.

The last service ended. The body was placed in the heavy sarcophagus and carried to the uttermost chamber deep in the rock. That door was sealed with muttered incantations; the doors to the other rooms were sealed.

For a long time the light of the torches played over the glittering treasure in the deserted tomb, then the flames flickered and died against the wall.

Outside, working with furious haste in the light of other torches, the professional gravediggers sealed the outer entrance. The priests spoke final incantations. The protective emblems were hung on the thick door which was then covered over craftily with stones and sand and all footprints swept away so that no man who did not know could say, A door is hidden there!

Still, it was known. The grave when discovered had been robbed of every article of value except the sarcophagus. That only was found, in a different place, and in it lay the body of Amenhotep III, a great and good king, and as impressive in its dignity as when mother and son had looked on it last before the coffin lid had closed over it, thirty centuries before.

The sealing of the tomb set Akhenaton free. Now he could leave Thebes with its resentful Amon priests and sullen subjects and its many gods in which he no longer believed. He returned to Amarna, his city of love, and to Nefertiti, his "lady of happiness."

Queen Tiy was left with one solace which Nefertiti, when her time of bereavement came, could not know. Nefertiti had wholeheartedly accepted the faith of Aton. Akhenaton's mother evidently worshiped Aton in company with several thousand other gods. Queen Tiy had not turned with her son against the ancient religion.

She kept her trust in the deities who, she knew, were guarding her newly dead husband through his first lost wanderings in the underworld.

It was one of the comforts supplied by Egypt's old religion
that the bereaved could follow in their thoughts the progress of
the dead person in that shadowy eternity where Osiris, the resur-
rected, presided as king of the dead. Queen Tiy knew exactly
which stage her dead husband was passing through, every hour
of the day or night.

Still in his natural body, for by some mystic power a man took
his body with him into death, King Amenhotep III had stepped
into the sun boat which Aye has said he prepared for his king
and sailed away from Thebes on the dark waters of the underworld.

The underworld, as all religious Egyptians knew, was that dark
passageway under the Nile through which the sun passed each
night, moving from the West back to the East that it might rise
again. (This was according to the religion of the sun god Ra at
Heliopolis, the faith which Akhenaton had incorporated into his
own worship of the sun.)

The sun god had two ships. One waited for him in the West,
and he entered it while setting and in it made his night's journey
back to the East through the twelve caverns of the underworld.
The Egyptians had been the first to divide the night into twelve
hours, one for each cavern. Arriving in the East, the sun entered
his second ship, rose in splendor over Egypt and sailed westward
again through the twelve hours of day.

For this reason the Pharaohs had built the funeral ships of
wood or stone in which after death they would make the underworld journey as representative on earth of the sun. And in his
ship, on this first night of his journey, Queen Tiy's dead husband
was making his way through the twelve underground caverns of
death.

Tiy could remark at a given moment, "My love is now passing
under Memphis," as a modern wife might speak of a husband
making a trip by subway.

Rites, prayers, incantations, and the burning of incense in the
temple followed the king on this perilous journey. Queen Tiy
encouraged her husband with her prayers, as following rituals
centuries old, the meanings of which have been forgotten, the
dead king made his way through one dark cavern after the other

until he met at last with that dread mysterious figure known as the Questioner.

Fixing the applicant with his awful stare, the Questioner demanded: "What is your name?"

And as meekly as any of his dead subjects, the dead Amenhotep III would pronounce his name.

The king passed on through the gates of the underworld and faced the dread jury of immortal gods who would decide whether he was worthy of eternal life, or must suffer eternal death.

There he stood in his body, exactly as he had on earth, in the terrible hall as large as space, where were waiting the most powerful and terrifying gods. Queen Tiy, safe in her painted palace on the Nile, asked for stronger prayers at this point, for she knew her husband's claim to immortality was being decided.

Facing the king was Osiris, who stood under the canopy that showed he was chief god of the underworld, and beside him was Anubis, the jackal-headed god who had presided over the king's embalming and burial. There was Thoth, Aye's patron god, scribe of all the deities, with his palette and pen on which he would tally all the good that could be told about this applicant for eternal life. The king's good deeds had been registered in his tomb and on many monuments, they were listed in the Book of the Dead, but there was no escape for him and he must plead his own case like any common man.

The king approached the scales, which were guarded by the sun god Horus, and beside them stood Maat, the revered goddess of truth, the tiny, prettily dressed but faceless woman-goddess who wore the ostrich plume of justice in her hair.

Set, the lean and fiendish god of evil, was waiting with slavering jaws to devour any applicant weighed and found wanting. Such an applicant could never live again, or enjoy the bounty in his beautiful tomb, or visit his funerary palace. Above all, he could never again look on the face of the sun.

Even as great and good a king as Amenhotep III would tremble as he advanced before the august jury and taking his heart from his breast laid it on the scales.

The goddess without a face moved. She took the long plume

from her hair and laid it on the scales, opposite the king's heart which was to be weighed.

The "heart amulet" his son had laid over the dead king's breast spoke: "Oh, my heart, rise not up against me." Then the king began his plea, with his breast empty, and behind him his "ka," his other self exact in every detail, imitated his movements, for it too would attain immortality with him or be damned forever.

The early Egyptians were the first to make a good character and righteousness the requirements of happiness in the next world. Breasted has called their period in history "the dawn of conscience." Parallels have been drawn between its ethics and those of Judaism. Now, facing the awful tribunal of the gods, King Amenhotep was forced in his own defense to relate the secrets of evil every human heart must know.

As humbly as the most common born, he made his confession, answering to the solemn questioning that required forty-two answers, for there were forty-two sins in the Egyptian ethical (hence legal) code.

His confession was made in the form of denials:

"I have not blasphemed. I have not murdered. I have not committed thievery. I have not slandered. I have not eavesdropped. I have not borne false witness. I have not committed adultery. I have not robbed the dead."

Sex relations in holy places, or entering such a place directly afterward, was listed among the sins. So, in certain districts, was homosexuality.

After answering the forty-two questions, the dead man was free to cite his good deeds:

"I clothed those who were naked. I protected widows and orphans. I gave bread to the hungry. I fed and sheltered animals. I gave to the temples of the gods . . ."

Queen Tiy in her palace had no doubts as to the final verdict in the underworld court. Clear in her vision she saw the rising of the heart on the scale and the trembling balance of the feather on the other side. All knew Amenhotep III had been one of the best of kings. And now came the final mystic transfiguration, for the dead king, having passed every test given by the gods, became Osiris! In that shadowy underworld, unreal as a dream and still part of life forever, the all-powerful personality of Amenhotep III, dead these seventy days, was now king of the underworld and ruler of all the dead.

This his rejoicing widow knew, and all Egypt.

In the magical old religion, this transfiguration was not only awarded to kings. The mysterious alchemy of death transformed every Egyptian into Osiris!

This was the divine privilege Akhenaton was trying to take from his people when he said, There is no god but Aton! In his new religion, all who died returned to the sun. What Egyptian wanted to merge with the sun, when by continuing his allegiance to the old gods he could become the supreme god after death?

There were other comforting attributes possessed by the old religion. For example, one was never actually separated from the dead. Queen Tiy resumed contact with her dead husband as soon as the priests gave her the joyful report that he had been accepted as king of the shades. Now she could give memorial banquets in his splendid funerary temple where his ka might feast surrounded by all their friends, dead and living, every anniversary of his death, and on the Day of the Dead.

Egyptians paid frequent ceremonial calls at the tombs. The necropolis, where those less than royal were buried, was as gala as a fair, with its funerary booths and graves trimmed with hanging baskets of flowers and palm branches, and filled with gifts for the departed—food and drink and ointments. Songs and prayer helped give joy to the scene, and relatives, standing before the doors of the tombs, bandied family gossip and asked advice of those sealed within. All family problems were discussed with the dead. Serious matters and affectionate messages could be printed in cuneiform on bowls which, baked and filled with food and left at the entrances of tombs, were certain to attract the attention of the dead.

Queen Tiy must have written many a letter to her powerful husband in the underworld in the troubled months that followed.

She stayed on in the Theban palace. There is some evidence that after her husband's death she acted as a subsidiary regent with Akhenaton. Certainly she did her best to serve his interests in Thebes. Her hold over him remained strong, and she was often pictured with Nefertiti and her son. In the background might be Aye, with his wife, the nurse.

These were the members of the royal circle now Amenhotep was dead. They were Akhenaton's devotees, his disciples and his only confidantes—his mother, his wife, and his wife's lowly born parents.

The little group faced an Egypt that was growing strangely threatening, and the threat emanated from the great Temple of Amon at Thebes.

Akhenaton, a sensitive man, observed the rising enmity. He must have returned to Amarna with a sense of escaping. He realized the Amon priests had not relinquished their hold on Egypt. They were as rich and strong as ever, taking more tribute than before from the people and artfully stirring up resentment against the young king and his new city of the sun.

Akhenaton must have realized that the average Egyptian saw no merit in his simplified faith. It offered only intangibles—goodness, kindness, love. The sun gave all and demanded nothing. Akhenaton found it worthy of adoration and wanted all beings blessed by the sun god to be grateful and good in return.

But this simplified faith left the god-ridden Egyptians uneasy. It offered none of the colorful pageantry, endless holidays, and public spectacles that had made the worship of Amon a perpetual festival. It showed no golden idols, performed no magical rites and miracles. It held no threats, no terrors.

The Egyptians found this religion hard to accept.

It had not been accepted in Thebes. The Amon priests had seen to that. They may have tried influencing Akhenaton during his visit to Thebes.

Akhenaton, back in Amarna, was thoroughly angry.

The pristine happiness of the seven past years had been cruelly interrupted. He had been forced to realize that he was unloved and plotted against in Thebes, and the experience had embittered him.

There was another reason for the lessening of joyousness. Nefertiti was no longer his "lady of happiness." Grief lay on her face like a delicate veil, for Akhenaton's prayers to Aton asking long life for his two first-born daughters had failed. Meketaton, their second daughter, died close to the time of the old king's death. She was probably six or seven years old. Her tiny mummified body was the first placed in the royal tomb in the new Valley of the Kings at Amarna.

A palette with Meketaton's name on it has been found, so that we presume the little princesses of Amarna were given a certain amount of education in preparation for the high places they were expected to occupy.

Now it was Nefertiti who carried the garlands of funerary poppies to the tomb, wore leis of cornflowers and nightshade and olive leaves, and cast dust on her lovely head; and the world's greatest king saw a queen's tears and could not stop their falling.

The birth of two more little daughters to Nefertiti completed what is known as Amarna's "garland of princesses." Setepenaton and Baqtaton were born in 1359 and 1357 B.C. All the children were named for the sun. But the shadow of grief would never again leave Nefertiti's sensitive, expressive features. It shows in the famous bust found at Amarna for which she sat for Thutmes the master sculptor at about this time of her father-in-law's and daughter's deaths. She was twenty-five or -six years old, it is believed, and she had lived through more than most women do in their entire lifetimes.

She was still Nefertiti, the all-beautiful, the sweet of love, but the childlike look was gone. The large clear eyes may have foreseen the future, with its hatred and enmity that were to pursue the Amarna dreamers from this time on. For it was shortly after, some say before, the death of the old king, that Akhenaton launched the crusade that made havoc of their perfect world.

Akhenaton issued his ultimatum. All the old false gods must go! Above all, an end to Amon! The chief god's temples must be emptied or destroyed, its priesthoods disbanded, their wealth confiscated and given to Aton. All worship must end in Egypt save that of Aton.

The shocking edict was followed by even more shocking action. His soldiers were sent into all the Amon temples. The priests were driven out into the streets and the wealth of hundreds of Amon temples was confiscated and carried to Amarna. The gold statues of Amon were melted down. Then in one final act of devastation, the king ordered hundreds of masons to smash all Amon statues and chisel away the name of Amon wherever it appeared in Egypt—even in the tombs.

To obliterate a name was a way of decreeing the owner's death. Akhenaton was ordering the murder of the chief god of Egypt.

The translation of hieroglyphic records is always open to controversy and the reports of this act of Akhenaton's definitely do not agree. Certain respected authorities believe he committed an unforgivable sin (as it would have been regarded in his time) by ordering the removal of Amon's name everywhere, even where it was part of his father's name (Amenhotep, for Amon). Other authorities, equally respected, deny this act of vandalism, or sacrilege and insist he limited the destruction to the name of the banned god.

Suddenly Akhenaton, the prince of peace, the teacher of love, had turned warrior. His crusade would never have been waged for worldly reasons. He had launched a religious war. Defiant of all the old gods, their priesthoods, and their power, he pitted his tremendous authority against theirs; his faith against Amon. He would never capitulate until he had driven every god out of Egypt except Aton, his single deity, source of all light and all life.

Egypt plunged into turmoil. Amarna alone remained unaffected by the resentment boiling in the other cities. Singly and in small bands, angry unfrocked Amon priests met in secret places in Thebes to plot retribution. Open war broke out between them and the triumphant Aton priests. According to their preachments, Akhenaton's move went beyond all human crimes. The Amarna Revolution was an attack on all the ancient gods, but all knew the king's motivation had been his hatred of Amon.

By this single decree Nefertiti's love, the dreaming poet, king, and mystic, had made himself the most hated person in Egypt.

In view of the curses heaped on Akhenaton and Nefertiti and the evil done them, it may be well to consider the opinions of more recent authorities.

Breasted, who paid special attention to the Amarna period and "the unparalleled religious revolution" of Akhenaton, considered him: "The first individual in human history . . . far in advance of his age . . . he gradually developed ideals and purposes which make him the most remarkable of all the Pharaohs." Pendlebury: "The first rebel against the established order . . . the first man with ideas of his own which ran counter to all tradition . . ." Woolley: ". . . who in the fourteenth century before Christ tried to impose a monotheistic religion on a people whose gods were legion." Petrie: "A great leader and thinker." Steindorff and Seele: ". . . the most fascinating personality who ever sat on the throne of the pharaohs."

And other masters of Egyptology: ". . . the world's first idealist" ". . . a superman born before his time . . ." ". . . the most remarkable figure in earlier Oriental history . . ." "The world's first pacifist" "The first to give the principle of monotheism to the world . . ." "Only a Pharaoh and a god sort of man could have effected such a revolution . . ." ". . . the Eighteenth Dynasty reached its apex under the supremely intelligent but unhappily reckless reform of Akhenaton. . . . to be intelligent then was to court disaster, even if one was an almighty king."

This sums up modern opinion of Akhenaton. While he lived, and for centuries after, his enemies used but two words of anathema to describe him. Rebel! Heretic!

These were the most terrible words the Amon priests could hurl against their ruler at Amarna.

CHAPTER TWELVE

Shadow on the Sun

Tell el-Amarna, 1361–1356 B.C.

On that night in the year 1361 B.C. in Thebes, when the funeral procession of Amenhotep III carried his body to the Valley of the Kings, one, and possibly two, little princes lay sleeping in the harem of the queens in the painted palace on the Nile. They were probably the last children sired by Amenhotep by one or more of his "extra" royal wives. They were half brothers of Akhenaton.

The two children were to play important roles in a nearing drama.

Both bore sun names, as Akhenaton had requested when he changed his own name to honor the sun. The oldest, Sakere (Smenkhkare), had been named for the sun god Ra. The other, either newly born or perhaps a posthumous child of the dead king, was named Tutankhaton in honor of Aton. It would be his tomb that opened to a twentieth-century world the glories of Egypt fourteen centuries before Christ. He may have been the last-born child of Amenhotep III.

These were no children of Tiy's, but they were reared in the Theban palace as her own. They played in the painted palace where Akhenaton and Nefertiti had played as children, and in time both little boys would become kings of Egypt.

Were their mothers princesses of Mitanni of which so much would be written in the Amarna Letters and who continued to arrive at Thebes until shortly before Amenhotep's death? Tiy amiably took part in these marriage arrangements, which were politically necessary and part of eastern tradition. Evidently she was kind to the new arrivals and fond of the children they produced. She could afford tolerance; her role as queen mother was secure. She had been great wife and great queen, and it was her son who now sat on the throne. And small princes, even though only half royal, could be valuable assets to Egypt as had been amply demonstrated in the past. So the two little boys were reared as befitted the sons of a great, dead king.

No sooner was the old king buried than Akhenaton's troubles began with the Mitanni in-laws. The Amarna archives filled with correspondence of a personal nature from Mesopotamia.

Up to the time of Amenhotep's death, a cordial relationship had been maintained between the kings of Mitanni and the royal family at Thebes. Akhenaton's father had married the Princess Gilukhipa, a daughter of Prince Shuttarna of Mitanni, who had sent along with the bride 317 ladies in waiting and an impressive dowry—"ten span of horses, ten chariots, thirty eunuchs"—and many other gifts, including personal presents for Queen Tiy. In fact, so extraordinary a friendship existed between Queen Tiy and the Mitannian kings—they even exchanged letters—that a family relationship has been suspected but never substantiated. Then Amenhotep married Tadukhipa, a daughter of Tushratta, King of Mitanni, and another dowry was sent to Egypt. The sacred image of the goddess of Ishtar had followed when news reached Mitanni of Amenhotep's last illness.

Now all Tushratta's gifts to Egypt, whether of brides or dowries, had always been accompanied by strenuous demands for return gifts of gold. And King Amenhotep had sent gold to his "brother," in lavish amounts. Now that Amenhotep was dead, the Mitanni king began a campaign to insure equal largess from Akhenaton, who had shown no interest in Mitannian brides nor in Tushratta. The first letter Akhenaton received after his father's death was honeyed with flattery:

"When I was informed that my brother Nimmuria (so Amenhotep was known on the Amarna tablets) had gone to his destiny, then I wept on that day. I sat here day and night; on that day I partook neither of food nor drink, for I was in sorrow. And I said, 'If only another in my land or in the land of my brother had died, and my brother whom I loved and who loved me were still alive! For our love would endure as the heaven and the earth endure.'"

Then, getting down to fundamentals, Tushratta explained that he was certain relations between Egypt and Mitanni would go on as before, because no sooner had he learned that the son of the Great Consort Tiy was king, he had exclaimed, "My friend is not dead, for his great son rules in his place. He will turn no word from its former place."

Tushratta's confidence was misplaced. Before long he was writing Akhenaton concerning two statues promised him by Amenhotep before his death. Tushratta's own envoys in Thebes had seen these statues and reported them to be of pure gold. But now, alchemy had wrought evil, for the statues had arrived in Mitanni and they were not gold at all, but of gilded wood!

To this complaint Akhenaton made no known answer.

Tushratta complained to Queen Tiy. Although she was a widow and an ex-regent he addressed her as queen of Egypt, and sent fulsome greetings from himself and his wife Iuni. He begged her to intercede with her son and insure the continuation of their friendship. (Meaning, may the flow of gold continue!) He recalled to her mind the matter of the gold statuettes promised by her late husband, and begged her to bear witness to Akhenaton that the statues might be sent.

To Akhenaton he wrote calling on Tiy as witness: ". . . in all matters negotiated with thy father, Teye (Tiy) thy mother knoweth them. None other besides knoweth of them."

While there is no evidence that Tiy interfered, the exchange serves to show the extraordinary confidence their royal consorts placed in Nefertiti and Tiy.

Akhenaton's reply to Tushratta reproved the King of Mitanni for his greed.

The Egyptian king may have decided it was time to put a stop to the Mitannian in-law's shameless demands for "gold and more gold . . . for gold is as dust in thy land." He may have decided the endless gifts of Egypt to Mitanni, a subject land, were a form of bribery to insure the peace, and what need had the world's leading power to pay tribute to a subject nation? Still, no one knows what Akhenaton was thinking when he permitted a friendship to dwindle that had lasted through three royal generations.

The rift over the two statuettes cast the first shadow on the Amarna sun. This was the first of the recognizable errors in diplomacy on Akhenaton's part that were soon to increase in a bewildering way. Tushratta was a minor king, but Akhenaton needed his friendship, for serious news was rushed down from Asia Minor: the Hittites were on the march again!

The Hittites were the most powerful people in Asia and the only ones feared by the Egyptians. Their kingdom, Great Kheta, in eastern Asia Minor was second in power to Egypt. The two nations had hated each other since the time of Thutmose III.

Until the Hyksos took over, all-powerful Egypt had never suffered an invasion. Thutmose had driven out the Hyksos and to emphasize the victory had soundly punished the Hittites, who had allied with the Hyksos. Egypt had been an impenetrable fortress since then. There had been a minor flurry during the reign of Akhenaton's father, when Prince Aziru, an Egyptian vassal but a Hittite ally, had attempted to stir up rebellion in Syria, probably encouraged by reports of the sybaritic nature of Amenhotep the Magnificent. Amenhotep had not even troubled to lead his armies against Aziru in person, but had sent troops into Syria who had subdued the "upstart dog," at least for the time being.

It would soon be revealed that Aziru was playing an important secret role in the new trouble starting in the north.

Any news traveled with amazing speed. The efficient courier service of Egypt had carried letters to every hamlet in the nation, revealing the rivalry between Thebes and Amarna and the growing resentment against Akhenaton and his one god. The priests of Amon had their own effective network of communication. They kept their fellow priests everywhere informed of the progress of their plottings against the king who had tried to destroy the gods.

The rumors ran like wildfire, south to Aswan, down the shores of the Red Sea, across the Mediterranean, through Canaan, over the Euphrates River. It reached the remote northern kingdom of the Hittites, Kheta, in the mountains of Anatolia. The Hittites were Indo-Germanic. They were great horsemen and mighty warriors; they loved war. They had nursed their hatred through an enforced and sulky peace of 150 years. They were enflamed with the new wild hope of revenge, for if there was a rift in Egypt's eternal power, now was their time to press in.

So they came swarming down out of the North, out of their

mountain fastnesses, by the hundreds, the thousands. Their appearance was as fierce as their ways of fighting. The foot soldiers bore formidable weapons—heavy battle-axes, spears, swords, and larger bows and arrows than the smaller-sized Egyptian archers could carry. Their armored warfare was irresistible, for great clumsy chariots, each carrying three warriors, rolled like modern tanks over the exquisitely fashioned gold and silver chariots of the Egyptians.

But it was their appearance that seemed to paralyze all who attempted to oppose them. The slender, smooth-faced, light-boned Egyptians regarded these apparitions from the North as monsters from another world. The "parrot-faced" Hittites wore tall, pointed, sinister-looking felt hats under which their large noses jutted like scythes. Their hair fell in long locks over their hairy cheeks and they strode the land in thigh-high felt boots that turned up at the toes. They wore long, tight-fitting tubular dresses of thick dark wool. The thinly clad, elegant Egyptians thought the Hittites the most hideous, uncouth, and frightening people alive.

And suddenly, there they were in Egyptian territory, pressing south, ever south, fired with new hopes of conquest, determined this time to be the subduers of the peace-loving Egyptians. They pushed into the lands of Asia Minor conquered by Akhenaton's ancestors. They pressed southward into Syria. There was no end to them.

Letters were rushed from northern Egypt to Amarna. The wooden filing cases in the archives began to fill with stacks of the cuneiform-covered tablets known to us as the Amarna Letters. Each was a cry of terror and despair, a prayer for protection, and a pledge of undying fealty on the part of the threatened vassal kings.

The first came out of western Asia. The Hittites were not only invading but they were being urged on by armies of Assyrians! This was war on a scale Egypt had never experienced. Help must be sent by King Akhenaton to enable the faithful to hold lands belonging to him! Beseeching messages were rushed to him from the kings of Syria, Palestine, Mitanni, and Babylon.

One of the first of the subject countries invaded was Mitanni. King Tushratta wrote in panic—no time now to recall the long history of friendship and intermarrying and exchanging of gifts. "I have routed the Hittite invaders," Tushratta reported fiercely. "There was none of them that returned to this land."

But the Hittites would return in greater numbers to Mitanni and King Tushratta's resistance against them was to weaken in ratio to his faith in the friendship of Akhenaton.

Akhenaton may not have believed at first in the Hittite threat. During the century and a half of peace, Egypt and Kheta had maintained a profitable trade relationship that at times almost approached amiability. At the time King Akhenaton took the throne he had many congratulatory messages from the heads of various nations, and among them one of the warmest came from King Seplel who at that time ruled over the Hittite kingdom. When Akhenaton had staged the Amarna Revolution and moved his court from Thebes into the great new beautiful palace at Amarna, among the first of the foreign ambassadors waiting there to pay him homage was the Hittite, bearing magnificent gifts and affectionate messages from King Seplel.

The Amarna Letters show the effort made by King Seplel to continue their correspondence and their friendship "as it was in the time of thy father." Akhenaton's reaction to this offer was curious, for a later letter from the Hittite king, contained a shocking charge—Akhenaton, in a letter to King Seplel, had the effrontery to put his own name first!

This was against all the rules of protocol. In diplomatic correspondence, and every other kind, the name of the addressed was always put first as a matter of courtesy, and this was followed by flattering protests of esteem. Akhenaton had received many such messages from the Hittite king.

Letters to Akhenaton began in such terms as these: "To the King, my Lord, my Sun, my God, say: Thus Suwardata, thy servant, the servant of the King and the dust under his feet, the ground on which he dost trod. . . ." (This was from the Indo-Aryan Prince of Hebron Suwardata to inform Akhenaton of his fear of the Hittites.)

And another to Akhenaton: "To the King, my Lord, my God, Sun of Heaven: I am thy servant, the dust of thy feet. . . . At the feet of the King my Lord seven times and again seven times I prostrate myself upon my back and upon my breast."

Another: "To the King, my lord, my god my sun: Yabitiri is
thy servant, the dust of thy feet. . . . a faithful servant of the
King am I. . . . I look to the King my lord, and there is light.
. . . I move not away from the king's feet . . . on my neck
rests the yoke of my lord the King. . . ."

And this from a prince of Hebron to Akhenaton: "At the feet
of the King, my Lord, the Sun of Heaven, seven times seven I
prostrated myself on my belly and on my back. . . ."

Akhenaton's breach of etiquette may indicate that he had
begun to refuse advice in the simplest matters of diplomacy.
Certainly he contributed nothing to the friendship sued for by
the Hittite king. Akhenaton had chosen for his subtitle "living
in truth." He may have thought lack of respect for a powerful
fellow king was a way of expressing truth. He may have dis-
trusted all Hittites; he had his reasons. Or he may have revealed
his growing lack of interest in anything going on in the world
outside of Amarna.

Why should he have been troubled?

His forefathers had conquered countries, cities, tribes of men,
hordes of wild beasts. He—Akhenaton—had conquered the gods.

He had taken the throne under the most beneficent of circumstances, when the Hittites had been safely pushed back in
Asia, and all Egypt and its vassal states had declared their
allegiance. Fortunes in treasure had been sent to him, and
tribute paid.

Mitanni—what threat could lie there? Had not King Tushratta
assured him of his devotion, and had not Akhenaton's own father
married princesses of Mitanni? As for the threatening Assyrians,
a former king of Assyria had permitted the sacred image of the
Euphrates' greatest goddess to be sent to Akhenaton's father when
he was dying.

Treasure continued to pour into Amarna. Tribute was still being paid, even by those Akhenaton was told were plotting against
him. He would not be troubled by letters from petty kings. He
was not interested in rumors or the making of wars.

All his interests now were in the city of the sun.

An astute observer of the political scene in Thebes, such as
Aye, might have paused before the tremendous door of the

deserted Temple of Amon. There, facing the two Colossi of
Amenhotep III, was the stele of Amon. The tabernacle was one
of the eight temples of Amon in Thebes emptied by Akhenaton.
He had sent armies of masons into the temples and sanctuaries
with orders to chisel away the name of the old god wherever
found. On this door in the very heart of Thebes was the most
conspicuous Amon image in Egypt.

The hand of the mason ordered to eradicate it may have
trembled at the desecration it was to commit, for the name of
Amon was only partially destroyed.

The half-erased carving still exists—a symbol of warning to
Akhenaton, if he had been willing to accept warnings. But he
ignored them all, including the rapidly developing Hittite threat.

Aye may have tried to let the headstrong king know of the
resentment growing in Thebes, through the queen mother. It
was doubtless Aye who urged Tiy to make her first and only
visit to Amarna and see for herself what was going on in the city
of the sun.

This was after the death of Amenhotep III. The rapid chariot
service must have carried excited correspondence between
Thebes and Amarna pending the queen mother's arrival! Thanks
to the Amarna artists and writers, we can picture the crowds
gathered on the pillared stone wharf crossed by picturesque
gangways and hear the shouts of welcome as the bannered Theban barge rode majestically up out of the south on the Nile's
tide. The widowed queen stepped onto the wharf where her son
and his beautiful Nefertiti awaited her, surrounded by their
"garland of princesses," her granddaughters—with tribute of flowers and song.

What pride Akhenaton and Nefertiti must have taken in showing the queen mother their city of the sun! All Tiy saw on that
day must have raised her respect for the regents—and perhaps
her fears. Queen Tiy had spent most of her years surrounded
by oriental magnificence but Amarna must have been over-
whelming even to the queen who had ruled over imperial
Thebes. Amarna's singers sang to her, Amarna's poets wrote of
her, Amarna sculptors modeled her, Amarna's musicians played,
while the queen mother's adored son, his family, and his court
showed her the great temple, the palaces, and her own palace

with its granary and treasury. There is one portrayal by an
Amarna artist entitled "Introduction of the Queen Mother to
her Sunshade," Tiy's own Aton chapel in her own garden.

The queen mother was shrewd and well informed. She must
have spoken frankly to Akhenaton and had many a talk with
Nefertiti as queen to queen. She knew that the subversive campaign launched by the Theban priesthood against Akhenaton
and his new city was well on its way.

Akhenaton's decree to make Atonism the state religion was not
being carried out in Egypt.

A faith that had made Egypt all-powerful could not be anni-
hilated by royal decree.

The people of Thebes had heard in a terrified silence the reading of the king's ban against Amon declaring the name of the
chief god should not again be spoken, or written or carved, or
worshiped in any form. They had seen the eight temples of Amon
in the city, (and heard of many others elsewhere) entered and
the well-fed Amonite priests driven out by thousands and
scattered like beggars in the city. The homeless priests could
only pronounce curses as their temples were looted, the images
of Amon broken and tossed through the doors, and the doors
sealed. The people saw the name of Amon chiseled even from
the royal tombs, and the fields and herds and all the treasures
of Amon confiscated and turned over to Aton. The king had
robbed the richest god in Egypt of all his worldly possessions;
he could not rob the god of the people's faith in its supernatural power.

The Amon priests remained in hiding, forbidden to appear in
public in their white robes and sandals and leopard-skin capes.
They were fighting in secret to regain their interrupted authority. Before contrived altars and hastily fashioned images of Amon
and the other gods, they prayed for the destruction of Amarna
and its king.

The priests of Amon were famed for the efficacy of their
curses.

Egypt was a country of magic. The Amon priests used magic
to cure or to curse. They could make a wax figure of one to be
cursed and do with it what they willed. It was particularly
effective if nail parings or clipped locks of hair from the doomed

one could be pressed into the wax. Then curses were poured upon it, it could be stabbed, maimed, or melted over a slow sacred altar fire, resulting in pestilential fevers to the subject and eventual death.

Spells and curses could be written on a wax shape of the serpent god Apepi (the archfiend whose coils were wrapped around the sun each morning to prevent its rising) and melted over the sacred fires. Or they were written on papyrus scrolls, to be burned. Many a curse carrying the name of Akhenaton was burned in Theban fires.

Such curses were accompanied with the incantations of the priests who stamped their white-sandaled feet as they chanted to give the rite greater strength.

Even the laity could curse. One magic way of outwitting an enemy was to inscribe a bowl with the hated one's name; smashing it, one did lasting damage to the hated. There were special curses and charms against snakes, and the sting of scorpions, and curses to protect one against curses!

But no curse equaled that of a Pharaoh. A royal curse was awful and comprehensive. It took in not only the principal subject but everyone connected with him in any way, including his women and his eunuchs. It soured the milk of his cattle and put a blight on his wheat. It was a terrible fate to incur the curse of a Pharaoh of Egypt.

Akhenaton did not trouble to curse his critics. He no longer believed in the power of the old gods to harm, and he considered his own god incapable of evil. He contented himself with forbidding the lighting of Amon fires in Thebes. It was apparent to all who knew the Amon priesthood that this order was not obeyed.

The Thebans had not been roused by the urgings of the priests to the actual point of rebellion against Aton. They merely continued the worship of all the old gods, but in their homes, or in small gatherings attended by one or more priests, who carried out for them on a reduced scale the prayers and rites and sacrifices once sacred to the temples. Still, this was the start of counterrebellion against the Amarna Revolution.

To the Thebans, whose youthful king and queen had deserted

them, Akhenaton and Nefertiti were the rebels, not they. And Amarna was far away.

So the Amon priests increased their pressure, and the worship of the old gods, begun in secret, grew, and with it hatred of Akhenaton and Nefertiti.

The priests conjured up for their support ancient deities the Egyptians had never ceased to fear. Akhenaton held against their dark terrors only the shining emblem of the sun. To him, it was all that existed. To his subjects, it was not enough. Amonism was rising with renewed power in Thebes, and threatening an authority that should be used to quell the Hittite threat in the north.

It was this Tiy told her son in Amarna.

Where was his failure? Why did monotheism fail to seize and hold the Egyptian mind as it did that of Akhenaton?

The average Egyptian simply could not grasp the concept of one god. In his world every existing object throbbed with divine life. There was a loneliness in the new religion that created a sense of fear. What protection could one deity offer against that given by thousands?

Osiris, Hathor, Bastet, and the beloved hippopotamus goddess, Opet, could not be forgotten.

Akhenaton's teachings, so often compared to those of Jesus, actually differed in important ways. The one god of Christianity laid down certain definite laws, and left orders that they should be obeyed.

Akhenaton's god had but one rule—universal love born of the goodness of man. Aton did not enchain or threaten or demand obedience. His religion did not demand that wars be fought in its name. It was simply life—the sun.

A king lost in the sun could not consider worldly laws a necessary part of religion.

But the religion he was trying to supplant was woven into Egypt's legal and social and moral code. The Egyptian pattern of human responsibility was based on the forty-two laws of ethics by which an Egyptian must live if he hoped to survive in the next world.

The only law made by Akhenaton was his adamant: Beyond all else, the truth!

With that he hoped to release Egypt from fear. But the Egyptians were not prepared to be good without being afraid. Had they been, a new civilization might have sprung forward, based on the Amarna concept, many thousands of years ahead of our own.

The world was not ready for Akhenaton and his single god. He had converted Nefertiti and their charmed circle at Amarna. Outside the city of the sun Egypt continued in its worship of the old gods. A thousand years after Christ was born Egypt was still worshiping its ancient gods.

Queen Tiy, certain of these facts, must have seen little in Amarna to insure the future of imperial Egypt. It was a capital ruled by a king and queen lost in a dream.

The queen mother was a practical woman. She was the last of the Eighteenth Dynasty feminine despots. As the wife of Amenhotep III she had known the advantage of an authority that inspired obedience born of fear. She and her dead husband had contributed much to the architectural grandeur of Thebes, but their love of beauty had never been allowed to weaken their grasp on reality. When rebellion threatened, they had been ready to strike, and swiftly.

Now she saw her son reluctant to defend his country. Or rather, to refuse to acknowledge that such a need could exist.

The queen mother was aware that Egypt was being threatened from without and within. She must have been fascinated and horrified by life in Amarna. She saw Akhenaton and his beautiful Nefertiti in their palace, the largest on earth, playing with their children as if they too were still possessed of the hearts of children. She watched their high spirits as the leaders of their youthful, lighthearted court.

In the North the scribes of the vassal kings toiled through the nights taking down the words of their terrified lords; messengers came and went between Amarna and many cities, bringing the clay pellets of threat and despair; royal envoys lay "on their bellies and their backs" at Akhenaton and Nefertiti's feet, praying that protection be sent to protect the invaded countries from the Hittites. All the messages were the same: Save us, for we belong to Egypt! Queen Tiy saw the envoys sent off and their protests filed away unanswered.

The old queen watched the royal pair at worship in their great temple of the Aton. Faces lifted to the emblem of the sun, upon them an almost holy innocence, they heard the deep voices of the Aton priests chanting the sonorous measures of the hymn written by the poet-king:

"The ships sail up and down the Nile
And the highways open because you have risen.
The fish in the river leap before you
And your rays drive to the depths of the great sea."

The family reunion at Amarna did nothing to help the cause of Egypt. Akhenaton and Nefertiti walked high and glittering over the earth, unaware of the tremors of earthquake.

Queen Tiy could see their devotion was no longer to the throne but to the altar and she was afraid for Egypt. And Aye and many others were afraid.

It was during or after Queen Tiy's visit that the two little princes from Thebes became part of the royal household in Amarna. They were welcomed into the family circle, for only in one way had Nefertiti disappointed her lord; she had not given him a son to inherit Egypt. Akhenaton's small brothers, being half royal, hence half divine, were insurance against possible future contenders for the throne.

Aye had his plans. He assumed responsibility for the upbringing of Sakere and Tutankhaton as once he had directed the youthful destinies of Nefertiti and Akhenaton. The roles these children were to play in Egyptian history would be owed to Aye.

Nefertiti added the little boys to her "garland of princesses" and brought them up as if they were her own. King Akhenaton showed a special preference for the older boy, Sakere, while Nefertiti was apparently fonder of the smaller Tutankhaton. The Amarna artists welcomed the newcomers. Life continued joyously in Amarna.

Let the Theban priesthood mutter! Let far-off enemies threaten! Egypt's armies and navies were strong. Akhenaton's country was still supreme. He was King of Egypt—and what he willed must be obeyed!

The beautiful city continued to grow. Tribute continued to pour into it.

The dreamer who had written the great *Hymn to the Sun* cannot be blamed for refusing to believe any earthly power would dare infringe on the domain of Aton.

The serenity of life at Amarna must have been shattered when word came from Thebes that Queen Tiy, who had returned to the old capital, had died. Akhenaton would have seen to her burial in the Valley of the Kings. His mother had not long outlived Amenhotep III.

Now their strongest support in Thebes was gone. Aye devoted himself after her death wholly to Amarna and to the interests of his beautiful daughter. Nefertiti had need for Aye's resourceful political knowledge. Evidently she recognized the hatred being built up against Akhenaton and his god.

Aye is modestly described as having been at this time "one of the most honored of the courtiers of Amarna." He was still a high-ranking army officer. But he was growing old and felt the need of a younger, stronger, and trustworthy aide. He had never been one to give the outer appearance of leadership. He preferred to operate behind the throne.

He chose the soldier and political leader Harmhab (Horemhab).

Aye had a will of iron and the ability to recognize in others the same determination to win. Harmhab was a man of destiny, cut to Aye's own pattern.

When Harmhab was a child, his horoscope had been read by a seer, not by the stars, but by the calendar, as futures were in Egypt. He was told: "You will come to great power."

He never forgot the prophecy. He shaped his life by it, and when he became a man he manipulated his way to the attention of Aye, who was impressed by Harmhab's powerful personality and brought him to Amarna.

At court Harmhab attracted the admiration of Akhenaton, who appointed him to a high office as a public administrator.

No sooner was Harmhab assured of his position than a loud

voice was raised in the land. It was Harmhab's, who lost no time in censoring the king for his refusal to order out his troops against the invaders in the north.

Also, as administrator, Harmhab saw the rise of corruption in an Egypt that had been singularly free of internal problems.

Harmhab was an early Egyptian Savonarola. He dared argue with the king, perhaps encouraged by Aye. He preached of danger. He argued that the wealth being poured into Amarna should be given to subsidize armies to repel the Hittite invaders —it was not too late! His brassy voice grew more stentorian as the danger grew; and more displeasing to a peace-loving monarch.

Akhenaton was unique in his loyalty. He continued to honor Harmhab as one of his "great favorites." He showered costly gifts upon him. But to Harmhab's pleas for national defense Akhenaton sealed his jeweled ears.

Akhenaton now held daily communion with the sun. He "identified," as the modern term is used, with Aton. The soaring lines of his great hymn had become part of him. His godhood was in the hymn.

There are times when even a king must be alone. When Akhenaton stood on his aerial platform with his long, fanatical face lifted to the sun, life had two levels for him, Amarna and his benefactor, the sun. The rest did not matter.

He celebrated the twelfth anniversary of his ascension to the throne.

Between the palace and the temple, over the fifty-foot-wide King's Highway, he rode in a gold sedan chair carried by eighteen soldiers high over the heads of a cheering populace. His narrow face was set as an idol's under the towering dual crown of the Two Lands. He glittered from crown to sandals with jewels, holding in his long slender hands the gold crook and flail. Nefertiti and the children followed in other chairs. Plumes waved. Music sounded. The magnificence of the procession awed even an Amarna accustomed to lavish spectacles.

The great temple toward which the procession moved was his first Amarna tabernacle and the supreme temple. There were several other temples of Aton in Amarna, and in Thebes, Heliopolis, Memphis, Hermopolis, Hermonthis, in Nubia and the Fayum, other cathedrals had risen at his bidding in honor of the sun. But his greatest offering to the one god was Amarna. No other Egyptian Pharaoh had ever built on so tremendous and magnificent a scale.

Remember Akhenaton on this day of jubilee, for it is the last clear picture of triumph history offers of Akhenaton, king of kings.

He was twenty-nine years old, Nefertiti twenty-eight.

Never again would Nefertiti be so proudly radiant, surrounded by her "garland of daughters."

The garland would not long remain unbroken. Behind the pomp and glory was Aye, busily weaving strong nets to secure the future. He had prepared the two little princes from Thebes as best he could for future responsibilities. Time was running out; Aye was no longer the man of iron.

And Nefertiti's daughters, like the princes, could no longer be thought of as children. Akhenaton and Nefertiti had married at sixteen and fifteen—ripe ages for tropical Egypt. Nefertiti's little daughters could not be permitted so many years of childhood. At this time of the jubilee Meritaton was twelve years old, with much of her mother's beauty, and twelve was a marriageable age for an Egyptian girl.

We can be fairly certain at least three of Amarna's "garland of princesses" were married before or shortly after they reached their teens.

Aye arranged their marriages with all the forethought he had given to that of Nefertiti to Akhenaton.

In 1356 B.C., when Meritaton was thirteen, she was married to Akhenaton's half brother, her uncle Sakere, thereby making her half-royal relative fully eligible to the throne.

Several years later Nefertiti saw her third daughter, Ankhe-senaton, married to the younger half brother, the child-prince Tutankhaton.

The Eighteenth Dynasty was now considered safe. Two authentic heirs were readied against any emergency that might come to the Egyptian throne.

Aye was well aware of the dangerous situation in Egypt. He was still the king's chief scribe and in charge of the Amarna Letters. Some were written by him, others mentioned him by name, pleading that he intercede and try to bring reason to Akhenaton. But there was no reasoning with the sun king. Aye watched the letters being packed away in the strong wooden boxes and knew that almost every clay tablet was an arrow pointing along the highway of doom.

CHAPTER THIRTEEN

Correspondence Between Kings

Tell el-Amarna, 1357–1355 B.C.

The letters being stored in the Amarna archives would not be read again for more than three thousand years. In the main they were from the vassal rulers ruled by Akhenaton, payers of tribute to him, protectors of his lands.

The clay tablets hold the darkening chapters in the history of Amarna.

Written by vassal kings, princes, governors, ambassadors, generals, officials, and officers high and low, the letters speak of plots and counterplots, charges and countercharges, accusations, scandals, complaints, evasions, connivance, and betrayal. All are expressed in courtly phrases; all pledge fidelity.

Akhenaton has been called a cynic because of his refusal to take action. The Amarna Letters might account for his growing lack of interest in man-made politics. Their writers must have wearied him with their endless cries for gifts and protection. Those who protested their loyalty the loudest were to be his betrayers.

Among these the outstanding Judas was Prince Aziru the Amorite, who, once before, when Akhenaton's father was living, had been supressed for attempting to start a rebellion in Syria. Aziru was one of the original fifth columnists; ostensibly a vassal of Akhenaton's, he was secretly allied with the Hittites. He was one of the sons of Abdiashirta, "the rebel of Byblos" (Gebal in Syria). These two petty princes had long records of attempted disloyalty.

Now warning reached Akhenaton that Aziru, emboldened by the unblocked invasion of the Hittites, had re-established himself as a dictator in Syria. Akhenaton ignored the warnings. Was not Aziru writing him flattering letters and sending tribute? Akhenaton refused to believe evil of Aziru, while the disloyal

vassal began undermining Egyptian rule in Syria. Aziru, encouraged by the Hittites, gathered an army, seized lands and
towns, and, founding an independent kingdom, set himself up as
its king.

Aziru worked hand in hand with the new king of the Hittites,
King Shubbililiuma, who made no attempt to carry on the token
friendship a former Hittite king had offered Akhenaton. Aziru
began a subversive campaign in Canaan (Syria-Palestine), urging other vassal princes not to resist, but to join with the Hittites.

Almost overnight Akhenaton's subject countries were swarming
with traitors urging the dominated peoples to break free of imperial Egypt.

The loyal vassal princes preferred the protection of Egypt to
alliance with the Hittites. They were frankly terrified by the
invaders who were sweeping through Canaan, taking city after
city. They were governing princes of countries that sent tribute
faithfully to Akhenaton; some were related to him by marriage.
In return they expected his protection against their common
enemy.

Letters poured into Amarna from the kings of Mitanni and
Babylon, the princes of Syria and Palestine, the governors of
Tunip, Simyra, and Gebal.

All were pleas to be saved from the Hittites. Many contained
warnings against "the dog Aziru."

One faithful supporter wrote Akhenaton in terms as strong as
ever were addressed to a king:

". . . when you ascended the throne of your father's house,
Abdiashirta's sons took the king's lands for themselves. Creatures
of the King of Mitanni are they, and of the King of Babylon,
and the King of the Hittites."

The charges are at cross purposes. Mitanni was still trying to
defend itself against the Hittites. Akhenaton may have lumped
the accusations together and ignored them all.

Aki-Izzi was governor of the Egyptian city of Qatna in Syria.
He was among those sending warning against Aziru. "Oh my
Lord," he wrote Akhenaton, "if the trouble of this land lies upon
the heart of my Lord, let my Lord send troops, and let him
come!"

This became the incessant cry, Come save us in person, king of kings!

From Biruta (Beyrout), Kadesh on the Orontes, Sidon, Akko, Megiddo (gloriously won by Thutmose III), Hazor, Gezer (Gaza) and so many other places, the beseeching letters came, and all in the same vein:

"Lord of the Two Lands, King of Kings, God-King on earth: lead your army to us in your own divine person, at the head of your vast army, with glittering chariots of gold, with warriors heavy with weapons far as eye can see. . . ."

So they prayed to Akhenaton, dreaming of him as their avenger and deliverer. And one wrote the king, ". . . if nothing can be given, take me to the side of my king."

And some sent tribute, the last they had to give, but the treacherous princes sent greater tribute to appease Aton, and Akhenaton accepted all that was sent and poured it into the continued building of Amarna, and no help went to those who prayed, and waited.

Akhenaton's refusal to smite the Hittites sparked fires of rebellion in his domain. The network of betrayal was being carefully laid and old resentments revived and utilized. The vassal kings conquered by his aggressive ancestors, notably Thutmose III, seeing Akhenaton's apathy to the encroachment of the Hittites and encouraged by Aziru, remembered ancient wrongs dealt them by Egypt and began reclaiming their own countries.

Mitanni, Syria, and Palestine were swept by small, flickering fires of rebellion.

Reports raced into Amarna, of countries ravaged, lands being laid waste, allies captured, loyal subjects lost in battle, ambushed, murdered, and deserters turning to the enemies of Egypt. It was the king's faithful subjects who were being robbed, mutilated, their homes and crops burned, their cattle driven away and they and their families slain or sold into slavery. The loyal kings were being driven from the subsidiary kingdoms and their names erased from their lands.

The endangered faithful sent their dearest, their brothers or sons, to plead with Akhenaton. They were sent away unanswered.

His officers raged at his inertia. His soldiers wanted to fight. The demands grew from the besieged, Send ships with warriors ready to fight. Send armies by land! Send aid, before your kingdom falls, Oh King!

The faithful sent gifts with their prayers for aid, and apologized for their small value, but it was all they had left.

The faithless continued to send rich tribute, often loot taken from the faithful. This may have influenced a king in need of endless treasure to complete his city of the sun.

In answer to their prayers the faithful were sent no help at all, or a small force that was useless. They were given strange and paralyzing orders, and always tribute was demanded of them, no matter how great their own need. Many deserted in despair and went over to the enemy.

It was for the king in person these helpless subjects prayed. A great, glittering, wrathful king in his golden chariot, leading his tremendous armies into the war that would save Egypt. Akhenaton had the best-organized military system on earth and unlimited wealth to amplify it. In its earliest stages the destruction could have been easily stopped, and even in its final stages a determined Egypt could have held its own. But only feeble efforts were made at intervals to stem the dissolution and no one knew what was going on in the mind of Egypt's king.

A powerful, aggressive Thutmose III was needed to gather his armies and sweep up into the north, to reinforce the subject princes, drive out the Hittite invaders, stamp down the fires of rebellion, and save Egypt. For it was becoming clear to Egyptians and vassals alike, (all save those in the enchanted inner circle of Amarna), that unless this was done, Akhenaton's reign would mark the collapse of the great Egyptian empire.

Their prayers met with silence. Akhenaton ordered out no armies. He prayed to the sun.

The Hittites held the plain north of the Orontes. Mile by mile they were conquering land that belonged to Egypt. Prince Itakama, one of the Syrian vassals, fired by Aziru's successes as a rebel, joined forces with him and seized the city of Kadesh on the Orontes, once conquered by Thutmose III. Three vassal kings loyal to Akhenaton dared oppose Itakama and were not heard from again.

Aziru marched forward, gathering forces and forcing his way through Phoenicia and Syria to the mouth of the Orontes, slaying the faithful kings, confiscating their wealth, killing, looting, and laying waste to the land.

At the river he joined forces with the Hittites, and the allied legions proceeded to march against Simyra and Tunip. The two cities sent terrified appeals to Amarna: "Bring help, before it is too late."

But Aziru was also writing Akhenaton, and so was his father Abdiashirta. The two traitors boasted in ardent words of their loyalty and continued to send the tribute so dear to Akhenaton's heart. In fact, while the most pitiful letters begging for protection against Aziru were arriving in Amarna, Akhenaton was writing Aziru asking for more tribute! Evidently the poet-king could not believe so generous a donor had designs on his kingdom.

Aziru and his legions surrounded the two cities and were mercilessly attacking them. Some of the tragic reports smuggled out of Tunip reached the archives. Until its last hour the besieged city hoped to be rescued by Akhenaton's soldiers.

There is one letter from the elders of Tunip. They recalled to Akhenaton's mind that Tunip's loyalty to Egypt had existed since the time of Thutmose III and that Tunip and Egypt worshiped the same gods. They wrote that twenty messagers carrying dispatches had been sent from Tunip to King Akhenaton, and that not one answer had been returned by the king, nor had any of the messengers returned and it was feared they had been captured by Aziru's forces. Now Simyra was falling to Aziru, and where were the king's chariots and warriors that would save Tunip?

Was this letter heeded? For there is another letter to Akhenaton from the wily Aziru, protesting his loyalty, and with no mention of the fact that the Amonite was at that moment storming Tunip and had made a hostage of its aged and respected Prince Yadiaddu.

One final letter came from Tunip, written by its governor: "Now we belong no more to our Lord, the King of Egypt. . . . when Aziru enters Simyra, Aziru will do with us as he pleases, in

the territory of our Lord, the King. . . . And now Tunip, thy
city, weeps, and her tears are flowing and there is no help for us."

So Simyra was taken, and Tunip fell.

Letters accusing Aziru came from Tyre, where Akhenaton's
governor, Abimilki, wrote pleas for aid that were never answered.
Abimilki reported Aziru's ally, Zimrida of Sidon, had delivered
Simyra over to Aziru and was now launching hostilities against
Tyre. The city was under blockade, and its wood and water
supplies were cut away.

Tyrians were dying of hunger; he, Abimilki, was hungry and
cold. No official retinue remained to him, and he apologized
for being obliged to send his letters to Amarna by an ordinary
soldier. Then, casting protocol aside, the faithful vassal pleaded:
"Send help to Tyre, or grant permission for me to recruit an
army . . . send water and wood that I may be warm."

But his next letter was written in a transport of joy, for not
only had King Akhenaton deigned to answer, but he had made
many promises of support to Abimilki. Abimilki sent tribute to
express his gratitude (the pathetic list includes "five talents of
copper") but was forced to beg for immediate help. He reported
other cities falling to the Aziru forces, but "if only the king will
send a few troops, all will be well with Tyre."

King Akhenaton's astonishing reply to this was to order
Abimilki to take his own soldiers to the aid of another belea-
guered town!

The despairing vassal tried again to make Akhenaton understand. Abimilki explained that he was being driven out of Tyre;
he couldn't remain in the king's city. He would go to Sumuro,
although he had heard there was revolution there. He would go
to Sumuro protesting undying allegiance to his king.

So Governor Abimilki fled for protection to a Sumuro raging
with civil war, protesting to the last his loyalty to Akhenaton,
and we hear no more of him.

Every charge brought against Aziru was being ignored by
Akhenaton. The "nobles of Irkata" wrote Akhenaton pledging
loyalty. They begged for protection against Aziru who was be-
sieging their city; they had shut the gates against Aziru, but

without help they could not hold. They sent Akhenaton thirty horses as gifts.

Aziru sent far more valuable gifts, taken from the captured city.

The governor of Gezer, in Palestine, wrote begging that soldiers be sent "as soon as possible to protect Gezer." Gezer was permitted to fall.

Sixty of the Amarna Letters were written by Ribbadi, the governor of Byblos (Gebal), an important commercial center in Syria. He was among the first to warn Akhenaton against the renegade prince. In letter after letter he detailed the crimes committed by Aziru. He wrote of loyal subjects killed or captured, of the king's ships being seized, of the king's lands and cities taken. He wrote that conspiracy was everywhere in the land. Then he wrote in desperation that Aziru's army was at the gates of Byblos.

"Send help to save Byblos," he begged again and again. "I am prepared to hold . . . help must come to me."

Once he pleaded for "only thirty or fifty men to hold the city."

When no help came, Ribbadi wrote Akhenaton that all the country around Byblos was in the hands of the enemy, but that he would hold the city "as long as the corn holds" (until starved out). But the corn was almost gone and the city was facing famine. Unless the king sent help Byblos would be forced to surrender. In this letter he begged someone close to the king to reason with Akhenaton and get help to Byblos.

Several of the Amarna Letters contain postscripts addressed to the "scribe of the Lord the King," begging his intercession. Evidently these were intended for Aye.

No help went to Ribbadi, who wrote again that the Aziru forces had offered him protection if he would ally with them and that Ribbadi's own wife and children had begged him to give up and fly with them to Egypt, but he would not leave Byblos, he would not desert the cause of his king.

"Only a little help," he pleaded, "and I can hold the city."

Akhenaton might never have read the pleas and warnings. He sent a dispatch to Ribbadi ordering him to send soldiers to aid the Egyptian Army! This order Ribbadi carried out to the best of his ability; then came a dispatch from the king asking for corn!

Corn—of a besieged city facing starvation!

Ribbadi's letters began to approach hysteria. For three years Byblos had been under siege "with little corn." Now the threshers were on strike (one of the first), they had driven their overseers from the fields and were refusing to thresh the grain. But let the king send him soldiers, since Ribbadi had sent his own garrison away at the king's order and Byblos was left undefended. The soldiers left to him and the people were hungry.

"Send help," he prayed again. "Only a little help, and your city can still be saved."

King Akhenaton's incomprehensible reaction to this came in the form of an order. Ribbadi was to take what soldiers and chariots were left to Byblos and go to the rescue of besieged Beyrout.

His but to do or die—the faithful Ribbadi set out with his remnant army to Beyrout. There Prince Ammunira, governor of Beyrout, closed the city gates against his would-be rescuer. Ribbadi reported Ammunira as one of the traitors who had attempted to win him over to the side of Aziru.

A series of accusations and counteraccusations began between the two governors. Ammunira was having problems of his own. Akhenaton had also ordered him to send troops and horses to the Egyptian Army. This he reported having done, adding a rather surly postscript to the effect that he expected to be compensated for his efforts when the rebellion ended. Now he had complaints to make against Ribbadi, whose soldiers he accused of mistreating some of his officials.

This charge did win the attention of Akhenaton, for Ribbadi was soon writing the king demanding to know who had spoken ill of him, and why the king gave ear to such slander? "I am faithful to the King," he wrote, as many times before. Ammunira was also writing Akhenaton, protesting his undying fidelity.

Was ever a king more harassed? It is understandable that Akhenaton preferred the beauty of Nefertiti and Amarna to a perusal of his official mail. Ribbadi's letters were particularly open in their devotion and their reproach.

The bewildered Ribbadi left Beyrout in the hands of the Aziru puppet, Ammunira, and returned to Byblos. His starving city was about to capitulate to Aziru. Ribbadi sent word to Akhenaton that he would not permit it to yield, he would be faithful to his king, and if only the king would send a little help, Byblos could still be saved.

Instead (this was preceding the collapse of Simyra), Akhenaton ordered Ribbadi to proceed with his remaining troops to the rescue of Simyra!

Ribbadi's replies are those of a man drowning: "Why does the king give such orders? What is being done to the faithful Ribbadi? He cannot obey the king that he loves, for he is shut up in Byblos, his city, and it is surrounded by foes . . . He is shut up in Byblos like a bird in a cage . . . help must be sent, quickly."

And still, so loyal was Ribbadi, that he did lead his starving soldiers in a quixotic attempt to save Simyra. They were ambushed on the road. Many of his soldiers were slain, others were scattered. Simyra had fallen to Aziru.

The survivors returned to Byblos. Ribbadi's tragic reports continued to be sent from a dying city. He wrote of the many cities taken, the territory lost, the hostility hemming him in. In Byblos the last of the corn was gone. The people were starving. The hungry soldiers left the garrison and went "where there is corn to eat." (They had deserted to Aziru.) And Ribbadi begged Akhenaton to send help, to save Byblos, the king's city. To the last he protested his loyalty.

No help was sent to him. A letter came from Akhenaton, but its contents are not known. Ribbadi wrote sorrowfully back that he could no longer be addressed as the governor of Byblos. The city had fallen; "Aziru has burned the King's city with fire." He summed up the infidelities and betrayals. "There remains not one prince to my Lord the King, every one is ruined . . . let the king take care of his land and let him send troops. . . . for if no troops come in this year, the whole territory of my Lord will perish."

He wrote that the infamy done him would bring tears to the eyes of the king, and adds sorrowfully: ". . . if no troops are to be sent, let the king send his officers to fetch me and all my brothers, that we may die in the presence of our Lord the King."

There are no more letters from Ribbadi.

Too little and too late, aid went to him. Akhenaton sent a token force under a General Bikhuru to bring order out of the

chaos Ribbadi had reported. The general's forces promptly allied
with the Aziru-controlled Bedouin mercenaries, who by this time
were fighting on both sides, and joined in the pursuit of Ribbadi.
The unfortunate prince fled to Jerusalem, which was another
center of trouble, and from there he fled to Gaza and is supposed
to have died in the attempt to hold that city. No more was heard
of this last of the northern princes faithful to Akhenaton.

Urusalim, City of Peace, as the Amarna Letters name Jerusalem, was at this time an important Egyptian stronghold in south
Palestine. Letters from its Egyptian governor, Prince Abdikheba,
reveal a revolution stimulated by the successful inroads of the
Hittites in the North. Encouraged by their victories, the success
of Aziru, and the steady weakening of the Egyptian empire,
there came swarming up out of the south and into Palestine the
Aramaean Semites, the Khabiri. They allied with the troops of
Aziru and harried the Palestinian cities. They razed or burned
the harvests and burned the towns. They were in Lebanon; they
held Mount Ephraim and Sheschem. Reports poured into
Amarna from Palestine: the cities cried out for protection to be
sent them. The Palestinians were fleeing in terror into Egypt, or
hiding in the mountains where they were "living like goats."
The displaced begged for help, or to be taken by the Pharaoh
into the protection of Egypt.
Prince Abdikheba wrote Akhenaton in desperation to report
that the Hebrews had not only invaded the Promised Land but
were settling there, evidently with the intention of remaining
forever.
The Amarna Letters at this point corroborate in every detail
the story of the Conquest as told by Joshua.

It was a long time before King Akhenaton took notice of the
many accusations against Prince Aziru. At last he wrote the rebel
demanding an explanation.
It came in the form of a glib denial. Aziru cleverly refuted the
charges point by point. Certainly he had raised an army! He
had been trying to beat back the Hittites. True, he had destroyed
Simyra—to prevent it being taken by the Hittites: he promised
to rebuild that city. As for all the other cities he had taken, such

as Tunip, his present stronghold, he had been obliged to take
them to keep them from the Hittites! These had been cities pay-
ing tribute to Akhenaton, and from now on he would collect
the same tribute and send it to Akhenaton. And he sent costly
gifts to the king and flattering protests of undying loyalty.

Akhenaton accepted the tribute and the flattery, and no more
was said at that time to Aziru.

But reports of Aziru's treacheries continued to mount in the
Amarna archives and the king's suspicions were finally raised
again. Akhenaton sent an official named Khani from Amarna with
orders to Aziru to appear in Amarna and stand trial. Aziru had
friends in Akhenaton's court. A fleeter messenger went ahead
of the king's to warn Aziru, who hastily left Tunip and hid in
the hills.

Khani returned to Amarna with the undelivered letter.

The king wrote a stern letter to Aziru reproving him for not
having shown the proper respect to his emissary.

Aziru's reply was prompt and, as usual, bland. He begged to
be forgiven for not having been in Tunip to greet the king's messenger, but he had been called away to fight Hittites; he cited
his victories. When word had reached him of Khani's presence
in Tunip he had "set out at once to meet him but had missed
him on the road." However, Aziru's friends had made Khani's stay
in Tunip pleasant and had given him fine food and gifts of
oxen, horses, and mules. And in turn Aziru was sending costly
gifts to the king . . .

For the first time King Akhenaton showed indignation: "Even
if thy actions be just, yet if thou dissemble in thy letters at thy
pleasure, the king must at length come to think that thou liest in
every case."

Aziru wrote back, protesting his innocence and his loyalty:
"I prostrate myself seven times and again seven times . . . I am
thy servant forever."

Akhenaton's reply to this is not recorded, but evidently he had
gone beyond the reach of flattery, for Aziru was forced to appear
in Amarna, bringing many chests of treasure stolen from the
king's subjects as gifts for his king, despite which he was forced
to stand trial. The final letter in his files is a tablet from one of

his followers condoling with Aziru for being in prison—we hear no more of the bandit prince.

But the damage he had done was beyond calculation. Aziru had helped undermine loyalty to the throne from the Euphrates to Nubia.

Aziru's main support in this treachery was the inexplicable weakness shown by Akhenaton. The king who had broken so many taboos seemed determined to break one by one with the strongest ties of the past. At a time when Egypt had need of every friend in Asia he succeeded in annoying another ally and relative-by-marriage, King Burraburias of Babylonia.

King Burraburias was one of the in-laws who took advantage of his relationship to demand gifts of the world's richest king. Akhenaton, who was never reluctant to accept gifts for himself, may have disapproved of the habit in others, for many of the Amarna Letters complain of his failure to send requested treasure. King Burraburias wrote frequently, reminding Akhenaton (as the king was so often reminded) of the friendship that had existed between their fathers, and making the usual request for gold.

He evidently felt free to criticize Akhenaton to a curious extent. Once he scolded Akhenaton for having accepted from Assyrians the gift of a silver chariot drawn by two white horses. The Assyrians were his subjects, the Kassite king declared (they were also in league with the Hittites), and Akhenaton should not have accepted a gift from the Assyrians as if they were his equals.

The carping of the Babylonian may have weakened the relationship between the two kings, which should have been close. One of Akhenaton's daughters had been sent to Babylon as the bride of Burraburias' son. The Kassite king had given her magnificent wedding gifts, including a necklace "set with one thousand precious stones," which he did not fail to call to the attention of Akhenaton. In the archives is a tablet from the king's daughter in Babylon to Akhenaton, and on it is written "before the face of my Lord let him come." This was a way of marking a letter "personal" and instructing that its carrier be permitted to deliver it only into the hands of the king.

The king of Babylonia's letters took on a new angry note as

inner and outer pressures made a shambles of what had been a secure and orderly Egypt.

The rebellion in the subject countries was soon reflected in Egypt. The result was a crime wave across the land. During this upheaval many gifts promised by the king to friendly vassals never arrived. They were taken by bandits or corrupt officials. Many reports of this nature were sent to Amarna.

Among the first to complain was King Burraburias, who always felt free to speak his mind.

"I have sent many gifts to King Akhenaton . . . none have come to me . . ."

This became his litany.

"If nothing is denied me," he tempted, "I will deny you nothing."

Then, with royal frankness: "Our fathers were friends. We should continue to be. Messengers have now come from you thrice, but you have sent with them no gift worthy of the name. I shall also desist."

Stung perhaps by this threat, Akhenaton sent word of valuable gifts on their way to Babylon with emissaries Burraburias had sent to Amarna evidently in the hope of collecting such tribute. Chariots and horses, a fine bed, other treasures, and much gold were being sent to Babylon through Syria. In time a wail of complaint came from Burraburias. Where were the gifts promised by Akhenaton? They had vanished, and with them the messengers from Babylon.

Burraburias was afraid they had been murdered.

"Canaan is your land and you are king of it," the king of Babylonia scolded Egypt's king. "It is in your land I suffered this injury. So restrain the do-ers of it, replace the stolen gold, and slay the murderers of my subjects to replace their blood."

Akhenaton had more serious problems. The correspondence between the two kings was allowed to die.

While enemies pressed deeper into the kingdom, in Thebes the priests of Amon strengthened their attack upon the dreamers of Amarna until all Egypt was in open rebellion against the king and queen and their god.

Akhenaton had been respected as more than a potentate. He

had been considered a god. With godlike disdain he had refused to act while the royal ships were being commandeered
and plundered, the royal caravans ambushed and robbed, and
from every side came reports and proof of organized treachery.
Now enemy ships patrolled the Red Sea and enemy troops occupied lands long faithful to Egypt. Akhenaton's inertia in the face
of the national catastrophe had resulted in a general breakdown
in the government.

The military in the occupied lands were among the first to
revolt. Egyptian soldiers turned against their officers and joined
the rebels.

Within Egypt the military began a systematic oppression of
the civilians. They robbed the people of their crops and cattle
and raped their women. They burned the homes of those who
tried to oppose them.

The government followed the military into the melee of dis-
integration. High-ranking officials began to use their authority
to demand unwarranted tribute. Tax collectors levied unjust
taxes on the citizens. The justice of Egypt, which had been
famed for centuries, ended, and it was reported that every judge
and court official had to be bribed, and no poor man could
obtain justice in the courts. The pettiest officials found ways for
thievery. The priests had always been noted bribe takers; now
they became extortionists. Suddenly every Egyptian seemed determined to take what he could wherever it might be found. In
Egypt, where civilization and an ethical code had developed
that would merit the admiration of history, graft and ruthlessness
and corruption took over, and a dog-eat-dog policy became the
law of the land.

An administration without decency or mercy developed in the
reign of the best-intentioned and farsighted of kings.

The collapse of integrity in high places was promptly imitated
by the people. Armies of bandits prowled the country, robbing
wayfarers and camel trains, and even the royal caravans of the
king. The weakest chieftain raided his neighbor and in turn was
raided.

One vassal wrote Akhenaton that an Egyptian official had
kidnaped his wife and children and begged that soldiers and
chariots be sent to their rescue.

The Amarna tablets detail the moral breakdown. The outrages were the king's responsibility and should have been recognized by him. Evidently a few weak attempts were made to bring order out of chaos. Officers were sent with soldiers to towns that begged for protection. The officers evidently shared in the growing contempt for authority; for complaints came back that the military were worse in their behavior than the enemy!

The stable, civilized government created by the Eighteenth Dynasty had collapsed.

Akhenaton, poet and dreamer and priest, closed his ears to the prayers for help rising in his troubled world. A believer in goodness may have found it difficult to see that hatred could grow so swiftly both outside and within Egypt, or that its principal objective was Aton the one god, giver of love and of light.

Breasted summed up the situation: "A religious revolution by the young and gifted King Ikhnaton [Akhenaton], caused an internal convulsion such as the country had never before experienced, while the Empire in the north gradually disintegrated under the aggressions of the Hittites . . ."

Akhenaton has been called a pacifist; the world's first prince of peace. Does this explain his silence when the security of his empire was threatened and his impatient armies longed for the word that would send them to the rescue of Egypt? Can it explain his lethargy while internal protest swept Egypt, almost to his palace doors, and he would not attempt to put down rebellion or clear the government of crime?

He had not wished to be a warrior conqueror. Now he was refusing to defend what had been conquered for him. It is evident that during these cloistered Amarna years the king was refusing counsel even of those he knew wished him well.

Aye had long been a general in the king's army. Harmhab was a general. Evidently both tried to persuade Akhenaton to give the orders that would save Egypt, and failed. Harmhab's voice was heard far beyond the confines of Amarna. He prophesied ruin was coming to Egypt.

Aye spoke softly from his secure position behind the throne. King Akhenaton remained with his face lifted to the one god and hymned the sun.

Harmhab was as determined as Aye but far more ruthless. He

conferred in secret with other military leaders and the scattered
Theban priests of Amon. All were agreed that strong measures
were needed if Egypt was to be saved. Thebes itself was a city
of intrigue, ravaged by factions struggling for power.

Obviously the first necessary step was to bring Egypt back to
a semblance of law and order. For this, Maat, goddess of order,
must be reinstated, along with all the other gods that had been
ordered banished by Akhenaton. For it was clear to all except
Akhenaton and his loyal Nefertiti, that Aton was responsible for
the collapse of Egypt.

So a decision had to be made to placate the gods, beginning
with Amon. But Akhenaton was king of Egypt and opposed to
all but Aton.

There were troubled conferences in Thebes. The throne had
to be given new authority if it was to survive. Would the abdica-
tion of Akhenaton be the answer? That would mean the end of a
great era; the end of a splendid dynasty. If only Nefertiti had
borne sons . . .

It is believed that Aye found the temporary solution to the
problem facing Egypt, and probably with the consent of Akhenaton.

The king was open in affection for his half brother, Sakere,
who was now fully royal, having married the Crown Princess
Meritaton. "The noble Sakere," so Akhenaton called him, in terms
given to those he trusted and loved. "The beloved Sakere, great
favorite of the King."

Sakere was in his late teens and Meritaton thirteen when they
married, and the royal game of chess began again with pawns
who were little more than children but who were of the royal
line. Time could not be wasted if the throne and the dynasty
were to be saved.

So the boy Sakere was named co-regent in 1355 B.C., and co-
regency rings with the names of Sakere and Akhenaton have been
found in the rubbish heaps of Amarna.

Akhenaton and Nefertiti were hemmed in on every side by
hatred. She had been his love too long to escape the campaign of
evil launched against him. She was wholeheartedly converted to
Aton and she would not change. They were children of the sun.
Perhaps they could not see into the gathering dark.

For a long night had come to Egypt. Akhenaton's conquering ancestors, even the great Thutmose, might never have lived. The lands they had captured were lost. Egypt's Asiatic empire was sacrificed. Phoenicia was lost. Syria had fallen to the Hittites. Palestine was gone. Megiddo, Tunip, Kadesh and Jerusalem were lost. The Bedouin were overrunning Egypt. In the South was anarchy.

Slowly the great Egyptian empire fell into ruins, leaving Akhenaton and Nefertiti imprisoned in Amarna. Sakere's appointment was an attempt to stem the avalanche.

A few letters continued to straggle into the archives from several vassal kings surviving in Asia, protesting their fealty. Such messages may have encouraged Akhenaton to believe he was still king of kings.

One may wonder, knowing no answer can be given, what was going on in Amarna at this time, and in the mind of Akhenaton. It is a temptation to let the imagination race among the known facts, which offer such tempting opportunities for speculation. They are important not only for what they reveal but for the questions they raise.

One may ask if Akhenaton's reactions during this period of dissolution were those of a normal man. What explains the conflicting orders, the refusal to defend his empire, the tolerance of traitors and rebels, the refusal to defend those loyal to him?

Flinders Petrie has described Akhenaton as "a man of determination, delicacy of feeling, kindness of manner, and a sense of humor, taking pleasure in popular enjoyment."

What had happened to this king that he refused to try to hold Egypt?

Sometime during this troubled period Nefertiti sat again for her portrait in the Street of the Sculptor. This second and last bust, far more touching, more human, more beautiful, is in the Museum of Cairo. A few years before she had been pictured as Nefertiti the all-beautiful, symbol of antiquity's highest romance, queen of queens. Now she was apparently in her thirties, and her beauty was shadowed by deep emotions. She had seen more of life than most women ever experience. She had given birth to six children. Of these, one lay dead in the rock cliffs outside Amarna, one was planning to usurp her place on the Egyptian throne, and another had married a foreign prince and was living in a far-off land now turned hostile to Egypt.

The king she had loved was discredited, ill, and betrayed. She was trying to hold a weak and failing ruler to the throne.

The quartzite bust in Cairo portrays a woman of many sorrows. The pride, the queenliness is there, but the expression of sadness makes us wonder, as all Egypt must have wondered then, what was taking place inside the city of the sun.

Nefertiti may have had one more deep and private grief, for who knows the true ending of any love story?

CHAPTER FOURTEEN

King Sakere

Amarna and Thebes, 1356–1352 B.C.

Maat, goddess of truth, scattered fragments of history she wished to have remembered through the storerooms and rubbish pits of Amarna. Wine jars were among her favored artifacts. By the jars stamped with their owners' names the archaeologists have identified many of the leading houses of Amarna, such as Akhenaton and Nefertiti's palaces and those of Prince Sakere, Princess Ankhesenaton, and Akhenaton's sister, Princess Beketaton.

According to the jars and other evidence, it was in 1356 B.C. (some authorities quote 1355) that Sakere married Meritaton and became co-regent with Akhenaton.

Even these reminders do not tell us how Nefertiti's life changed after her young son-in-law Sakere took the place she had held beside Akhenaton. Suddenly his name was on the documents and letters of state where hers had been written all the years of her marriage. Akhenaton and Sakere cartouches would be found by Howard Carter in Tutankhaton's tomb.

Sakere even took for his own the special title Akhenaton had given Nefertiti, "Beautiful is the beauty of Aton."

Much imaginative writing has been given over to this curious interruption in the hitherto idyllic romance of Nefertiti and Akhenaton. Apparently Akhenaton's twenty-ninth year marked some kind of climacteric in his life. He would never again appear as the devout and devoted king of kings. Apparently this was his last year as an active regent, although the co-regency would continue while he lived.

Meritaton assisted her husband in supporting her father. Much has been made of an alleged rivalry between Nefertiti and her oldest daughter. At thirteen Meritaton evidently had her mother's strength of mind and much of her glamour. The wine jars indicate a family rift in 1356 B.C. Akhenaton left the king's palace on the royal estate and moved to the North Palace, that jewel-like building in the northern residential suburbs, the walls of which, decorated with Amarna's finest murals, are now among Egypt's most valued artistic treasures. Meritaton and her new husband went with her father. Wine jars of this year with Nefertiti's name have been found in her own palace "against the wall."

The great palace in the heart of the city, still the largest non-religious building in the world, was left empty. Within a year its elegant rooms became storage places for produce and stables for small domestic animals. A few years more and the walls began crumbling; no one repaired them. The king's palace was never used again.

There is much speculation as to this abrupt division in a family that had been famed for its devotion. It has been suggested that Nefertiti was banished from the king's side in disgrace; again that it was she who left Akhenaton, baffled by her failure to cope with his increasingly strange behavior.

We are free to imagine Nefertiti's proud withdrawal to her own palace. As if in defiance of the growing Theban pressure in favor of Amon, she named her palace the House of Aton and set up what was virtually a rival court. She was not alone. Aye came and went between the Amarna palaces and Thebes, but his loyalty was to her. And sharing her life in the bijou palace with its charming walled courtyards and gardens were three, and perhaps four, of her smaller daughters—Neferneferuaton, who was five and had been given Akhenaton's own special name for Nefertiti; Setepenaton, aged three; and Baqtaton, last of the Amarna "garland of princesses," who was one year old. Since it was after her birth Akhenaton and Nefertiti separated, there may have been state reasons; it may have been known Baqtaton would be their last child. Nefertiti was twenty-eight; her woman's life had begun when she was very young.

With the other children in the Aton house was Nefertiti's favorite, Akhenaton's small half brother. Sturdy-appearing and handsome, the seven-year-old Tutankhaton gave no indication of his innate physical frailty.

The only proof of this alleged separation is in wine jars owned by Akhenaton and Nefertiti, which placed the royal pair in sep-

arate households after the birth of Baqtaton. Since every member
of a royal family was supposedly given his own establishment,
we cannot place entire credence in the testimony of the jars.

Still, there is evidence of some high-handedness on the part of
Meritaton, who was installed as mistress, if not regent, in the
North Palace with the two kings.

It could not have been with the proud Nefertiti's approval
that her name was chiseled from certain Amarna buildings and
monuments and Meritaton's name substituted. King Sakere's
name already replaced hers on the royal documents. Hints of
mother-daughter rivalry exist in such places as the so-called Sunshade House of Meritaton, where the original queen-owner's
name was cut away and that of Meritaton substituted. John
Pendlebury writes that there is no doubt the erased name was
Nefertiti's. The Sunshade was built for a queen. Sakere was co-
regent, but Meritaton was never made queen. She was Crown
Princess, no more.

It may be that Nefertiti's beautiful oldest daughter, excited by
her sudden elevation to power, assumed certain privileges and
possessions of her mother's. Now it was Meritaton who reviewed
the queen's cavalry squadron, and Meritaton's wine jars would
be found in Nefertiti's palace.

Sakere and Meritaton evidently usurped the privileges of
regency with few of the responsibilities. Amarna artists portrayed them as a charming young couple, in the same affectionate
poses in which Akhenaton and Nefertiti had been so often shown.
In every way they imitated Meritaton's royal parents. And in
many ways they failed; the most notable failure being that three
years of the co-regency passed and no child of theirs appeared
to serve as heir to an endangered throne.

Can this be the reason for the incident, so often cited, so alien
to our modern ethical code, that took place at Amarna at this
time?

The evidence is on a fragment of stone found in the ruins of
Hermopolis. On it is carved: THE SUNSHADE OF THE KING'S
DAUGHTER, WHOM HE LOVES, ANKHESENATEN THE YOUNGER, THE
DAUGHTER OF ANKHESENATEN AND AKHENATON.

This siring of a child by his and Nefertiti's third daughter took place in 1354 or 1353 B.C. and is virtually the last known act of Akhenaton's life.

Intermarriage to preserve the purity of the blood strain was considered particularly desirable in royal Egyptian families facing extinction. Prevalent earlier in the Eighteenth Dynasty, it may have accelerated extinction. Nefertiti, who had given only daughters to the throne, and whose daughter Meritaton had given no child to Sakere, may have approved this as a last desperate attempt to produce a male heir to continue the Eighteenth Dynasty. The effort failed; the child was a little girl.

But the fragment from Hermopolis has cast a long shadow over the memory of a great king.

There were other incidents in the great palace that must have held Nefertiti in proud silence in her smaller palace by the wall. Still, as had her mother-in-law Tiy before her, Nefertiti must have continued to shoulder grave responsibilities, for Akhenaton was a man exhausted by the burdens of state. His last sculptured portraits show him slumped in lethargy. He had never been physically strong. He had never wanted conflict for himself or for Egypt. And Sakere, the boy he had chosen to be his heir to the throne, showed no sign during his brief reign of having a will of his own.

But even if, as has been suggested, Nefertiti spent a few months or even several years in banishment from the great palace, she was never submerged as a personality. And always behind her slender, proud figure was to be seen the shadowy figure of Aye, aging but indomitable, the man of destiny still. Harmhab was close to Aye, and the two kept her informed as to the disturbing events in North Palace and in Thebes.

Harmhab, with his vulture croakings against the attempt to enforce worship of Aton, his demands to be permitted to lead his soldiers to the recovery of Egypt, and his prophecy that unless Amon was restored to Egypt the country was facing certain doom, must have become increasingly repugnant to Akhenaton, who became less willing to hear criticism of his faith the more it endangered Egypt. Sakere had been chosen to divert Theban antagonism from Akhenaton and Nefertiti. He was of little use to the crown as long as he remained in Amarna. Harmhab harbored reservations against Aton. These he confided to certain highly placed Amon priests in Thebes.

It is not likely that he told them to Aye, or to Nefertiti, who remained faithful to Akhenaton's religion.

She continued to worship the sun god. As Akhenaton seemed to withdraw into the shadows, her image came forth brighter and bolder until she became in the public mind the representative of Aton and drew the steadily growing distrust of Thebes.

It is now that the strength of Aye begins to show clearly through the miasma gathering over the throne. The Amon priesthood began reorganizing, secretly encouraged by Harmhab. Sakere's appointment and his continued residence in Amarna with the heretic king was not enough to silence the priests. They did not want a king who continued to live in Amarna, that center of heretical outlawry. Aye and Ramose recognized the gathering menace of revolution.

The Amon supporters had to be appeased; Sakere must leave Akhenaton and his dream life in Amarna and go to Thebes, to conciliate the Amon priests and restore order to the city.

Sakere and Meritaton sailed away to Thebes and evidently established court in Queen Tiy's colorful old palace on the west bank, in the very heart of the Amonite opposition. Who approved this move on Sakere's part, and who disapproved, we do not know. We do know the good-looking young couple were surrounded by enemies.

Aye may have sent them there, not only to conciliate the Amonites, but to return Akhenaton to the ministrations of Nefertiti. Aye was always on her side, and would have known any reasons behind her separation from Akhenaton. But it is absurd to speculate. The facts and artifacts contain satisfying drama.

Sakere may not have been the handsome weakling prince his portraits suggest. For even in Thebes, in the center of his enemies, he maintained a certain fidelity to the teachings of Akhenaton in which he had been reared. He must have been under pressure from the Amon priests to adopt an Amon name, as Tutankhaton was later. But Sakere and Meritaton retained to the last the Aton names given them by Akhenaton, and Sakere also kept the title he had borrowed from Nefertiti, "Beautiful is the beauty of Aton."

There was no actual capitulation to Amon. Still, the ban against Amon was partially lifted, for it was during Sakere's co-regency that some of the beautiful articles manufactured at Amarna, which had always carried the stamp of Aton, now appeared with the name of Amon.

The fact that Sakere did not actively oppose Amonism was not enough for the Amon priests. They maintained an unflagging resistance to the crown and a poisonous campaign of antagonism against Akhenaton.

They were fighting a myth—a great king who was only the emptied shell of his greatness. During the three uneasy years of Sakere's co-regency Akhenaton gave no sign of being alive. But he did live.

Evidently he rejoined Nefertiti after Sakere and Meritaton left for Thebes. They lived in the North Palace or in hers. A sad little queen had reclaimed the semblance of authority. Now she was nurse and caretaker and Akhenaton's fierce defender. There is a final picture of Akhenaton at Amarna. Ill and lined, looking twice his years, he is shown sitting slumped and staring into space, looking very much as his father did in his last days. And as Queen Tiy had stood guard beside King Amenhotep, so Nefertiti is shown in sad attendance on the king whose love and inspiration she had been during his splendid years.

Shell of a king though he was, he still had the kingdom and Nefertiti and Aye. Evidently the reunited family were living in the great North Palace. And in Thebes there was Sakere, charming and futile but loyal to Akhenaton. We may never know how much Akhenaton sensed of this, or how much he knew of what was happening in Egypt and to him.

Guesses are always hazardous, but many attempts have been made to explain the curious collapse of this brilliant young king and his kingdom. The Amarna Letters contain proof of Akhenaton's growing strangeness. What can be deduced when a man under thirty sinks first into an abyss of contemplation, then, when his world falls into collapse around him, refuses to make any attempt to save that world?

A legend has outlasted the centuries in Egypt of a heretic king who was poisoned by enemy priests. Many believe Akhenaton was that king. This would account for the period in which his once brilliant mind was apparently drained of its ability to reason, when no letters were answered, and no decisions made that might have saved much of his empire. Certain Amon priests were medical men adept in the use of poisons. Prolonged poisoning over a number of years could account for the period preceding Akhenaton's death in which he permitted Egypt to touch the brink of ruin.

Certain authorities have suggested Akhenaton turned against humanity in despair of its behavior, of the wars starting everywhere in the empire, the hatred of the religious representatives, and the cynicism of state politics. But he made no effort to stem the wars or repair the political situation.

It has been suggested that Akhenaton lost interest in living when his world refused to accept his faith in the one god, and that he turned from that world to the sun.

Medical experts have suggested physical reasons were behind his obvious collapse. Some point to the overly large Akhenaton skull.

There have been many theories concerning the strangely shaped head of Akhenaton, which was so often and frankly portrayed by the uninhibited Amarna artists. Its earliest known portrayal has been found in the tomb of Akhenaton's Grand Vizier Ramose in Thebes and was evidently made shortly after Akhenaton took the throne. Medical authorities have several theories concerning this type of head with the heavy bony overhang at the back. Several believe it due to generations of inbreeding; others that it may have been deliberately shaped or molded in infancy, as is still done by certain primitive people.

Photographs of such cranial deformations are to be found in medical textbooks, including Nelson's authoritative *Textbook of Pediatrics* and Boyd's *Surgical Pathology*. The Akhenaton-type skull is described as "one of the forms of cranial synostosis of the scaphocephalic type." In such cases the skull has been pressed into boat-shape by the premature ossification of the sagittal suture. In rare cases this can be hereditary. Although such inheritance is usually through the male, the portraits of Nefertiti's daughters show the same strangely shaped heads.

In such cases loss of intelligence is inevitable, and with it loss of vision. It is sad to think of a blind Akhenaton. Such a victim may live a vegetable existence for many years before the release of death; others die young.

Akhenaton died young, which is offered as just one more of the many attempts to explain the strange last days at Amarna, when a king sank deeper into lethargy, and a saddened and still beautiful Nefertiti nursed him through his last illness. The record is obliterated in places, but we know she was there, she was strong, and that care rested heavily upon her. The Amarna Letters reveal that Akhenaton ceased to lead an active existence for several years before his death, but when that took place, or how, nothing is known. We only know he died at Amarna.

He had not completed the building of his perfect city.

According to recently approved dates, he was thirty-two years old when he died in 1353 B.C. (one authority believes him to have been forty-two), and had been a king for sixteen years, or half his lifetime. Before that he had ruled four years as co-regent.

Thomas Peet and other authorities believe that Akhenaton's body was taken by night, as royal mummies always were, to the new tomb in the valley east of Amarna, but that later, with equal secrecy, it was removed to another tomb in the Valley of the Kings at Thebes. We can picture Nefertiti, worn but still beautiful, going through the demanding ceremonies of burial in the Amarna grave.

We can imagine her as returning to the palace surrounded by her weeping children and her mourning retinue and with her small head still held proudly under its burden of dust from the grave. She could give no time to mourning. On her rested the terrible responsibility of Egypt.

Nefertiti was not yielding to Akhenaton's enemies. She prepared to defend his memory and to hold Egypt to Aton. She had Aye on her side.

The grave Akhenaton prepared for himself at Amarna was ransacked and the king's handsome sarcophagus pounded into fragments. His mummy is supposed to have been hidden there for a brief period before it was smuggled to Thebes. Canopic

jars were found in his Amarna tomb, but they had not been used.
The lids of such jars were usually shaped to resemble the heads
of the gods of death; Akhenaton's were copies of his own head.

Aye would have been the logical attendant at the final interment of Akhenaton in the Valley of the Kings at Thebes.
There is no record of this burial; Akhenaton's enemies saw to that
when they wrecked his tomb. Sakere would have been present if
he were still living. It was Aye's destiny to attend to the death
ceremonies of many of the Eighteenth Dynasty's kings and
queens. Tutankhaton's tomb, which Aye was shortly to prepare,
was magnificent; how much more splendid must have been the
grave Aye prepared for the greatest of all the Eighteenth Dynasty
rulers.

We can only be certain the furtively hidden body would have
been surrounded by magnificent furnishings and treasures representing the art Akhenaton had brought into being, with statuary
and carvings and paintings by Amarna's greatest artists, and
faïence and pottery made by its great master craftsmen. Aye and
Nefertiti would have required worthy tribute for Akhenaton's
grave. Then, fragrant with incense and fresh flowers, with lamps
still burning on the walls, it was sealed by Aye that Egypt's
most outstanding Pharaoh might rest forever surrounded by the
riches of his world under his emblem of the sun.

This grave at Thebes when found had been brutally plundered. The vandalism was beyond that of grave robbers. It expressed hatred and the need to annihilate. We have no need to
guess who hated the memory of Akhenaton to that extent. Nothing was left but the mutilated walls.

A mummy that may be his was found crowded into another
grave with those of several other kings, including that of his
grandfather, Amenhotep II. The royal mummies were often
shifted from one hiding place to another in a futile attempt to
keep them from their enemies, or from robbers.

Nefertiti may not have been present at the second burial. She
had assumed Akhenaton's legacy of hatred; Aye would have
warned her not to risk the fury of the Theban priests. She did not
have her father's ability to avoid enmity. She was too fierce a
devotee of Aton and had openly shared Akhenaton's denial of
Amon. Aye, the skilled courtier, walked like a charmed man be-

tween the two opposing factions. He kept his eminent position in Amarna while managing not to incur the enmity of Thebes. He was protected by his reputation for wisdom and piety. Priests of Aton and of Amon alike respected Aye.

But as powerful as Aye was, he could not provide Akhenaton with a permanent resting place. Akhenaton's burial like his death remains shrouded in mystery.

Any comment other than Breasted's on the great Pharaoh seems feeble, for he wrote with depths of understanding after years of intensive study of Akhenaton and his world. Of the king's death, Breasted wrote:

"Thus disappeared the most remarkable figure in earlier oriental history . . . however much we may censure him for the loss of the empire . . . the fanaticism with which he pursued his aim . . . there died with him such a spirit as the world had never seen before—a brave soul, undauntedly facing the momentum of immemorable tradition."

And Breasted wrote again that seven or eight hundred years after Akhenaton's death his type of man might have been looked for among the Hebrews, but that he was unique in his time, while the modern world has yet to know and evaluate Akhenaton "who in a world so remote and under conditions so adverse, became the world's first idealist and the world's first individual."

Akhenaton and Sakere vanished at about the same time.

Sakere left no imprint on Egypt. He may not have been permitted; stronger personalities than his were at work behind the throne. Perhaps he was ill-advised. He may have refused to accept advice. Shortly before Akhenaton's death Sakere made a futile attempt to restore polytheism to Egypt and became noticeably friendly with the Amon priests. This was in 1352 B.C., in the third year of his co-regency. In that year Sakere suddenly and mysteriously died.

Carter, in his report of the discovery of the Tutankhaton tomb, wrote his belief that Sakere "came to his death at the hands of a rival faction."

This faction may have been led by Aye, Nefertiti, or that rising grim-faced man of ambition, General Harmhab, who, frustrated by Akhenaton's refusal to permit him to become the military avenger of Egypt Harmhab longed to be, was nursing long-range plans of his own.

A mummy has been found that may be Sakere's. It was hidden in what is called "Tiy's Tomb," a crude, undecorated cave, under thirty feet of sand and broken stone. The royal coffin in which the body lay had evidently been made for Akhenaton, but the shattered catafalque entirely covered with gold and gems was Queen Tiy's, and it was surrounded by funereal articles also marked with the name of Akhenaton's mother. The body, wrapped in gold leaf and the thinnest of clothing, was taken at first to be Queen Tiy's, but scientific tests proved it to be that of a young man.

The royal half brothers were evidently buried as hastily and furtively as if they had been criminals.

Whether Sakere was dethroned, and then died or was murdered, and why he was buried in so strange a fashion are among the minor mysteries of Egypt. Some believe he and Meritaton were murdered together by Amon priests in Thebes as soon as the news of Akhenaton's death reached the former capital. The death of an inadequate king would mean little when balanced against the dire need of Egypt. And Egypt was in danger, and a strong leader was needed if the Eighteenth Dynasty was to survive, for the greatest of all the dynasties was threatened with total extinction by the sudden mysterious disappearance of both Akhenaton and Sakere.

Yes, a leader was needed, and for the first time we see Nefertiti as Aye's daughter, with his iron determination. That hitherto unrevealed strength had supported Akhenaton through the golden years and the dark. Nefertiti had been a creature of romance, devotion, and mystery. There had been no indication that her personality and her sense of loyalty were as strong as Aye's.

She knew, no one knew better, the royal game of Egypt. She had been pushed into it as a child pawn by the relentless ambition of Aye. It was like the game of checkers she and Akhenaton had played when they were children. She had learned it in the palace at Thebes and the palaces of Amarna. She had watched the skillful moves of that queen of players, Tiy.

There are authorities who believe Nefertiti was responsible

from the first for Akhenaton's attempt to make Atonism the national religion. Others suspect that before his death she ruled in his name. Certainly she had shared Akhenaton's problems and his power. Now she knew every danger threatening Egypt. She who had nursed the great king through the last years of illness, dissolution, and perhaps blindness, knew how foolishly he had played the royal game.

The next move was up to her. It had to be boldly played. She had the courage. She had Aye's support and Aton's. She had the best of informants in Harmhab.

The Amon priests in Thebes hated her, but they had no reason to suspect her plans. To them she must have seemed a forlorn and weary woman, still a queen, but living in virtual banishment far from Thebes as the widow of a dead and discredited king.

So the impact on Thebes must have been tremendous when Nefertiti showed she had no intention of conceding the royal game.

She was Queen Nefertiti and—she still held a king.

CHAPTER FIFTEEN

King Tutankhamon

Thebes, 1352–1344 B.C.

He was a very small king. He was only nine years old. There are touching pictures of the boy Tutankhaton in Amarna. Nefertiti, an affectionate mother, brought him up in her Amarna palace as if he were one of her own children. Evidently his boyhood there was happy and normal. The toys he played with, even his sling-shot with its pebbles, would be found in his tomb.

Who was he?

According to William Stevenson Smith, and others, both Sakere and Tutankhaton were of obscure origin. "Both based their claim to the throne," Smith wrote, "upon their marriages to daughters of Akhenaton."

Percy E. Newberry wondered if Aye, who acted as mentor to both princes, had not been their father. Rudolf Anthes has expressed what has been believed by many authorities when he wrote of Tutankhaton: "His mentor was Aye, a high-ranking officer, a relative of the royal family (Anthes evidently believes Aye to have been a cousin of Akhenaton's) who had been one of the most honored courtiers at Amarna . . . he led the boy successor wisely into the period of restoration and took over the office of vizier."

Immanuel Velikovsky, in his startling *Oedipus and Akhnaton* theorizes that both Tutankhaton and Sakere were the sons of Akhenaton by his own mother, Queen Tiy, and that Akhenaton was the original Oedipus.

Others have studied the relationship of Sakere and Tutankhaton to Akhenaton. The two princes have been generally accepted as the half brothers of Akhenaton, the sons of his father, Amenhotep III. Tutankhaton at least laid claim to the blood royal by claiming Amenhotep III as his father and describing his mother as "the mother of a king." He may have meant King

Sakere's mother was also his. A woman named Merytre (princess, concubine, extra wife?) bore that title. We can be no more certain of the ancient royal relationships than of the dates. Egypt reveals only tantalizing glimpses of some of her most fascinating secrets.

We only know that Tutankhaton was living with Nefertiti when the news was made public that both Akhenaton and Sakere had died. Nefertiti was ready with her queen's checkmate. Aye was the boy's sponsor and guardian, Harmhab his champion, Nefertiti the catalyst who brought him into history.

She summoned all the queenly authority left to her and named Tutankhaton the new king of Egypt. She made him fully royal and divine by hastily marrying him to her third daughter, Ankhesenaton. The marriage stopped any protests that might have been made as to Tutankhaton's right to the crown.

The boy-king of Amarna was between nine and twelve when he took the throne in 1352 B.C. His wife was thirteen; she had already given birth to a child, the mysterious little girl whose existence was registered on the rock fragment at Hermopolis. Until that time they had been two of the children playing in Nefertiti's palace at Amarna. They had been as brother and sister—terms that as used by the Egyptians are confusing to modern minds. They were still children, as shown in affectionate poses by the Amarna artists who had so often portrayed Akhenaton and Nefertiti in like poses. Tutankhaton's queen, according to the pictorial works in his tomb, was a lovely, graceful creature in her pleated transparent robes, fond as was her mother before her of many colorful jewels and flowers. The married couples of the Eighteenth Dynasty clung to youth and despite their many dark problems continued to show a touching affection and playfulness.

Nefertiti may have served in the beginning as co-regent with her child son-in-law. In the splendid North Palace at Amarna objects have been found bearing her name and Tutankhaton's.

They might have been happy and lived long in Amarna, but Thebes would have its will. It had been too long the deserted capital. High priests of Amon conferred with Harmhab; their representatives came in formidable array to Amarna bringing an

ultimatum; the throne must be removed from Akhenaton's city
of the sun and back to Thebes.

Nefertiti tried to hold the new king and queen to Amarna.
She knew they were her last hope of retaining her husband's
vision of the one god for Egypt. As long as Tutankhaton lived
in Amarna the memory of Akhenaton could not die.

The Amon priests knew that too. They knew Nefertiti was fighting to hold an imperiled empire to her husband's faith. As powerful as her hold was over Tutankhaton, it was not so strong as the
arguments of the Amon priests. For a blight had fallen on the
Eighteenth Dynasty. The boy-king of Amarna had inherited a
tarnished throne. He was handicapped by his association with
Nefertiti, his relationship with Akhenaton, and his own youth.
He was not a dominant king-image, as Akhenaton had been.

The Amon priests evidently spoke bluntly to the boy-king.
Since Nefertiti would not yield, Amarna must. Akhenaton's revo-
lution had ended. Tutankhaton must either move the court to
Thebes, or give up his throne.

Aye knew Tutankhaton could not rule without the support of
the priests and he could not rule from an exiled throne, so far
removed from Thebes. He was the boy-king's chief adviser. Even
against his daughter's wishes, Aye knew, the move must be made.

Once more, by land and by the Nile, a great royal trek began.
Nefertiti may have watched from the windows of her own palace
the progress of the bannered royal barge being rowed slowly
upstream toward Thebes in the south. How different was this
pilgrimage from the joyous expedition she and Akhenaton had
led to the barren site of Amarna, only a dozen years before!

She might have gone South with the others and deserted
Amarna. The revolution against Amon ended when the royal
barge with the throne chairs aboard left for Thebes. She could
have returned on that barge to her former city that had loved
and worshiped the beautiful girl-queen-goddess Nefertiti. She
could easily have rewon its love, for she was mother of the new
queen and daughter of Aye, and the dynasty she represented
was still in power. She might have lived out her days as revered
queen mother, as Queen Tiy had in her palace at Thebes.

Nefertiti was the proudest of queens. She would not sue for the affection of the country that had refused her husband's faith. Gentle, sad, and disillusioned, she remained in Amarna. It was no longer the capital of Egypt. Its supremacy vanished up the river with Tutankhaton. And with the boy-king—she must have known —went the last worship of Aton as the state religion.

But it was still the most beautiful city in the world, and it was Nefertiti's city. She lived on in her palace with her remaining small daughters, the wine jars testify, and around her the never completed city of Amarna began the inevitable deterioration that overtakes a neglected city. According to Anthes the craftsmanship of Amarna and the life of the common people continued for another ten years or more after Tutankhaton's desertion. The Amarna potters and faïence makers continued to produce the most beautiful wares made in Egypt.

In Thebes, two awed and excited children wearing the royal emblems on their foreheads were borne in royal procession through a jubilant city and proceeded to take possession of Queen Tiy's former palace, where Nefertiti and Akhenaton had lived as children. There the full weight of the Amon hierarchy fell upon them. It was not enough that the court had been restored to Thebes and it was again the capital, No-Amon. Sakere had made it that in a token transference of power, when Akhenaton had still been living, and still Sakere had vanished. Now a boy-king had his orders—he was to change the state religion back to Amon.

Aye, his adviser, knew it must be done.

The boy and girl from Amarna had been given Aton names at birth, and been reared by Nefertiti in the faith of Aton. But now they were beyond Nefertiti's protective care and in the hands of Amon. They yielded, and with that yielding, Aton fell.

Sakere and Meritaton had not changed their "sun names." The priests of Amon demanded full measure of Tutankhaton in exchange for the support the child-king needed. Akhenaton's first unpopular act had been the changing of his name to honor Aton. Now, since everything must be done to discredit Akhenaton and Aton, the Amon priests insisted that the new king and queen change their Aton names.

Tutankhaton became King Tutankhamon. His wife changed her name to Ankhesenamon.

It may have been at this time that Aye, hitherto designated as
Aye, son of Hapu, assumed the name of Amonhotep in honor of
his first royal patron and the reinstated god. He retained the
identifying "son of Hapu." He is confusingly known in histories
under either name. His mortuary temple built in the name of
Amenhotep at Thebes contains some of the finest examples of
Amarna art.

Aye could not afford Nefertiti's single-mindedness. He had to
compromise; Tutankhamon must compromise. Once Aye had
been a high priest of Amon. He had left Amon to serve Aton.
Now to support Tutankhamon, he reverted and became a high
priest of Amon.

It is during King Tutankhamon's reign that we see most clearly
the strong hand of Aye. The former scribe whose iron personality
had served to steady so many thrones was now devoted to
Tutankhamon's. Under Aye's guidance the restoration of
Amonism began in Egypt.

Acting on Aye's advice, Tutankhamon began the same type of
crusade against Aton that Akhenaton had waged in behalf of
Aton. He restored the Amon temples, conducted the revived
Amon festivals in person, and re-engrave the name of Amon
wherever it had been removed from walls and monuments all
over Egypt. He sent masons and painters to destroy all memora-
bilia of Aton and Akhenaton. Those names were chiseled away
and the names of Amon and Tutankhamon substituted. Sculptors
and artists were recalled from Amarna, and all over Egypt—
except in Amarna—the emblem of the sun was substituted by the
kingly figure of Amon.

The last of the Amon priests burst joyously from their hiding
places and took possession of the long deserted Amon temples.
The great Temple at Karnak was reopened, a new gold image of
Amon was raised on its altar, and the great hall filled with
processions of white robed priests burning incense and chanting
the old hymns before the idol and, seated under it, the childish
bejeweled figure of the new king.

Thebes took to its heart the amiable young king who had
returned to the city its chief god and its former position as the
Egyptian capital. Once more its busy streets filled with Amon
priests.

To Tutankhamon and Ankhesenamon it evidently meant little that they now answered to new names and worshiped a new god and were the means of restoring a lost kingdom. In a sense they, too, were lost. Aye was the true king; Harmhab his right hand. The Temple of Aton built by Akhenaton between Karnak and Luxor was permitted to stand, and it is believed that between his public appearances in behalf of Amon, Tutankhamon continued to worship there the sun god of Amarna.

Thebes would have allowed the boy-king this latitude; he had restored its god. Tutankhamon was given full credit for all that was being done to return Amon to its former supreme power. His most important work was that of restoring the Amon temples that had been ruined during the "Amarna heresy."

A stele in the Temple of Amon at Karnak describes his work: ". . . the temples of the gods and goddesses . . . had gone to pieces. Their shrines had become desolate, had become mounds overgrown . . . their sanctuaries were as if they had never been. Their halls were a footpath . . . their gods had turned their backs upon this land.

"One prayed to the old gods, but they did not come. They did not come when the army went forth, and failed."

Then, the boasting continues, his majesty had appeared upon the throne of his father, Amon, and this king was Tutankhamon. And now "there are thirteen splendid carrying poles where formerly there were only eleven bearing the holy image of Amon-Ra in fine gold and every costly stone . . ."

The ruined sanctuaries were cleansed by priestly ritual of the lingering presence of Aton, the shrines restored, the altars replaced. Back to their deserted temples came the images of the cat Bastet, the hippopotamus Opet, the ibis-headed Thoth, and all the other curious animalistic gods that had formerly been worshiped in Egypt. All were welcomed home with prolonged festivals by the Egyptians for whom one god had never been enough.

Tutankhamon began the work of restoring and completing the great Temple of Amon which Amenhotep III had begun and which his son Akhenaton had never finished. "I restored the fallen temples of Egypt; I suppressed wrong doing in the land,"

Tutankhamon continued his account, in words doubtless dictated by Aye.

The gods were placated, the Egyptians content. The priests of Amon were restored to power and "the property of the gods and the temples doubled, tripled, quadrupled." Tutankhamon's reign was proving to be the most popular since that of Amenhotep III. As his popularity increased, the memory of Akhenaton became more abhorrent. The hatred had not ended with Akhenaton's death; it increased.

Tutankhamon, reared as the "small brother" of Akhenaton and Nefertiti, was being forced to render poor returns for the affectionate care given him by the queen and her "heretic king."

As for Aye, to paraphrase the words of another great national leader, spoken centuries later in another land, he had lived to preside over the liquidation of the spiritual and temporal kingdom of Akhenaton. Much that King Akhenaton had built Aye was forced to order destroyed in the process of restoring Amon.

"Clearly . . . there must have been a power behind the throne," Pendlebury wrote of this period, "and we can be tolerably certain who this power was . . . Ay, (Aye) Chief Priest, Court Chamberlain . . . the most powerful court official . . ."

Aye had charge of the boy-king's household, as he had presided in turn over those of Nefertiti and Tiy. His tomb at Thebes shows him welcoming in King Tutankhamon's behalf an official delegation of Nubians bringing tribute. The black men are decked with ostrich feathers; one is leading a giraffe.

Aye was a politician, an opportunist, a compromiser, adept at the most dangerous game, that of advantage on the level of supreme power. His loyalty to those who advanced him might make wide detours, but in the end he was strangely faithful. If he advised those in his charge to yield to certain pressures it was to save their crowns, or their lives.

It may well have been he was saving both for the two married children from Amarna.

According to Rudolph Anthes, Aye led the boy Tutankhamon "wisely through the period of restoration and took over the office of Grand Vizier."

Aye had been a powerful political figure for more than fifty years and this was the first public acknowledgement of his long sustained hold over the throne.

Only Amarna held out against the restoration of Amon. Amarna was Nefertiti, and it would not change while she lived. Aye kept her informed of the work of restoration in Thebes that had to be done if Egypt was to hold for the Eighteenth Dynasty.

She could picture—no one more clearly—the day memorable in Thebes when King Tutankhamon took his place on his gold throne under the image of Amon on its thirteen new carrying poles and rode the sacred barge from Karnak to Luxor in the revival of the great annual procession of the celebration of Opet. The return of this most beloved of all the sacred festivals served to convince the Thebans that Amon had been fully restored to Egypt. Commemorative reliefs on the wall of the temple at Luxor showed King Tutankhamon as a glittering motif with the god in the long water processional, while from the banks thousands of cheering Thebans hailed the progress of the god and the king up the river.

Such scenes were faithfully reported to her by Aye.

Aye may have found time to remember Akhenaton in his prayers, but in spite of his age he was still the busiest man in Egypt. He and Harmhab had determined to further cover the memory of the pacifist King Akhenaton with a brave portrayal of Tutankhamon as an aggressive warrior king in the tradition of the Eighteenth Dynasty ancestors. Egypt had turned a cold face to the prince of peace; Egypt should have a conqueror image as its ruler. So the fledgling king was portrayed in ferocious scenes, most of which must have been based on sheer fantasy. Tutankhamon could not have advanced beyond his middle teens when he was shown as dashing into battle in his chariot and conquering entire tribes of Asiatics and Nubians. He may have taken part in one battle with General Harmhab as his guard, but even that is doubtful. Still he is depicted as nobly trampling on the faces of his enemies and slaying those he captured—one picture shows him sacrificing a Syrian prisoner in the presence of his "Divine Father Aye."

He was also portrayed as a mighty hunter, as all Eighteenth Dynasty kings had been until Akhenaton. Still in his chariot, armed with bows and arrows, Tutankhamon was shown pursuing and slaying droves of gazelles, ostriches, and lions. In some of these hunting scenes his young wife appears.

Harmhab had his reasons for building up the boyish image as the doughty warrior-king. For in his own portrayals of himself, he was at the king's right hand when these valiant deeds were done. He would make use of such claims later when the opportunity came.

Harmhab had his plans. Aye must have known. He was the wise man of Egypt, and he recognized a man made in his own ambitious mold. But his was still the strongest hold on the throne. He could curb the fierce demands of his ambitious protégé.

Among Aye's more pleasant tasks was that of preparing King Tutankhamon's tomb. Aye always kept an eye on the future, and it was shortly after the arrival of Tutankhamon at Thebes that Aye began supervising the construction of the magnificent grave in the Valley of the Kings. This did not indicate any foreknowledge on Aye's part that the young king's life would be brief. Royalty always began preparing early for the afterlife; Aye had begun building Amenhotep III's when that king and Akhenaton's mother had been quite young. Akhenaton had ordered the building of his own tomb, and Aye's, at the start of the building of Amarna.

So, although Aye was often credited with second sight, it was probably with no expectancy of an early need for it that he began the construction of what was to become the most famous tomb in history, and ordered magnificent furnishings made for it in Amarna.

Tutankhamon was the least of the Eighteenth Dynasty kings, but his reign was satisfactory to the Egyptians, who were tired of turmoil, rebellion, and war. General Ramose had driven back the Hittites and their allies and was diligent in holding the country that remained to Egypt against further invasion. Aye kept the ship of state on an even keel. There was not enough time to bring Egypt back to its former condition of internal integrity and external power, for Tutankhamon's reign ended abruptly with his death in 1344 B.C.

He was eighteen or nineteen years old. For a long time it was believed he was murdered, but scientific studies of the mummy in the Cairo Museum have fairly well established that he died of tuberculosis.

The end was evidently unexpected. Aye, facing the reality of that slight dead body in the palace at Thebes, knew that more was involved in this tragedy than the death of a boy.

Tutankhamon was the last male of the powerful line of Ahmose, founder of the Eighteenth Dynasty. Aye's granddaughter, weeping beside her dead husband, had only produced for him two stillborn children. Unless an heir could be found, and at once, the Eighteenth Dynasty would end with Tutankhamon. The splendid, powerful Theban family that had ruled Egypt for almost two and a half centuries would pass out of history.

Where could a legitimate heir be found to fill the empty throne? Nefertiti was only thirty-three, but she had no husband to act as king, and she was too tainted with the Akhenaton heresy to be of actual use to the crown.

There were her daughters, among them the grieving girl-widow, Ankhesenamon. There was Harmhab, pushing his way upward ruthlessly, as once Aye had climbed. Aye may have had reasons by this time for mistrusting him.

Who else remained of the brilliant royal circle that had revolved around King Amenhotep and Queen Tiy?

The indomitable Aye who had maneuvered his way through so many state crises had to think fast. The royal game was almost played out. The next move must as always be swift and sure and probably made before Egypt woke to the fact that it was again without a king.

It must be remembered that at this time Aye was incredibly old for an Egyptian of that period. He was well into his eighties; some believe he was over ninety. Again and again he had maneuvered Egypt's through crises, chosen the best material available, shaped it for the throne, fought and connived to hold it there. He had been ruthless for himself and for others.

He was still Aye the incredible, master of destinies. But no royal pawn remained for him to play across Egypt's imperial board.

Stern-faced, Aye accepted the truth. All the great figures he had served had vanished. He remained.

For the first time the mysterious Aye had to come from behind the throne and publicly accept the burden of Egypt.

It may be he had only a few hours to act in before Thebes
learned of Tutankhamon's death. There was no time to found a
new dynasty.

As grand vizier, Aye was only a step from the throne. Old
and tired as he was, he took that step. In the great Temple at
Karnak, the former scribe announced the death of Tutankhamon
and took his place on the gold throne, under the image of Amon,
as King Aye of Egypt.

One of Aye's first responsibilities as king was the burial of
Tutankhamon. There is much that is unexplained about this
interment. As in the cases of so many other kings whose mummies were shifted about in the Valley of the Kings, Tutankhamon's hastily mummified body was not placed in the great tomb
Aye had been preparing for the young king, which was still
incomplete. Instead it was placed in a tomb that may have originally been prepared by Aye for Amenhotep III, or for Sakere, or
even for Aye himself. One of the gold canopic jars holding the
embalmed viscera of Tutankhamon has on it Sakere's name. It
is believed that both Akhenaton and Sakere were secreted in
tombs other than their own to keep their bodies safe from the
followers of Amon and this may also have been the reason for
Tutankhamon's mysterious interment. None of the three were
buried with the pomp and ceremony and long-drawn-out public
mourning usually attendant upon the death of kings.

We do not know why the boy-king of Amarna was buried so
swiftly and so furtively, but we do know the proceedings were
carried out under the direction of King Aye, and so skillfully
that Tutankhamon's would be the only royal grave left unvio-
lated in the Valley of the Kings.

Sir Leonard Woolley has commented upon the fact "that it
was the grave of one of the most insignificant of Egypt's rulers,
found intact, that has astonished the whole world by its riches."

By the treasure found in the Tutankhamon tomb we can dimly
guess at the fortunes that must have been hidden with the greater
kings, of which to date no trace has been found.

Woolley, Carter, Breasted, Cottrell, and many others have

written in glowing terms of the discovery of the Tutankhamon tomb. Its fabulous contents have been often described. Still the oft detailed story remains one of the magic legends of our time.

This richest of all archaeological discoveries was made on November 4, 1922.

By then the discoveries made at Amarna and the translated Amarna Letters had prepared archaeologists for an understanding of historical events in Akhenaton's, Nefertiti's, and Tutankhamon's time. The missing gap in history had been bridged; their faces and lives were known. But no one was prepared for the background of their Eighteenth Dynasty splendor that would be revealed by the opening of this last tomb in the Valley of the Kings.

For seven seasons the archaeologist Howard Carter had been excavating for Lord Carnavan in the valley entrance of the Theban necropolis. A drearier and less hopeful setting can scarcely be imagined. The rock façade was pierced by more than thirty empty graves that once had held the mummified bodies of the kings of the Eighteenth, Nineteenth, and Twentieth Dynasties. All had been ravaged centuries before by grave robbers. Their stone mouths gaped open to the sun.

Until this time the leading discovery in the Valley of the Kings had been the tomb of Queen Tiy's non-royal parents, Huya and Yuya. Even that tomb had been robbed.

Still the Carnavan expedition probed the cliffs at the entrance of the valley in the hope of finding one unplundered tomb.

Carter had directed the slicing of parallel trenches into the cliffs. It seems strange that he chose to cut directly under another tomb that had once belonged to the Twentieth Dynasty Pharaoh Rameses VI. The trench was forced through tons of rock rubble, which, when cleared away, revealed stone steps leading down into the cliff to a door that had not been opened for more than three thousand years.

How many times have we read of that moment when Lord Carnavan, waiting outside the long sealed door, permitted Carter to enter first. And calling impatiently to learn what the archaeologist's flashlight was showing within, could only wring from Carter the cry: "Marvels! Marvels!"

Marvels they were, but what Carter glimpsed was a mere hint

of what lay beyond the gold-glittering entrance; a fabulous palace deep under the earth, with corridors and colonnades and treasure rooms and storerooms crammed with wealth and beauty it would take years to clear away, and deepest within and most secret the burial chamber where the small body of the boy-king of Amarna had lain undiscovered in its triple coffin since the day it was left there by his Divine Father Aye.

Breasted has described the opening of the tomb, the falling of light upon the almost unbelievable splendor, and the soft strange sounds entering into the thousands of years of silence "as the ancient jeweled furnishings, responding to the first change of air in all those years, began their long postponed process of decay."

Room opened upon room, holding everything intended to give pleasure and delight to a young king in another world. Unimaginable, to those who have not seen them, are the contents of the tomb of Tutankhamon—the gold chariots, the funerary furnishings, the beds and chairs and household ornaments, and, burning like flames in the treasure chambers, the fabulous gold articles and the jewels. There were many beds. One was a hinged folding camp cot, one was red, others were massive gilded affairs decorated with animal gods to protect the sleeper, for many gods were represented in this tomb; but the one most portrayed was Aton.

This presence of the outlawed Aton in the necropolis of a city consecrated to Amon and populated by his jealous priests, may have explained why the last rites of King Tutankhamon were hurried and why King Aye took such care to make this tomb deep and secret and safe.

In the rooms were handsome chests and coffers and caskets, all made of the rarest of woods, inlaid with gold, gemmed with fine stones, and filled with the king's clothing, and his household linens and personal treasures. There were chairs with lion feet and carved backs, and folding stools with legs shaped like the necks and heads of geese; one chair studded with gold had carved on it a squatting scribe offering the young king the conventional wish of devotion—a million years of life—an ironic touch in the tomb of a lad who had died aged eighteen.

There, jeweled and golden, was his throne and on it a scene

showing him seated on a chair while his young queen anointed
his body with oil from a jar—the rayed sun of Aton is over them.
The throne, made in Amarna, is in the Cairo Museum; it is one
of the greatest treasures of antiquity. On its back, with Amarna
artistry, are portrayed the child-rulers as they had been in the
brief years of their regency; sharing intimate carefree moments,
playing games, shooting wild duck on the Nile. Over them is
Aton. The tomb holds the bright moments of their brief, troubled
lives. All they possessed together, even the toys and games they
had shared as children, Nefertiti's daughter left with her dead
husband.

With Tutankhamon were buried superbly carved vases and
statues and lamps and boxes of alabaster; pottery and faïence
from the studios in the city of the sun; his hunting equipment,
his shields, and his Syrian spear; his great fan with its ivory
papyrus—stem handle and spray of white ostrich plumes; and
gold objects of many kinds—scepters, walking sticks, trumpets,
daggers with sheaths that were jewelers works of art, headrests,
and fans. There was one iron headrest and an iron dagger—iron
was far more valuable than gold. Gold was everywhere, catching
the light of the flashlights as the discoverers moved in awe from
room to room—gold that had flashed under the light of Aye's
torchbearers, thirty centuries before.

The light fell on a small pair of linen gloves that could be
worn today. Each finger was carefully outlined with tiny stitches.
How very small were Tutankhamon's hands!

All these objects King Aye, driven by some unknown need for
haste, succeeded in cramming into that hurriedly completed
tomb.

The great hour of the discovery came when the last door was
unsealed and cautiously entered and Carter and his group stood
at last in the actual tomb. It contained only an immense wooden
chamber, or shrine, encased in gold. In fact it resembled nothing more than a large gold packing case. This disclosed another,
and still another, until four funerary boxes had been opened,
each dazzling with gold leaf. The wonder was how these immense boxes had been passed through the narrow entrance of
the tomb, until it was noticed that every panel and part of each
shrine was numbered. Aye's burial crew had carried the pieces

through separately and fitted them into place inside the tomb. This may have been the first prefabricated job in history.

Then, in the last of the gold-encased shrines, they found the sarcophagus of King Tutankhamon. It was carved from one piece of yellow quartzite. Its lid of rose granite weighing half a ton was so heavy four workmen were needed to lift it. It was removed and the gold face of Tutankhamon looked up at them, wearing the asp and vulture signs on the forehead and the divine gold beard on the boyish chin, and looking as bright and young as on the day of his burial more than thirty centuries before.

This was the first of three coffins shaped to the king's semblance. The two outer ones were of wood encased in gold, the inner of solid gold. Two are in the Museum of Cairo; one has been left in the Valley of the Kings. All were alike, of diminishing size, fitting snugly together in the stone sarcophagus. On the forehead of each mask are the king's emblems of the asp and vulture. Vulture goddesses spread their wings along the body to protect the king, and at the feet sits Isis, mourning for Osiris.

They found him in the last of his three gold coffins, dressed in his finest garments and wearing his most precious gems. The false gold beard was on the mummy's mask, the scepters were crossed on his bandaged breast, and on his head was the crown of the Two Egypts with emblems inlaid with cornelian, lapis lazuli, sardonyx, and malachite. More than a hundred pieces of jewelry were buried with Tutankhamon's body; on one arm he wore thirteen bracelets. Around his neck were the jeweled protective pectorals. He wore gold rings and gold toe and finger guards; even his small sandals were of gold.

To those who looked first on this glittering treasure one object touched them most, for on the dead boy's forehead, over the kingly emblems, lay a small wreath of dead flowers, placed there, it is believed, by the grieving girl he left widowed. Ankhesenamon, Nefertiti's ill-starred third daughter, must have placed them there at the last moment as the dead boy lay in the last of his gold coffins, before her grandfather, King Aye, led her weeping from the tomb for the last time. She left behind her the mummies of the two babies born dead, who, had they lived, might have saved the dynasty.

Aye's presence to the last moment in the tomb is attested by a painting on its wall in which he is shown administering the final rites to the dead Tutankhamon. This was without precedent; never before in Egypt had a living king performed the burial rites for a younger king. That was traditionally performed by a son for his father. But the boy Aye had tutored and trained for the throne died first, leaving no son or brother to perform the awesome ceremony of the Opening of the Mouth.

In this ceremony, usually long-drawn-out, more than one hundred separate rites were required. There are signs that at this funeral the ceremony was hurried through.

The painting shows King Tutankhamon as the mummified god Osiris, wrapped in white from head to the soles of his feet, and holding the royal crook and flail. He is wearing many jewels, the false gold beard, and the tall white crown of Upper Egypt that was favored by all the Theban dynasties.

King Aye presents a dramatic contrast to the white-clad figure of the dead man. Looking curiously virile, considering his years, he is wearing the white kilt and sandals a priest always wore for religious services and, thrown gracefully over his shoulders, the priestly leopard-skin cape with its trailing paws, head, and tail. On his head he wears a towering black headdress with the kingly emblems. He offers the dead king the stone fork that will reanimate the mummied body with its vital force and enable it to eat and drink again.

There was anointing, burning of incense, and prayers—an old king was carrying out the last requisites of death. As priest, Aye went into trance; he had gone to rescue the soul of the dead king. When he came out of his trance the soul had returned to Tutankhamon. Aye could do no more.

The doors were sealed on the tomb of the last scion of the Eighteenth Dynasty, the last king of the Golden Age of Egypt. A tired king, too old for tears, directed the sealing of the tomb.

Aye stood under the flaring torches before the tomb, and pulled his leopard skin closer about his throat against the cold desert winds. His voice and eyes were weary as he watched the door sealed and the steps covered with tons of rubble and sand. Fortune watched with him that night, for no robbers peered down from the higher cliffs and no member of the burial crew dared betray King Aye, who was purported to read minds, could foretell the future, and was believed to be a wizard. King Aye may have wept inwardly as he led the weeping young widow, his granddaughter, and the sad procession over the night desert back to Thebes. Slaves followed after them with palm fronds to sweep away the imprints of their steps. Now no man, walking there the next morning, could know of the burial procession or that the crowned body of a boy-king lay hidden in an underground palace in the rock cliff.

The tomb in which Tutankhamon lay was saved by Aye's precautions. Aye had done his work well. His long life did not hold many failures. Still he could not have known the magnitude of this night's success as he plodded across the sand to face the exhausting task of ruling over a ruined empire.

Although Tutankhamon's was the first and only one of the royal Theban tombs to be saved from the grave robbers, it was entered shortly after the burial, but the robbers were either frightened away or killed before they penetrated into the treasure-filled rooms.

Aye placed no special curse on King Tutankhamon's tomb. Much has been written about a purported "Curse of the Pharaohs" promising "death to him who touches the tomb of the king," and much publicity has been given to the deaths (including two suicides) of the members of the first group to enter the tomb, or their relatives. It contained only such amulets as were always placed with the dead, which gave solemn warning to any daring to intrude on the peace of the grave. On the boy-king's throat and breast were the amuletic collars with the charms of the funerary god Anubis, and on his crown and coffin masks the amuletic emblems of Egypt—the vulture head of the goddess Nekhbit and the serpent head of the goddess Wazit. In the inner coffin, wrapped into the linen body bandagings, were more than a hundred other protective amulets and devices, and sacred emblems and images of many gods were everywhere in the tomb.

Aton stood guard over all.

Still even the most scientific have testified to the awe, even dread, that accompanied the excitement of the discovery of that tomb. One cautious archaeologist has commented:

"The number of strange deaths suffered by those who took part in the opening of the Tutankhamon tomb have been, to say the least, beyond the bounds of mathematical probability."

The Tutankhamon treasure is a testament of Aye's devotion. His motto may well have been: "Beyond all else—Egypt!" If he yielded certain advantages for himself and for those whose careers he guided, it was to gain more for the throne.

And still, viewed in the long range of history, Aye's loyalties are clear. They were given to the regents he served. He molded his royal pawns, guided them, bullied them, protected their thrones, their lives, their reputations, and, when he could, their immortal names. To serve them he paid lip service to Amon and consorted with enemies as all great politicians must; but he guarded those he loved in life, and when they died he placed them under the emblem of the sun. The old man lived to bury four of the bright and beautiful kings—Amenhotep, Akhenaton, Sakere, and Tutankhamon, and he defied their enemies, and his, to insure their eternal life under the sign of Aton. As grand vizier of Tutankhamon, in a Thebes savage with hatred against the one god, he buried the boy-king of Amarna under Akhenaton's sign.

In the august presence of death Aye showed where his loyalties lay. The kings and queens served by Aye had no reason to regret the trust they placed in the ambitious scribe who had made himself grand vizier and who now was king.

A period of historical confusion followed Tutankhamon's death. The records are blurred by the ruin the enemy would shortly make of all reminders of the dead King Akhenaton. The only complete picture left of royal life in the Eighteenth Dynasty was hidden in the Tutankhamon tomb.

Everything found in that grave was a memorial to Nefertiti and Akhenaton and to Aye who created it in the cultural tradition of their city, Amarna. With its art, its furnishings, its wall paintings and inscriptions not only the dead boy, but those who shared his brief destiny, were made immortal. The grave held safe the essence of Amarna centuries after that most glorious of cities had been returned to the dust.

Statues found in the tomb mark the final stages of the development of Amarna art. Such funerary equipment as the famed gold mask, the magnificent throne chair, the coffins and much else of the tomb's furnishings are believed to have been made in Amarna's Street of the Sculptor, where Nefertiti sat for the portrait that made hers the most widely recognized face in history.

The opening of that tomb revealed for the first time the wealth of the Pharaohs of her time. "Marvels!" Carter exclaimed, seeing the merest hint of the gold objects heaped within, for as an ancient king once wrote Akhenaton, "the gold in your country (Egypt) is as dust."

Marvels indeed, as delighted museum visitors in many world cities attest, as Americans were to see for themselves when in 1961 the Tutankhamon Exhibit began showing in the principal museums of the United States by permission of the government of the United Arab Republic. The exhibit gave the merest glimpse of the Tutankhamon treasure, just as any Egyptian history now written can show only a glimpse of the vast hidden treasure that is the Egyptian past.

Of all who have been dazzled by the Tutankhamon treasure, how many know its preservation is owed to Aye?

One of the first visitors to the Tutankhamon tomb after its discovery reported seeing footprints left in the sand by mourners or priests who had been dead for thousands of years. Was one small narrow footprint Nefertiti's? The image of Aton blessed that secret and hasty burial, and under its protection and her powerful father's the exiled queen may have been given secret escort from Amarna to attend the last rites for the boy who had been her small brother, her son-in-law, and her son. Aye was king of Egypt. He could have called out his Commander-in-Chief Harmhab's armies, if necessary, to protect Nefertiti from the fury of Thebes.

Nefertiti and Amarna would be safe while Aye was king.

CHAPTER SIXTEEN

King Aye

Thebes, 1344–1342 B.C.

Egypt probably learned of Tutankhamon's death at the same time it was told it had a new ruler. The small body of the boy-king was still undergoing mummification in the Pavilion of the Dead when Aye crowned himself with the double crown and proclaimed himself king of Egypt.

This was the last title won by the determined man who had begun his career as a scribe in the Theban court. The tomb (not the temple) he began for himself in Thebes records Aye's phenomenal rise to power from Amenhotep III's reign to his own.

"Acting King's Scribe. Fan-bearer on the right hand of the King. Master of the King's Horses. Chief of the Bowmen. Priest of Mut. Leader in the Festival of the Cycle of the Gods. Chancellor of the King of Lower Egypt. Mayor of Thebes."

Then, although his claim to being related to the royal family was vague: "Hereditary Prince of Thebes."

And now, lastly, "Aye, King of Egypt."

Final honor would be paid Aye after death, when he was acclaimed and worshiped as a god.

Aye could not add to his new title the boast of former regents: "king of kings." There were no royal vassals left to send their ambassadors with congratulatory messages and gifts to the new monarch.

Much had been lost under Akhenaton. Egypt had suffered change, rebellion, and war. It is not to be supposed that the coronation festivities of King Aye were as riotously celebrated throughout Egypt as others had been. Aye was an old man, and the country was sunk in lethargy.

This lethargy does not explain why a man of humble birth was permitted to take the throne after the death of Tutankhamon. Egypt took fierce pride in the bloodlines of its kings. Aye, who had shaped so many destinies, had no difficulty in reshaping his own. His lowly birth was concealed under the claim made in his and Tutankhamon's tomb:

"Father of the God-King, Divine Father Aye."

This has been translated in meaning that he was the father-in-law of Akhenaton, and that it was as the father of Queen Nefertiti that he made his bold bid for the throne.

There are other possibilities. A blue glass ring has been found with Aye's name and that of Nefertiti's third daughter, Ankhesenamon. Such a ring hints at a co-regency. Aye may have shared the throne with the girl widowed by Tutankhamon's death. The more popular assumption is that it was through Nefertiti he became king.

The fact that no one stepped forward to dispute his move shows the hold Aye had on Egypt. He was universally revered for his wisdom. He had been able to steer his course between the warring factions of two rival gods. Priests of Amon and Aton alike respected him. All knew how faithfully he had worked to steady the throne under the weakening line of Eighteenth Dynasty kings. When at last he stepped into the open all Egypt recognized his value and knew his assumption of the crown was Aye's last attempt to save the dynasty.

Age was his enemy. Aye came too late to the throne. Forty, thirty, even twenty years before, Aye might have revived Egypt. Now he was a venerable, dignified patriarch. He had not enough time or strength left to save the Egypt shattered under Akhenaton. As King Aye he accomplished one tremendous victory—he did not let the Eighteenth Dynasty die out in his or Nefertiti's time.

This could not redeem Egypt. The country had degenerated to a third-rate power. Its economy was wrecked, its fighting legions decimated, its fleets captured by the Hittites, most of its Asian empire lost. Egypt needed a young, aggressive king-defender.

This was the situation faced by a stern-faced patriarch as he took his place on the tottering throne. Aye was no longer the man Egypt needed. But he knew such a man. Aye had recognized him as a youth, reared him in his own image, brought him to power.

Harmhab was cast in the same mold as Aye. Both were men of iron. Both had climbed, one following the other, out of humble beginnings.

How do we explain these victorious ones who come to supremacy out of nowhere? Such men possess inexhaustible energy and constant vigilance. They never allow ambition to waver; their eyes are always on the next move, the nearest opening, the main chance. They know when to flatter, when to attack. Aye had been such a man. Now Harmhab, "that simple official" was the man of the hour.

There was this difference between the two men. Harmhab's progress would never be interrupted by a sense of gratitude.

Aye had schemed and maneuvered his way to power and swept along with him many destinies. The only destiny that concerned Harmhab was his own.

There is a revealing statue of Harmhab in New York's Metropolitan Museum. He is an Iago of a man, hunched and narrow-eyed, a mousehole watcher of opportunities. Egypt, *in extremis*, was in need of such a man, ruthless and capable of desperate action.

Beware the grand vizier! The ancient Pharaohs had been warned against giving too much power to those who served them. Aye, the all-wise, must have known Harmhab was determined—and dangerous. But Aye was struggling with his last strength to protect the throne and Akhenaton's memory and Nefertiti and her city. What other than a Harmhab could support a weakened throne under an aged but valiant Aye?

Aye could not have taken the throne without Harmhab's assistance. His reign shows Harmhab's growing power. He placed responsibilities in Harmhab's hands that other kings had once entrusted to him.

Breasted traced the rise of Harmhab. According to Breasted, Harmhab came from a family that had once belonged to the petty nobility. Every act of his life showed his determination to return to the exalted position he evidently felt should be his. While King Akhenaton was living, and Harmhab was his courtier and singer of his praises, Harmhab was building an impressive tomb for himself at Sakkara near Memphis. The tomb revealed his drive to power. His image there is majestic, as if Harmhab, even then, knew he would eventually have engraved upon its forehead the symbol of the royal serpent.

Harmhab chose his opening well in the army which many defeats had robbed of morale. The Hittite victories had sapped the strength of the great military machine built up over the centuries by so many Egyptian kings, especially by Thutmose III. Harmhab, as a trusted favorite of Akhenaton's, had no difficulty getting himself, a civilian scribe, appointed to the rank of general. He made a good officer. He had an exact, nonimaginative, military mind.

When Akhenaton was dying, and with him the Amarna Revolution and the spirit of Aton, Harmhab made his first appearance as the strong man. He had been reassembling the armies, urging further conscription, clamoring for war, and failing to rouse the dying king at Amarna to resistance. But Harmhab was on the rise, irresistible as the sun's rising. All he was doing was credited to Amon, and upon him were pinned the revived hopes of the Amon priesthood in Thebes.

Not much is known of Harmhab's activities during Sakere's brief reign. Perhaps Aye was too close to the young king, who never gave full satisfaction to the cause of Amon. The boy-king of Amarna followed, and it was with Tutankhamon that Harmhab came into his own.

Now, looking clearly at Harmhab, we can see how the boy Tutankhamon was forced to change his name from an Aton name, move to Thebes from Amarna, and make peace with the priests of Amon. Akhenaton, Sakere, Tutankhamon, all were steps for Harmhab. All gave him advancement and gifts. Harmhab was one of the richest men in Egypt by the time Aye became king. Tutankhamon, who had most needed his strength, had given him most. He named General Harmhab his chief royal councilor and commander in chief of all the Egyptian armies.

This could not have been done without the consent of Aye, who was even closer than Harmhab to the boy-king. Aye was never the warrior. Tutankhamon needed a powerful aide; when he arrived in Thebes he was still little more than a child. So Aye gave full support to Harmhab, who, as commander in chief, was doing his best to restore morale and power to the demoralized army. With this revitalized army, Harmhab set forth to defend the invaded boundaries.

In the privacy of his tomb at Sakkara Harmhab boasted of his victories as "Chief Commander of the Egyptian Armies, Bearer on the King's Right Hand, Attendant of the King in his footsteps in the foreign countries of the South and the North, King's Messenger in the front of His Army to the Foreign Countries, and the King's Sole Companion who is at the feet of his Lord in the battlefield on that day of killing Asiatics."

This last relates to an alleged battle in which Tutankhamon was supposed to have taken part.

Harmhab went on to relate how as king's messenger he set out "as far as the sun disk shows to capture the rebellious countries, and take forever from Syria," and he is seen boasting to Tutankhamon: "The countries which knew not Egypt, they are under thy feet forever and ever, for Amon has decreed them to thee."

It is not likely that Harmhab had recaptured any of the lost lands of Asia, but he did prevent further invasion and was able to hold what remained of Egypt. He was permitted to assume titles of a kind that had never been used before in Egypt, "Greatest of the Great, Chosen of the King, General of Generals of the Lord of the Two Lands."

So Harmhab was the most powerful man in Egypt except for the monarch, when, after Tutankhamon's death, King Aye sat on the throne.

While Harmhab was building his fine tomb near Memphis, Aye was at last starting work on his own tomb at Thebes. He had waited through the Amarna Revolution before that final pleasure. Now he was king and could build as he chose, and in that tomb he placed all the statements he wished to make while living. And in defiance of all around him Aye placed in it the symbol of Aton, that the voice of his divine son Akhenaton might speak forever in Aye's tomb.

Even as king, Aye did not openly antagonize Amon. He accepted the former god as he did Harmhab; both were necessary evils to the continuation of Egypt.

But he did not capitulate to Amon. He did not allow the power of the Amon priests to expand. He kept Harmhab from extending power to Amon; although Amon was given credit for all Harmhab's victories.

Tired and old as he was, Aye began a brave and unpopular task—he added to the Aton Temple Akhenaton had built at Thebes between the Amon temples of Karnak and Luxor! Even this Aye did not build for his own credit but to the memory of Akhenaton.

While he lived, the memory of Akhenaton lived, and Nefertiti could continue to hold court in her city of the sun. Sometime during these last years in Amarna, she posed for what may have been her last portrait. In the Amarna Collection in University College, London, a relief shows her careworn, with a heavy line of age chiseled from nostril to mouth. But the small head is high and the slender throat arched and the exquisite bony structure shows her face as that of a still-beautiful woman. Instead of the blue headdress she made famous she is wearing a thick wig and on it are set the horns and disk of Iris.

Isis, the goddess-wife who mourned for her dead Osiris!

Some crisis in Nefertiti's life may have caused her to wear again the symbols of a goddess renounced by Akhenaton.

Nefertiti was edging into her forties and Aye over twice her years. How long could they hold Egypt?

King Aye's was not a happy reign. He did not have the strength to stem the spreading evils of corruption inside Egypt. Harmhab knew of them and could have stopped them; Aye had given him unlimited power when he turned the armies over to Harmhab. But Harmhab made no attempt to return control and order to Egypt while Aye was king. Instead he permitted the priests of Amon to lay full blame for the dissolution of Egypt on the dead Akhenaton and his one god. Aye was respected by the priesthood, but he was also resented for his persistence in honoring the policies of the dead heretic king.

The development of hatred being built over these years was only part of Harmhab's far-reaching plans for himself. He knew exactly where he was going.

It is well to remember that Harmhab's ambition was curtailed as long as Aye lived. But even the wisest of men cannot live forever. A younger man, as strong and ruthless as Aye had once been, was pressing harder now on the heels of the venerable king. Meanwhile, the world's greatest civilization seemed about to collapse.

During some troubled time such as this, when in Thebes King Aye struggled for the country's survival and dread lay over the partially deserted city of Amarna, a queen of Egypt summoned her court scribe and dictated the strangest and saddest of all the Amarna Letters. A record of this correspondence would be found, not at Amarna, but in the royal archives of Hittite capital of Boghaz-Keui in Asia Minor. The series of letters were between King Shubbililiuma of the Hittite kingdom and the Egyptian queen.

For a long time it was assumed the pleading letters were written by the young widow of Tutankhamon. But, eminent authorities such as Steindorff and Seele and A. H. Sayce, believe they were written by Nefertiti.

What dread must have been hers, that she wrote in such pitiful terms to Egypt's most hated enemy! King Shubbililiuma was the invader who had led his shaggy-headed, peak-hatted warriors into the Kingdom of Mitanni and on into Canaan and the rich country adjoining Lebanon and taken all these lands in defiance of Egypt, while Akhenaton, lost in dreams in Amarna, had done nothing to prevent him. Now the Hittite king was the conqueror of much of the lands taken from Egypt, and his was the power to snub, as once he had been snubbed by Akhenaton.

Now a desperate queen sued for mercy to one of her own rank in the only way open to a queen.

The incident was recorded by Prince Mursilis, one of the sons of the Hittite king. There is first a description of the amazement in the Hittite stronghold when an ambassador arrived from the Egyptian queen bearing "rich bridal gifts" and the following cuneiform letter:

"My husband is dead and I have no son . . . your sons are said to be grown . . . send me one of your sons; I will make him my husband and King of Egypt."

According to the prince, the Hittite king's first reaction was distrust of the startling offer. "Never in my life have I heard of anything like this!" he is reported to have said. Evidently he

suspected a ruse on Egypt's part to lure away one of his sons to
be held as a hostage. He ordered his chamberlain Hattu-Zitis to
go to Egypt. "Find out if what she says is true. This may be a
trap . . . there may be a Prince . . ."

The chamberlain went to Egypt and evidently reported the
king's exact words to Nefertiti. Her return answer to the king
was regally indignant: "Why do you say I may be trying to de-
ceive you? If I had a son, would I write a foreign country in a
manner humiliating to me and my people? . . . He who was my
husband is dead and I have no sons. Am I to take one of my
servants and make him into my husband?"

Was Harmhab the scorned "servant" the haughty Nefertiti
was refusing to marry? She had known him first as a petty official in her husband's court. The letter may have been written
when Aye was dead or dying and she learned Harmhab was determined to take the throne. If so, the offer to the enemy regent
was a last pitiful effort on the part of a proud empress to continue the Eighteenth Dynasty.

Whatever the letter's intention, it almost worked. Prince Mursilis, continuing his story, wrote that the Egyptian queen pleaded
without shame to the Hittite king.

"I have written to no other country," she wrote. "I have only
written to you . . . Give me one of your sons and he shall be my
husband and king over the land of Egypt."

Evidently the ambassador sent by the Hittite king returned a
good report of the Egyptian queen's sincerity and need, for
Prince Mursilis wrote proudly:

"My father, a fine king, complied with the queen's request and
sent her the son she asked for."

The Hittite prince never arrived in Thebes. His bridal party
was ambushed before it reached the Egyptian frontier and the
young man murdered. "By Egyptians with many horses," the
Hittite report ran, "the Prince was captured and poisoned . . ."

Was this ordered by Harmhab? He had the power. Massed
behind him now was the Army, the civil authorities, and all the
priesthood of Amon. He was a vengeful man, as history would
show, and if he was the lover scorned, and by Nefertiti, it could
explain Harmhab's action after Aye's death.

The Aye who had reached the throne after his long climb was

only the ghost of a Pharaoh. Harmhab was the actual ruler, as Aye had been to other kings. King Aye reigned only for two to four years. The recently accepted dates are 1344 to 1342 B.C.

His reign ended in mystery. Some believe Harmhab unleashed the Army against Aye and either had him killed or driven from the throne. An Egyptian belief is that Harmhab had both Aye and Nefertiti poisoned. Harmhab's subsequent actions were to show him fully capable of such crimes.

Aye may have died a natural death, even of old age. We do not know his ending. When his reign ended in 1342 Harmhab moved swiftly, as Aye had so many times after the death of kings. Once more Egypt learned the gold throne had been left vacant and was as quickly filled. The resourceful Harmhab made himself eligible by marrying Akhenaton's sister, Princess Bekataton.

How Harmhab succeeded in marrying the sister of the great dead king has not been discovered. The Princess Beketaton was not only the sister of a king but the daughter of a king.

Nefertiti had maneuvered two half-royal princes, Sakere and Tutankhamon, onto the throne with Aye's assistance by marrying them to her two daughters. Harmhab had no authentic claim to noble blood. That did not deter him. By marrying the princess he laid claim, as Aye had before him, to the title of Hereditary Prince.

The marriage was obviously made for religious and political reasons. Harmhab was only a general, but he had control of the military and government, and when Egypt allowed him to act as king he was actually putting it under martial law. Harmhab dramatized the marriage as a romance for the official records. According to his account, the princess was introduced to him by the great god Amon in person, a claim that shows how the political wind had veered. Harmhab went on to describe the effect of this meeting. The princess was so overwhelmed that she bowed to the ground, and then, casting modesty aside, she "embraced his pleasant form."

This is in Harmhab's own words.

Harmhab always played to the gallery. He had been an ostentatious figure at all Amon events, and now his marriage was dedicated in all its splendor to Amon. It was staged during the most popular of all the Theban festivals, during the great feast of Opet that had been revived by Tutankhamon, due to the urgings of Harmhab. The bride and groom were escorted from the Temple of Karnak to the Temple of Luxor by thousands of Amon priests, and thousands of the royal troops, and all the cheering citizenry of Thebes that crowded the banks as the royal barge swept upstream on its brief journey between the temples. All throats were hoarse cheering the complete restoration of Amon to his role of chief god. At last Egypt could celebrate a coronation with revived hope; this one meant a return of all the divinities.

The ceremony took place in the Temple of Luxor under the image of Amon which in that temple was magically transformed into the lettuce-eating god of sensuality, Min. There the former scribe and his bride went through the long-drawn out rituals of marriage and coronation.

The jubilant Amon priests acclaimed Harmhab a true son of Ra, the original god of the sun, and his name was solemnly entered in the list of Pharaohs as King Harmhab. (In almost the same fashion, through Amon priests, Thutmose III had acquired the throne.)

Apparently little attention was paid to the small, begemmed figure at his side. History has little to say about Beketaton, Nefertiti's shadowy little sister-in-law, to whom the new King Harmhab owed his throne.

CHAPTER SEVENTEEN

Crowning Victory

Tell el-Amarna, 1342 B.C.–*As of now.*

The record fades with Aye's death. A gigantic hand might have swept the board of Egypt of all the glittering players of Akhenaton's time. Only Harmhab was left crouched in surly triumph on the throne.

We look for Nefertiti, with Aye gone. He was her first protector. He had been her last. She would have been safe in Akhenaton's city while Aye lived.

The incredible events following Aye's death brought Harmhab into the open as her enemy.

Whether she lived through them or died, we do not know. The records were destroyed on Harmhab's orders. There are leading authorities, including Steindorff and Seele, who believe she lived into the Nineteenth Dynasty and saw Seti I come to power, in which event she would have seen a recovered Egypt. She may have inherited Aye's longevity, and lived to see imperial Egypt return full cycle and restored to power.

The last clear glimpse of Nefertiti shows her in the magnificent North Palace at Amarna, fiercely dedicated to the worship of Aton and her memories of Akhenaton. She was the last of the Amarna revolutionaries.

The new king was a brooding, malignant man. Harmhab owed all he had achieved, including his crown, to the four preceding kings. Now Harmhab was free to show how beneath the lickspittle fawning he had hated those who trusted him.

He determined to wipe their names from the earth as if they had never lived. He would murder them after their deaths.

The power Harmhab had accumulated from his four patrons was now unleashed against all they had loved and believed in and all they had hoped to achieve that would keep their names illustrious forever.

He began with their names. His crusade of vengeance started
when he ordered out armies of stonemasons to obliterate, wherever found, the names of Akhenaton, Sakere, Tutankhamon, and
Aye, and replace them with his own name. Everywhere in Egypt
their names were carved away. Harmhab excused his vandalism
by damning Akhenaton as a heretic and the other kings guilty
by association. He ordered his name to replace Tutankhamon's
on the stele in the Temple of Amon, but the hand of the mason
faltered and enough of the inscription remained to testify that
the child-king of Amarna had assisted, under Aye's guidance, in
a partial capitulation to Amon. Thousands of years later this stele
would help restore this destroyed section of history.

If Nefertiti lived she would have seen her own name struck
out wherever Akhenaton had set it beside his own. Their statues
and monuments were hammered into fragments.

Now Harmhab, having wiped the four heretic names from the
list of kings, set his own name far back in the lists so that it followed that of King Amenhotep III, as if the four kings had never
lived. All his official documents and records gave the date of his
reign as starting in 1369 B.C., which had been the year of Akhenaton's coronation, so that according to his own records King
Harmhab, on the day he ascended the throne in Thebes, had already been king for twenty-seven years!

This loop taken in history would puzzle historians until the
discovery of Amarna.

It was only the beginning of King Harmhab's revenge. Every
trace of the heretic kings (and his own treachery) had to be
wiped away. To do that all references must be destroyed to the
religion of the one god Akhenaton had tried to impose upon
Egypt—the god in which the four kings had never lost faith.

The masons had orders to chisel away the emblem and name
of Aton, wherever found, and replace it with the holy name of
Amon. The last battle in the world's first religious war was won
by Amon when Akhenaton's rayed sun was forbidden to be displayed or worshiped in Egypt. All Akhenaton had built was destroyed, or re-dedicated to Amon.

In Nefertiti's city the order from Thebes was ignored. The
Aton emblem remained in the homes, on the doors, in the public

buildings and in the tombs. Who in Amarna dared attempt to obliterate the sun!

Harmhab dared. To wipe out the last memory of the heretic king and queen Amarna would have to be destroyed.

Once again an expedition made its way down the Nile from Thebes. King Harmhab may have led this pilgrimage to Amarna, for his is the last royal inscription found in the city of the sun. His pilgrims were not builders but destroyers.

Hundreds of demolition workers with bronze sledge hammers and chisels and wooden battering rams disembarked at the stone wharf of the most beautiful of cities. They had their orders from Harmhab: Destroy Amarna!

We are not certain as to the year this happened but it could not have been while Aye lived. The razing of the city probably began in 1344 B.C., when Harmhab took the throne, and it was carried out with the violence of a man whose hatred had gone beyond control.

The destruction began with the great Temple of Aton, which had been the first Amarna building raised by Akhenaton. The tremendous edifice was hammered down to earth level. The great archaeologists who would excavate in its ruins, including Howard Carter and Sir Leonard Woolley, would not find a single wall remaining of the "heretic temple" that had once been the center of religion for all Egypt.

Woolley reported that its walls had been pulled down, their ornaments defaced, and only splinters and scraps found of rock carvings. ". . . not a single stone remained in position," he wrote, "scarcely a stone remained on the site."

The ruins were used as a quarry. The broken stone was taken to Memphis and Thebes to be rebuilt there into temples dedicated to Amon by King Harmhab. This was Harmhab's supreme insult to the memory of Akhenaton.

His demolition squadrons moved on through the silenced city. One by one the other temples of Aton were torn down. The palaces were demolished—the North Palace with its never to be surpassed wall paintings, Nefertiti's palace, Akhenaton's. The Sunshade Houses and the pavilions in the royal gardens were destroyed.

The handsomest public buildings in Egypt were being leveled

when someone remembered and hid the Amarna archives in the floor of a wrecked building under a concealing layer of sand.

The famous glass and pottery and faïence factories that had produced so much beauty had never ceased operating. They were destroyed and the artists and craftsmen ordered away to Thebes. Their productions were stolen or shattered. By chance a few of these priceless art treasures were left unbroken under the debris of destruction.

Harmhab's despoilers did not cringe in their task of destroying all that was beautiful in Amarna. The bronze hammers splintered the flowing-lined marble statuary that had set Amarna sculpture centuries before its time. The wall murals of Amarna's greatest artists were brutally shattered.

The gangs moved without compunction into the Street of the Sculptor. In the studio of Thutmes, Akhenaton's master sculptor, even the dullest may have paused for a moment with arrested hammer, awed by the beauty surrounding him. In these rooms was concentrated the greatest collection of art studies the world would know until Greece reached its creative peak. Here Thutmes and his talented pupils had reproduced the lifelike heads of all the great who had lived in Amarna. Among them one stood out, poised and serene. It was Nefertiti's.

The order rang out. The hammers crashed. Amarna's heads burst into shards and dust. Somehow Nefertiti's bust fell only partially broken and in the fury of destruction no more harm was done to it.

Did a workman, moved by that pleading face, hold his hand? Dust and chips of limestone and marble covered the delicately tinted features. They left her there and moved on through the tree-lined, gardened streets into the residential sections. The Amarna families were driven out of their homes with orders to make their way to Memphis or Thebes and start new lives under Amon. Nobles, civilians, officials, clerks, workmen of every kind, were ordered to the wharf and the waiting barges. The exodus was carried out to the sounds of lamentation.

Evidently the Amarnians had been given no warning. Many left their family treasures, their furnishings and clothing. In the workmen's village walls collapsed over tables set for meals that would never be eaten, and pots of food were left on hearths that would not be seen again for thousands of years.

In the excavated ruins of Nefertiti's palace would be found the remains of two oxen, trussed in preparation for sacrifice. They might be evidence of an interruption as violent and unexpected as that which would later overwhelm Pompeii. The sacrifice may have been prepared on Nefertiti's orders in an effort to hold back the ruin threatening her beloved city.

The demolition squads marched into the Valley of the Kings where Akhenaton had chosen to duplicate the royal burying place at Thebes. The fury of Harmhab's passion for revenge is shown in the vicious despoliation of the tomb prepared by Akhenaton and Nefertiti for their final sleep. The underground rock palace they had planned was ravaged. Chisels ripped away the delicate reliefs showing the royal lovers in their moments of public triumph and domestic happiness. The handsome sarcophagus Akhenaton had ordered for himself and never used was reduced to splinters. Every act of Harmhab's against the memory of Akhenaton revealed the manic rage of the hater against the man who dares dream ahead of his time.

The tombs Akhenaton had built for his nobles were left in ruins.

The destroyers moved on to the public burying grounds in the valley. The mummied bodies of those who had died at Amarna under Aton were removed from their graves and shipped to Thebes to be reburied there in the necropolis under Amon. There could have been no greater insult to an Egyptian king than this removal of the bodies of those who had died in Akhenaton's city.

Harmhab may have been present at the destruction in Akhenaton's tomb at Amarna. Why, in his frenzy for obliteration, did he overlook the tomb Akhenaton had begun for Aye near his own, and never completed?

Harmhab could never have been shown that tomb. He was an educated man, a scribe, and he would have known what its preservation would do to his plan for wiping out all memory of Akhenaton. Aye's second tomb, which he began at Thebes during his brief reign and did not live to complete, would be brutally plundered by Harmhab. But for unknown reasons the workmen entrusted with the demolition of the Amarna valley tombs dealt lightly with Aye's. It may be they gave it only passing attention because it had never been completed or furnished or occupied— no mummy had been concealed there. They may not have considered the wall paintings and cuneiform inscriptions worthy of destruction.

Or it may be that someone, the gang foreman perhaps, respected the memory of the recently dead King Aye more than he feared the formidable wrath of the living King Harmhab. For although Harmhab chiseled Aye's name as a king from all the records and destroyed all he could that pertained to him, he did not succeed in removing Aye from the memory of the Egyptians. Aye was forgotten as a king, but he was remembered as the scribe and seer and architect who added so much to the brilliancy of the Eighteenth Dynasty. His fame grew, as all recognition of Akhenaton and Sakere and Tutankhamon and their city faded. Hundreds of years after Harmhab's siege of destruction ended, Aye had his own shrine at Thebes where he was worshiped as a god. His association with the heretic kings, Nefertiti, and Amarna was forgotten; only the man of wisdom remained. Nefertiti and her kings and her city had dropped out of history.

In death as in life Aye retained the respect of Egypt. To this we may owe the preservation of Akhenaton's great *Hymn to the Sun* which Aye inscribed on his tomb's walls at Amarna. The workman entrusted with the wrecking of the valley tombs may have been afraid to mutilate a tomb that might at any moment admit Aye's powerful ka.

Amarna was deserted. Little remained of the city that had been the most beautiful in the world and the capital of the great Egyptian empire. If Nefertiti was still living there, and it is believed that she never left Amarna, she and her remaining followers occupied a ghost city. The famed Amarna gardens and the orchards on the west bank had been uprooted. The doors of the deserted houses were left open to the jackals that prowled through rooms that had once known feasting and music. Termites devoured the painted woodwork and the straw in adobe walls that folded together and collapsed. Roofs fell and floors crumbled. Owls and bats nested in the halls. The wide King's

Highway could not be distinguished from the level sand of the desert.

Shu, the ancient Egyptian god of the winds, took over the city of Aton. He drove sand from the Arabian desert in the east, over the cliffs, over Amarna. The wells in ruined courtyards filled with sand. The lotus plants shriveled on Nefertiti's lake, which dried to a dusty plain. Wind and sand aided King Harmhab in blotting out the city of the sun.

Amarna had been built and destroyed in approximately a quarter of a century. Once more, and not for the first or last time in history, hate had triumphed over love.

Harmhab's destroyers had worked well.

Petrie wrote of the destruction of Akhenaton's Amarna: "Such was the fall of one of the great movements of human thought, carried out by a single idealist who set himself against the traditions, the religion, the hatred of his country."

Judas Iscariot slept unborn in the womb of time but his predecessors were active in Egypt. King Harmhab was an archingrate, and he was not alone. There were other Egyptian leaders who had wearied of a dynasty of poetic dreamers and were pleased to have an aggressive businessman-type executive take the sagging kingdom in hand. Harmhab raised men as ruthless as himself to power. All were dedicated, with him, to the complete eradication of the Amarna Revolution and the worship of Aton. All these Akhenaton betrayers had been raised to power by the dead king. One was Patonemhab. He had been a courtier and a favorite of Akhenaton's. His sudden elevation made Patonemhab one of the most zealous destroyers of the name and fame of Akhenaton.

Now that Amarna was deserted and damned, one might think Harmhab's thirst for vengeance satisfied. Instead, he and his cohorts launched one final attack against the dead king. They could not entirely destroy his place in history, but they could place him there as a nameless, faceless ogre.

Through the remaining years of the Eighteenth Dynasty and on into the Nineteenth, Akhenaton was never mentioned by name in the official documents. When it was necessary to refer to him he was invariably described as "the heretic king of

Amarna, the criminal of Amarna, or, the conquered one of Amarna." So his fame grew, not as the poet and worshiper of truth and prince of peace, but as a monster too terrible to be named. No insult to his memory was overlooked, but his memory was made anonymous, so that within a few years, since they could not be spoken, the names of Akhenaton and Nefertiti were forgotten.

The old temples of Amon were restored. The priests resumed their former luxurious lives. Splendidly robed, they placed new gold and silver statues and vessels on the altars, and all the lands and herds and revenue confiscated by Aton were returned to them. The new King Harmhab, who had chanted flattering hymns to Akhenaton and Aton in Amarna, now was seen in attendance at all the religious festivals honoring Amon.

The Egyptians returned joyously to the polytheism of their ancestors. All the old gods Akhenaton had denied were back—the smiling cat-faced Bastet, the hippo-goddess Opet, the hawk-headed, dog-faced, bird-faced gods, the monstrous, bloated beast-woman-goddess who devoured wrongdoers after death. Egypt had never ceased to believe in them and worship them in secret. Egypt felt secure again with its more than two thousand deities under the all-god Amon, and for this they gave thanks to King Harmhab.

The truth was that Harmhab, the archingrate, proved to be one of the best of the Egyptian Pharaohs. His eagle eyes had studied the darkening situation in Egypt since his start as a petty official under Akhenaton. He had seen the failure of the priest-god-king image, and he did not represent himself as such before the people. He was the administrator. He placed all responsibility for public welfare squarely on the military, the government, and the priests whose gods he had restored. To insure their diligence he supplied them with revenue and high rank, as when he made Patonemhab high priest of Heliopolis.

Having reinstated the gods, Harmhab wielded the first big stick in history and set about the redemption of Egypt. No man knew better than he how deeply corruption had eaten its way into the government and judiciary. Never before had he attempted to halt the evil, although he had the power. Now he was king, he traveled in person about Egypt, making friends with the local officials wherever he went. He invited them to visit him in Thebes, where in the palace he feasted and entertained them and sent them away burdened with gifts and singing the praises of their host, the king.

He awarded them rich revenue in their own right so they were not tempted to rob the people.

Then, to further insure their integrity, Harmhab passed laws to prevent bribe taking by any official or priest. He became Egypt's greatest lawmaker since Amenhotep III, whose Akhenaton had passed no laws, depending on the goodness of Aton to preserve Egypt. The acceptance of a bribe was held to be a crime against the state and anyone suspected of bribe taking was forced to stand trial. The penalties were loss of position and confiscation of property.

There was no legal code before Harmhab. Ethical rules had served. Now a great body of law was created at Karnak known as the native law. Harmhab set up the new code, "To recreate respect for law in Egypt, to prevent the practice of injustice, to eliminate crime, and to destroy falsehood."

The new laws dealt not only with civilians, but with the military and the government. No one was exempt. Ever since Akhenaton's failure to hold Egypt the soldiers had been openly oppressing the people, looting their homes, and stealing their crops and cattle. Now a soldier caught robbing a citizen was given "one hundred blows and five open wounds and whatever he has stolen shall be returned."

The new laws had no mercy on government employees who oppressed the people. A tax collector caught cheating had his nose cut off and was banished to slave labor in the mines.

One of Harmhab's severest laws controlled landlords who were cheating their peasant tenants.

Once more Maat's feather of justice was raised in honor in the Egyptian courts. Now the poorest could expect a fair hearing. There were civil trials as before and special commissions for special crimes, including tomb robbing, that decreed such penalties as exile or death or nose-cutting or whipping or banishment.

King Harmhab not only passed these laws but traveled about the country seeing that they were enforced. Judas though he was, he was one of the first to fight to outlaw oppression and legislate for justice. He was one of the outstanding kings of the Eighteenth Dynasty, and he would be the last of that line. There are authorities who deny his marriage to Nefertiti's sister entitled him to a place in the Eighteenth Dynasty, and insist upon his being placed as the first Pharaoh of the Nineteenth Dynasty. Wherever his rightful place, he was the salvation of an Egypt the gentle Akhenaton had brought to the brink of ruin.

He lived long. The end of his reign is disputed; he may have died in 1303 or 1314 B.C. He was not able to restore Egypt to the imperial position it had held when Akhenaton became king. The fall of Amarna marked the beginning of the collapse of the Eighteenth Dynasty, a collapse so inevitable even a Harmhab could not prevent it. Breasted has explained that "internal disorders had caused the fall of the Eighteenth Dynasty, an event which terminated the First Period of the Empire." Less than half a century after Akhenaton's death the greatest dynasty in the East ended.

But out of this sad ending came a strong beginning, for the great Pharaohs of the Nineteenth Dynasty were to revive Egypt, and these leaders came from the farsighted shrewdness of Harmhab. As Aye had been, Harmhab was a molder of destinies. One of his military aides who had been useful in helping to liquidate the spiritual kingdom of Akhenaton was General Rameses. Harmhab made him his chief of staff and was so impressed by his ability that he named Rameses his successor to the throne. Rameses recaptured Kadesh and became the founder of the great Nineteenth and Twentieth dynasties known as the Ramesside, which began with his siring of a truly great king, Seti I.

Seti I would invade Asia and win back more of the vassal countries lost under Akhenaton, and return to Thebes with bounty and slaves to divide between himself as king and Amon, and as was proper, he sacrificed some of his prisoners before the face of Amon. So the empire was eventually reassembled under Amon, and great monuments and buildings were constructed, and once more the Hittites were driven back and gold became again as dust in the land of Egypt.

Egypt would be great again, a fact Nefertiti could never have doubted, for was she not Egypt?

In his travels about the kingdom King Harmhab made many trips between Upper and Lower Egypt. Each time his bannered royal barge was rowed between Thebes and Memphis he passed the sandy crescent on the Nile that once had held Amarna. On each trip Harmhab noted that the sand had drifted higher. Where the world's most beautiful city had stood there was only wasteland, with here and there a broken wall.

The king knew the satisfaction of the Pharaoh who beheads his enemies in the presence of the gods. He had eradicated a king and queen he envied and hated and all who had shared their lives. There was nothing along that stretch of the Nile to indicate that a poet-king and a glamorous woman had lived in a city named Amarna. There was no indication of a child-king named Tutankhamon, who had ruled there briefly in the shadow of their greatness.

In the gold chair on the deck of his decorated barge, King Harmhab knew the swelling triumph of the avenger, for to his kind of man no emotion equals the sweetness of revenge.

He did not know that under that tawny stretch Akhenaton's hymns and poems and letters and the Amarna paintings were defying the termite-infested centuries. He did not know that the marble dust of Thutmes' studio was concealing the death mask of a king and the face of the woman he had loved.

King Harmhab could sail on down the river to Memphis and forget Amarna as the rest of Egypt was forgetting.

The attraction that brought Harmhab often to Memphis was his tomb being built at Sakkara. He had started it years before, when he was a minor official, and it was taking a long time to complete because Harmhab was a particular man who demanded the best of everything. The paintings on the tomb walls were by the finest artists he had been able to find in Egypt.

Here fate played an ironic trick on Harmhab the Destroyer, for his tomb was to help perpetuate the art of Amarna. He insisted upon the best artists—the best were of the school of Amarna. Their paintings represented the finest in Amarnian art, so his tomb, and Tutankhamon's, and Aye's (two kings Harmhab had hoped to annihilate) immortalized the flowing-lined, naturalistic art of Amarna.

Harmhab would never know that through such oversights his

crusade of annihilation had failed. Time would rewrite the pages of history he had torn away and restore the great destroyed ones to their rightful places.

Amarna had fallen, but its art and influence remained.

King Harmhab was a stern king and enforcer of laws for everyone but himself. He demanded the severest penalties for grave robbing, and he himself was one of the most monstrous grave robbers of all time. He had ordered the brutal plundering of the Amarna graves, and probably those of Akhenaton and Tiy and Sakere at Thebes. He robbed Egypt of much of its history when he destroyed those tombs, and only Aye's ingenuity in hiding the Tutankhamon grave kept it safe.

Harmhab's example may have helped encourage the professional grave robbers, for as has been said, by the time a commission was finally appointed in the Twentieth Dynasty to investigate the plundering of the tombs in the Valley of the Kings, every royal grave except Tutankhamon's had been plundered.

Aye had hidden the boy-king's tomb from Harmhab but he could not save his own.

Aye had recorded a plea he made to King Akhenaton:

"Grant me a good old age as thy favorite. Grant me a goodly burial . . ."

The years were granted, for Aye outlived all of Akhenaton's circle. In a sense his second wish was also granted, for although his tomb at Thebes was methodically ransacked, its furnishings stolen, his sarcophagus shattered and his mummy and that of his good wife, Tiy the nurse, mysteriously lost, the tomb Aye left unfinished at Amarna escaped vandalism.

The Amarna grave is the true shrine of Akhenaton and Nefertiti.

On its walls, with Akhenaton's permission, Aye preserved the only complete edition of Akhenaton's immortal *Hymn to the Sun*. One hammer stroke—and Egypt's greatest literary treasure would have been lost.

The *Hymn* held the essence of Akhenaton's being, his vision and his religion and his love, so that more than thirty centuries later we are still moved by his words to Nefertiti, his beloved: "Mistress of the Two Lands . . . Living and flourishing forever and ever."

Akhenaton failed in much that he tried to do, but his wish for Nefertiti has not failed. Nefertiti survived to become the personification of the ideal woman in many lands and centuries. To those who lived in her time in Egypt, three and a half thousand years may well have seemed forever.

She regards us with gentle dignity across the space of those years, in art shops and book stores and museums—the most widely known and reproduced bust in the world. We meet her serene gaze with a sense of recognition; she seems familiar because she is Woman. Every lovely tinted line seems to proclaim her identity. Her look is pleading as if, so many thousands of years after hers and Akhenaton's world was lost, she asks that their lives be justified. The head is held proudly on the lotus-stem throat, the delicately-colored mouth seems to speak, echoing Akhenaton's words:

"I am Nefertiti and I live forever. I was co-regent of imperial Egypt fourteen centuries before Christ, in the richest and most cultured dynasty Egypt has ever known. Long before Cleopatra lived, long before Helen of Troy, I was the fabulous one, the all-glamorous, the most beautiful woman of my world. My power was maintained through the love of five kings. Beyond all others I was the love and inspiration of the greatest, Akhenaton, King of Kings."

Nefertiti saw no visions, led no armies, claimed no authority save through the men she loved and who loved her. But she was the last of the great revolutionaries and she was Amarna. She had the trust and admiration of the last five Eighteenth Dynasty regents—Amenhotep, Akhenaton, Sakere, Tutankhamon, and Aye. She shared in every reign, until Harmhab's.

Harmhab, who betrayed them all, betrayed her.

But it is easier to kill the dreamers than the dream. Nefertiti's bust is her cenotaph.

Aye who was her defender while he lived, corroborated the testimony of her bust from his tomb. Out of his grave at Amarna has come Akhenaton's religious teachings of the one god that would find acceptance in a later world. Out of it came the Amarna vision of a brave new world ruled by beauty, peace, and love, which would be responsible in time for such utopian dream communities as Brook Farm, Oneida, and Philadelphia. Akhena-

ton was one of the first men to glimpse that vision. He looked
ever further into it, deeper into time, while around him his
world fell away.

Out of Aye's tomb, and Tutankhamon's, and even Harmhab's,
would come the memory of the vision and the love story immortalized by the greatest artists of its time. The recording is owed
to the tombs, but the vision and the glory were Akhenaton's.
Nefertiti's bust is a gift to us, from him.

Amarna's artists and sculptors created a pictorial album of
Amarna. The recovery of many of their works, even damaged,
restored the personalities of Akhenaton and Nefertiti and helped
return them and their times to history.

Petrie wrote of the finding of Akhenaton's death mask at
Amarna:

"In his remarkable position, the greatness of its changes, the
modernity of his thoughts, the wreck of his ideas, this strange
humanist is one of the most fascinating characters of history; and
into his face we may now look, as if we had seen him in the
flesh."

Aye was one of the truly great men of ancient Egypt. Most
of his life was spent as a mysterious power behind the throne.
One must hunt through many histories and under many names
to glimpse this elusive man. We know at last of the lives he
shaped, the kings he held to the throne, and his hold over
Akhenaton and Nefertiti. We know Amenhotep III and Queen
Tiy and the boy-kings Sakere and Tutankhamon owed much
to Aye. Nefertiti and Nezemmut, his daughters, and his granddaughters, the Amarna garland of princesses, owed their existence to him.

During his long lifetime Aye prepared and furnished tombs for
many of Egypt's kings and queens.

Why, during all this building, did Aye construct no tomb for
Nefertiti?

She would have been the most valued of all his dead. She was
Aye's creation, his daughter and Egypt's most beautiful queen,
and he would have planned her eternal home with more devotion than he gave to any of the others. The fact that Tutankhamon's would be the only tomb left unmolested in the Valley

of the Kings shows how skillfully Aye could hide what he did not wish stolen. We look at the riches from that tomb and wonder, what treasure went into Akhenaton's, and into hers?

Hers is one of the best documented lives in ancient history. The Amarna artists portrayed Nefertiti from her marriage at fifteen until she was in her forties. Soon after the last sad portraits were made, Amarna fell.

It is believed that she died in Amarna, but the date of her death and the place of her burial is unknown. She lived while Aye lived. After his death no record is found of her.

Nefertiti's life ended as it began, in mystery.

A belief persists in Egypt that Akhenaton and Nefertiti and Aye were poisoned. Some authorities think she died with Tutankhamon, others that her life ended with Aye's, while others are convinced she lived on for another half century after Amarna was razed. If her death occurred in Aye's time, we may be certain she was buried with all honor and wealth worthy of her station as a king's wife and daughter, but with even greater secrecy than had been given any of the others of the heretic strain, to keep her safe from her enemies, Harmhab and the priests of Amon.

If Aye prepared Nefertiti for eternal secrecy, the secret may still hold. Aye's life held few failures.

Somewhere in the rocky cliffs along the Nile, between the ruins of Thebes and the leveled site of Amarna, those who probe Egypt's past may some day find themselves with pounding hearts in the entrance of Nefertiti's tomb.

For the miracle is that with so much stolen, lost, and destroyed, so much remains. No other city in history was more completely ravaged than Amarna; none other has managed to give so much of what it was. Termites devoured, looters ransacked, but the dry preservative sands kept the secrets of Akhenaton and Nefertiti. Thebes, Heliopolis, Nubia yielded fragments of their lives. Discovery after discovery by the great archaeologists contributed to their story, and still the work goes on. Amarna consisted of a single level, but its dedicated area covers seventeen miles, and bits of evidence are still being found that fit into the colorful mosaic of Egypt's past.

Time, the supreme knapper, chipping away at the edges of

antiquity, has worked faithfully and long to bring into outline
the images of Akhenaton and Nefertiti.

The Eighteenth Dynasty ended in the half century after
Amarna's destruction. By that time the site was a strip of tawny
sand. Not a ruined wall remained to show that humans had once
occupied the desolate curve on the east bank of the Nile.

A century went by, then a thousand years, and three times a
thousand, and more centuries. No one remembered Amarna and
the names of those who had built that lost city. No history had
record of it nor of them.

But a legend persisted, like a drift of myrrh, of a woman who
had been beautiful beyond all women and who had lived in a
city beautiful beyond all cities, somewhere along the Nile.

New dynasties began and ended. Cities were built and vanished. Civilizations reached high levels and collapsed. Tyre fell,
and Babylon and Nineveh. Other Egyptian cities followed
Amarna into ruin, among them a ransacked Thebes.

In other parts of the world, Europe, Asia, and North America,
other cities and civilizations were rising.

The land of the Nile resounded with new and powerful names
—Alexander the Great, Ptolemy, Caesar, Cleopatra, Napoleon.
The wings of the twentieth century threw long shadows over
Egypt.

At Amarna, with her face in the dust, Nefertiti waited.

GLOSSARY OF NAMES OF IMPORTANCE IN
THE LIFE OF NEFERTITI

Newcomers to Egyptian history are often puzzled by the varieties of ways in which the ancient names are spelled, and by a habit the ancient ones had of changing their names. This confusion reached a peak in Nefertiti's time, when during the Amarna Revolution many changed their names. Akhenaton is used here as the name of his choice, although in other histories he may be found as Amenhotep IV and Amenophis IV. Aye may be found in other books spelled in a variety of ways, or as Amenhotep, Son of Hapu. Tutankhaton, who began life under that name, ended it as Tutankhamon, an act which has been bewildering newspaper readers since the discovery of his tomb.

In this book the simplest and most modern-appearing, unhyphenated forms will be used.

Nefertiti's name may be found spelled in a variety of ways, but she never changed it. It honored no goddess or god. It was her own distinctive name; as identifying as the blue headdress (blue for Egypt) she made her own. It was the essence of herself as woman and queen. Archaeologists dispute its spelling but all agree on its meaning:

"Behold! The beautiful woman comes!"

Akhenaton, King of Egypt. Originally Amenhotep IV or Amenophis IV. Also Amenothes, Ikhnaton, Echnaton, Achenaton, Akhunaton, Akhnaton, Khuenaton and Khunaten. In the Amarna Letters he was addressed in cuneiform as Napkhuria or Neferkheprure.

Amenhotep III, King. Father of Akhenaton. Also Amenophis, Amenothes. In the Amarna Letters he was Nimmuria.

Amose, King. Founder of the Eighteenth Dynasty and first known ancestor of Akhenaton. Also Amosis and Kamose.

Ankhesenaton, Princess. Third daughter of Akhenaton and Nefertiti. Married Tutankhamon. Anknespaaten and Enkhosepaaton. Later known as Ankhesenamon, Ankhesnamun.

Aye, son of Hapu. A scribe. Also known as Amenhotep, Son of Hapu. Eye, Ay, Eiy, and Huy. In the Amarna Letters he is Haya.

Aziru, an Amorite Prince. "That upstart dog."

Baqtaton, Princess. Sixth daughter of Akhenaton and Nefertiti.

Beketaton, Princess. Full sister to Akhenaton.

Gilukhipa, Princess. Daughter of Shuttarna.

Harmhab. Another scribe. Horemhab.

Meketaton, Princess. Second daughter of Akhenaton and Nefertiti.

Menes, King. Legendary founder of the Egyptian dynasties. Also Narmer.

Merire, High Priest of Aton. Also Ramery.

Meritaton, Princess. First daughter of Akhenaton and Nefertiti.

Neferneferuaton, Princess. Fourth daughter of Akhenaton and Nefertiti.

Nefertiti, Queen of Egypt. Wife of Akhenaton. Also Neferneferuaton, Nefretiti, Nefertete, Nofretete, Nefertythi, Nefretete, Nefertuthi and Nefertithi.

Nezemmut, Princess. Younger sister of Nefertiti. Also Mutnezmut, Mutnezem.

Rameses, General. Aide to Harmhab. Ramses, Ramesses, Uraeus and even Re, Ra.

Ramose, Grand Vizier of both Amenhotep III and Akhenaton. Originally known as Ptahmose.

Ribbadi, Governor of Byblos. The faithful one. Also Ribhadad.

Sakere, King. Son-in-law of Nefertiti. Smenkhkare, Sekenre, Rasmenkhka, and Rasmenkhkaserkheperu.

Setepenaton, Princess. Fifth daughter of Akhenaton and Nefertiti.

Shubbililiuma, King of the Hittites.

Shuttarna, Prince of Mitanni. Another persistent in-law.

Tadukhipa, Princess. Daughter of Tushratta.

Thutmes, Master Sculptor at Amarna. Another form of Thutmose.

Thutmose III, King. A conqueror, ancestor to Akhenaton. Thutmes, Thutmos, Tuthmosis.

Tiy, Royal Nurse. Wife of Aye. For variants see Tiy, Queen.

Tiy, Queen. Wife of Amenhotep III and mother of Akhenaton. Tyi, Ti, Ty, Tai, Tii, Teye, Thyi, Tuaa, Thuya and Thua.

Tushratta, King of Mitanni. Related to Akhenaton by marriage. Also Dushratta and Dushrata. Tushrata.

Tutankhaton, Child King of Amarna. Son-in-law of Nefertiti. Tutenkaton, Tutenkhaten, and Nebkheperure. Later known as Tutankhamon, Tutenkhamon, Tutenkamon.

Yuya and Thuya (See Tiy). Parents of Queen Tiy.

Names of places have changed.

Amarna was first Akhetaton.

The Land of Canaan has become Syria and Palestine.

Kush is now Aswan.

Mitanni was somewhere in northern Mesopotamia and probably in Assyrian domain.

Nubia is the Sudan.

Punt was probably Somaliland at the southern end of the Red Sea.

The names of the Egyptian gods take various forms. Those that most concerned Nefertiti were:

Amon, chief god of Thebes and Aton's rival. Also Amen, Amun, Ammon and in combination, Amon-Ra.

Aton. Akhenaton's one god. Also Aten and Atun.

Hapy, God of the Nile. Also Hapinou, Haapy.

Min, God of sensuality. Another transfiguration of Amon.

Maat, Goddess of Justice.

Ra, Heliopolis sun god. Also Re.

Set, God of Evil. Also Seth.

PROBABLE DATES OF IMPORTANCE IN THE LIFE OF NEFERTITI

Based upon the latest archaeological discoveries and the opinions of leading authorities.

Years B.C.

1372   Amenhotep III names his son Akhenaton co-regent.

1369   In this year Akhenaton is crowned full regent and marries Nefertiti. He is sixteen, she fifteen. In the same year he is converted to Atonism and her first child, Meritaton, is born.

1368   Beginning of Amarna.

1367   Birth of Meketaton, second daughter, at Amarna.

1366   Building of the tombs at Amarna. Somewhere is these years Akhenaton writes his *Hymn to the Sun.*

1365   Ankhesenaton, third daughter born.

1363   Fourth daughter, Neferneferuaton, born.

1361   Amenhotep III dies.

1359   Birth of fifth daughter, Setepenaton.

Somewhere in here, Meketaton dies, Tiy visits Amarna, Tiy dies.

The hatred in Thebes against Akhenaton and Nefertiti is growing.
1357   Baqtaton, Nefertiti's sixth and last daughter is born.
Another mysterious little princess is born, sometime in these years.
1356   Sakere marries Meritaton and is co-regent with Akhenaton.
1353   Death of Akhenaton.
1352   Sakere vanishes and Tutankhaton is made king.
Nefertiti is evidently acting as his co-regent.
1344   Tutankhaton dies. Aye is king.
1342   Death of Aye. Rise of Harmhab.
Harmhab 1342 to 1303 or 1314 B.C. The Eighteenth Dynasty ends.

BIBLIOGRAPHY

Anthes, Rudolf, *Tutankhamun Treasures*. Circulated by the Smithsonian Institution, The University Museum, University of Pennsylvania, 1961–63.

Anthes, Rudolf, *Bust of Nefertete*. The Berlin State Museum, Egyptian Department.

Bezold, Charles, *Oriental Diplomacy*. Luzac and Company, London, 1893.

Bibby, Geoffrey, *Four Thousand Years Ago*. Alfred A. Knopf, Inc., 1961.

Borchardt, Ludwig, *Excavations at Tell el-Amarna*. Orientalia, 1915.

Breasted, James H., *A History of Egypt*. Charles Scribner's Sons, reprint 1959.

Breasted, James H., *Ancient Records of Egypt*. University of Chicago Press, Chicago, 1929.

Carter, Howard, *The Tomb of Tutankhamon*. George H. Doran and Co., London, 1927.

Ceram, C. W., *Gods, Graves and Scholars*. Alfred A. Knopf, New York, 1956.

Cottrell, Leonard, *The Anvil of Civilization*. New American Library, 1960.

Cottrell, Leonard, *Life under the Pharaohs*. Evans Brothers, Ltd., London, 1955.

Daniel, Glyn E., *A Hundred Years of Archaeology*. Gerald Duckworth Company, Ltd., 1952.

Egyptian Museum, published by Egyptian State Tourist Administration.

Encyclopedia Brittanica.

Frankfort, Henri, *The Birth of Civilization in the Near East*. Anchor Books, Doubleday and Company Inc., Garden City, New York, 1956.

Frankfort, Henri, editor, *Mural Paintings at El-Amarneh*. Egypt Exploration Society, London, 1929.

Frazer, Sir James George, *The New Golden Bough*. Criterion Books, 1959.

Freedman, David Noel and Wright, G. Ernest, editors, *The Biblical Archaeologist Reader*, Anchor Books, Doubleday and Company, Garden City, New York, 1961.

Glanville, S. R. K., M.A., *Daily Life in Ancient Egypt*. George Routledge and Sons, Ltd., London, 1930.

Huxley, Julian, *From an Antique Land*. Crown Publishers, New York, 1955.

Keller, Werner, *The Bible as History*. William Morrow and Company, New York, 1956.

Lloyd, Seton, *The Art of the Ancient Near East*. Frederick A. Praeger, New York, 1961.

Musée Du Caire, *Description Sommaire des Principaux Monuments*. Imprimerie Nationale, Le Caire, 1956.

Newberry, Percy E., *The Journal of Egyptian Archaeology* (May 1932).

Niebuhr, Dr. Carl (pseudonym for Carl Krug), *The Ancient East* II—*The Tell El Amarna Period*. Translated by J. Hutchinson. David Nutt, London, 1903.

North, Leigh, *Predecessors of Cleopatra*. Broadway Publishing Company, New York, 1906.

Pendlebury, J. D. S., *The City of Akhenaten*. Egypt Exploration Society, Oxford University Press, Amen House, London, 1951.

Pendlebury, J. D. S., *Tell-el Amarna*. Lovat Dickson and Thompson, Ltd., London, 1935.

Petrie, William M. Flinders, *Tell el-Amarna*. D. C. L. Methuen and Co., London, 1894.

Posener, Georges, with the assistance of Serge Sauneron and Jean Yoyotte, *Encyclopedia of Egyptian Civilization*. Tudor Publishing Company, New York.

Pritchard, James B., editor, *Ancient Near Eastern Texts Relating to the Old Testament*. Princeton University Press, 1955.

Smith, William Stevenson, Ph.D., *Ancient Egypt*. Museum of Fine Arts, Boston, 1960.

Steindorff, George, and Seele, Keith C., *When Egypt Ruled the East*. University of Chicago Press, 1947.

Velikovsky, Immanuel, *Oedipus and Akhnaton*. Doubleday and Company Inc., New York, 1960.

Weigall, Arthur, *History of the Pharaohs*. Thornton Butterworth Ltd., London 1952.

White, J. E. Manchip (M. A. Contab), *Ancient Egypt*, Allan Wingate, London, 1562.

Wilkinson, Sir John Gardner, *Ancient Egyptians*, Volumes I & II. John Murray, England, 1871.

Wilson, John A., *The Culture of Ancient Egypt*. Phoenix Books, The University of Chicago Press, 1951.

Woolley, Sir Leonard, *Digging Up the Past*. Penguin Books, Baltimore, Maryland, 1961.

INDEX

F